hugo
in 3 MONTHS
GERMAN

Sigrid-B. Martin

LONDON, NEW YORK, MUNICH,
MELBOURNE, AND DELHI

This edition first published in Great Britain
in 2003 by Dorling Kindersley Limited,
80 Strand, London WC2R 0RL
Penguin Group (UK)

First published in Great Britain by
Hugo's Language Books Limited, 1990

2 4 6 8 10 9 7 5 3 1
001 – HD033 – Sep/12

A CIP catalogue record for this book is available from
the British Library.
ISBN 978-1-4053-9160-3

Hugo German in Three Months is also available in
a pack with three CDs, ISBN 978-1-4053-9156-6
001 – HD018 – Sep/11

Written by
Sigrid-B. Martin
Lecturer in German
School of European Culture and Languages
University of Kent at Canterbury

Printed and bound in China by South China Printing Co.Ltd

Discover more at
www.dk.com

Preface

Tschüss

Hugo German in Three Months has been written for us by Sigrid Martin, whose experience in teaching her native tongue ranges from beginners to post-graduate level. She has drawn on this expertise to produce a simple yet complete course for students aiming to acquire a good working knowledge of the language in a short time, and who will probably be studying alone at home.

The book begins with an explanation of German pronunciation, as far as this is possible without going too deeply into all the nuances and varying sounds involved. If you are working without a teacher, you should find that our system of 'imitated pronunciation' simplifies matters considerably. Using the book together with our CDs (allowing you to hear the German text at the same time that you read it) is an ideal combination, giving another dimension to the course.

The rest of the course is divided into 13 parts, each of which should take roughly a week to complete. It has always been a principle of the Hugo method to teach only what is really essential for a firm grasp of practical, up-to-date German; the sections contain those rules of grammar that will be of most use in this respect. Constructions are clearly explained, and the order in which everything is presented takes into consideration the need for rapid progress. Week 1 concentrates on pronunciation. Weeks 2–13 include exercises and conversations; later in the course you will move on to the use of idiom and colloquialisms, necessary for a thorough grasp of conversational German. The reading passages following Week 13 provide an introduction to written German, to prepare you for reading German books and magazines. Answers to the exercises, and a full vocabulary list, appear at the back of the book.

Ideally you should spend about an hour a day on your work (slightly less, maybe, if you do not have the CDs), although there is no hard-and-fast rule on this. Do as much as you feel capable of doing; if you have no special aptitude for language-learning, there is no point in forcing yourself beyond your daily capacity to assimilate new material. It is much better to learn a little at a time, and to learn that thoroughly.

When studying each week's lesson, first read each numbered section carefully and reread it to ensure that you have fully understood the grammar, then work through any following exercise(s) as they occur by writing down the answers. Check these by referring to the key at the back of the book; if you have made too many mistakes, go back over the instruction before attempting the same questions again. The conversational exercises and conversations should be read aloud and their constructions carefully noted. If you have the CDs, you should listen to these at the same time as you read. Listen also to the spoken German of each exercise, both before you complete the written work and again as you check the answers. After you have listened to the conversations and read them aloud, see how closely you can imitate the voices on the recording. It is best to keep your own running list of new words; this way, you will remember them better.

When you think you have completed a section satisfactorily (alternatively, just before your daily study period is over), go back over what you have recently done, to ensure that it is firmly committed to memory. When the course is completed, you should have a very good understanding of the language – more than sufficient for general holiday or business purposes, and enough to lead quickly into an examination syllabus if this is your eventual aim.

If time allows, you can experiment with what you have learned – and consolidate your learning – by tackling the passages in the Reading Practice section, most of which are typical examples of popular journalism. Each passage focuses on the new material covered by two chapters and should only be attempted after these have been completed. Do not make a written English translation but, at most, take a few notes and from these attempt to re-tell the contents (to yourself, to a teacher, or to someone learning with you) to check that you have grasped and can convey the sense of the passage. Any vocabulary not found in the German–English Mini-dictionary, which covers only the lessons themselves, is given below the passage concerned.

We hope you will enjoy *Hugo German in Three Months*, and we wish you success with your studies. If you would like to continue studying German, our Advanced German Course will develop and extend your fluency in both spoken and written German and contains reading passages from authentic sources, lively exercises, vocabulary lists and essential grammar notes.

ACKNOWLEDGEMENTS

The author would like to thank especially her husband John Martin, for many years Director of the Institute of Languages and Linguistics in the University of Kent at Canterbury, without whose help she could never have written *Hugo German in Three Months*. Thanks also to Naomi Laredo whose expert editing and calming influence in times of stress ensured that the text remained 'on course', and to those others who gave their encouragement and made comments on various drafts of this book.

Contents

Week 1   9

Speaking German
The alphabet and spelling
Spelling and pronunciation
Vowels
Consonants
The hiatus or stop
Stressed syllables
Punctuation

Week 2   25

Word endings and word order
Greetings, everyday phrases
'the' and gender
Plural of 'the'
Plural of nouns
Exercises and vocabulary

Week 3   32

'the' and case
Pronouns; 'I, me, we, us', etc
Useful verbs: 'to be',
  'to have' and 'to make'
Exercises, vocabulary &
  conversation

Week 4   39

'a/an' and gender
Numbers
Prices
The indirect object case
Verbs using the indirect object
  case
Exercises, vocabulary &
  conversation

Week 5   53

Asking questions
Negative sentences
Instructions and requests
Adjectives and adverbs
Exercises, vocabulary &
  conversation

Week 6   67

Prepositions; in, by, of, etc
The expression 'es gibt'
  ('there is/there are')
Exercises, vocabulary &
  conversation

Week 7   76

Words following the same pattern
  as 'der', 'die', 'das'
My, your, his, her, etc
Adjectives before nouns
Ordinal numbers, fractions
Conversation between friends
Word order
Exercises, vocabulary &
  conversation

Week 8   90

More on word order
Auxiliary verbs: will, can, must,
  may, etc
Using auxiliary verbs
Conversation
Measurements and quantities
The expressions 'es ist' and
  'es sind' ('there is/are')
Verbs expressing location
How to say 'put'
More about prepositions
Exercises and vocabulary

Week 9   107

More about 'der,' 'die', 'das'
Verbs: the present tense
Irregular verbs
The pre-present
The 'ge_(e)t' form
Time expressions, seasons,
   months, dates, time of day, etc
The expression 'nicht wahr?'
Exercises, vocabulary &
   conversation

Week 10   133

The possessor case
Prepositions taking the
   possessor case
Irregular masculine nouns
Using Type II verbs
'Zu' plus the infinitive
Expressing purpose
More useful expressions
The obverse process (passive)
More on the pre-present
Introducing the past tense
Exercises, vocabulary &
   conversation

Week 11   155

Quantifiers and identifiers
Making adjectives into
   nouns
Attached sentences
Joiners affecting word order
Reflexive pronouns
Reflexive verbs
Exercises, vocabulary &
   conversation

Week 12   179

More on the past tense
Verbs that change stem in the
   past tense
The pre-past ('I had been')
The oblique past tense
The conditional: 'if' sentences
More about the obverse process
Affective words
Exercises, vocabulary &
   conversation

Week 13   199

Translating the English '-ing' form
   ('by doing' 'in spite of doing')
Line-of-thought pointers
Conversation between intimates
Attached sentences with two
   '-en' forms
Impersonal expressions
The oblique present tense
Reported speech
Word order in reported speech
Enclosed attached sentences
Exercises, vocabulary &
   conversation

Reading practice 223

Hier geht es um die Wurst
London auf die Schnelle
Wein ist im Kommen
Versteigerung bei der Lufthansa
Leistungstest für deutsche
   Schulen
Jeder vierte Deutsche ist
   Allergiker
Die Sucht nach dem Handy
Erdbeeren: hoher
   Gesundheitswert
Größeres Drogen-Risiko
Reizende Leute
Was Männer abtörnt
Autoklau nahm deutlich ab
Unruhestand: jeder elfte
   Rentner geht zur Arbeit
Türkei diskriminiert Deutsche

Key to exercises 246

Mini-dictionary 253
German–English

Index 271

Week 1

- *the German alphabet and spelling*
- *pronunciation and its relation to the written language*
- *the hiatus or stop*
- *where the stress falls in German words*
- *German use of punctuation*

1 SPEAKING GERMAN

Although there are a few sounds in German which will be unfamiliar to you as a native speaker of English, on the whole English speakers find German easier to pronounce than French. Since the main thing is to be understood, don't worry if your pronunciation is less than perfect; to correct it, keep listening and practising, particularly with the CDs, which are an optional extra to this course. Some concepts introduced here will seem strange at first, but as you work through the course they will become familiar. You will find it worthwhile to refer back to Week 1 at frequent intervals for practice and revision.

2 THE ALPHABET AND SPELLING

1 The German alphabet contains all the 26 letters of the English alphabet. In addition, three of the vowel letters appear in the form **ä/Ä, ö/Ö, ü/Ü**, which represent entirely different sounds from the same letters without the 'umlaut' symbol (¨) above.

2 Note that double **ss** must be written **ß** (which never starts a word and occurs only as a small letter) when the preceding sound is either a long vowel (see section 4A) or a vowel combination (see section 4B):

Kuss	*but*	**Gruß**
floss	*but*	**Floß**
blass	*but*	**fraß**
	and	**Fleiß**
		Strauß
		äußern

1

3 All nouns, not just names, begin with capital letters. The pronoun **Sie**, the formal word for 'you' (see section 15), and related words (e.g. **Ihr** 'your') always begin with capitals. On the other hand, the first person singular pronoun ('I') starts with a small letter (**ich**).

4 Here are the letters of the alphabet with their names given in our imitated pronunciation, which is explained in the following sections. These are the names used when spelling out words.

A	a<u>h</u>	**J**	yot	**S**	es
B	b<u>eh</u>	**K**	k<u>ah</u>	**T**	t<u>eh</u>
C	ts<u>eh</u>	**L**	el	**U**	<u>oo</u>
D	d<u>eh</u>	**M**	em	**V**	fow
E	<u>eh</u>	**N**	en	**W**	v<u>eh</u>
F	ef	**O**	<u>oh</u>	**X**	iks
G	g<u>eh</u>	**P**	p<u>eh</u>	**Y**	**uep**sillon
H	h<u>ah</u>	**Q**	k<u>oo</u>	**Z**	tset
I	<u>ee</u>	**R**	e*er*		

3 SPELLING AND PRONUNCIATION

There is a greater consistency between spelling and pronunciation in German than in English. However, some letters are pronounced differently from the same letters in English, and some letters appear in unfamiliar combinations, so we need to mention these before looking at the sounds of German in detail. Try to say each of the examples in this section and in sections 4, 5, 6, and 7 aloud, preferably with the aid of the CDs.

Note that no English meanings are given for the examples in this first week of the course. We want you to concentrate on the sounds of the words, so resist the temptation to worry about meaning for the moment.

The following letters are pronounced differently from their English counterparts, or are subject to different rules of pronunciation depending on their position:

	Imitated pronunciation		
b	[b],	[p]	At the start of words and syllables
d	[d],	[t]	pronounced as in English. At the end
g	[g],	[k]	of words and syllables (standing either
	[*h*],	[*k*]	alone or in a cluster of consonants of

which they may not be the last) these letters MUST be pronounced as **p, t,** and **k** (or **ch**) respectively: this means that **habt** rhymes with **klappt**; that **wird** sounds exactly the same as **Wirt, Rad** like **Rat**; that **Erdöl** is spoken **Ert-öl**; and that **folg** could sound like **Volk, Krieg** like **kriech**. (All these words actually exist and some are therefore 'homophones': words spelt differently but sounding alike.)

c   Is used constantly in the combinations **ch** and **ck** but is rarely found on its own except in foreign words.

j   [y]   Is almost always spoken as English y at the start of a word (yet, yonder), thus **Junge, Jammer**.

q   Is always, as in English, in combination with **u**, but the combination is spoken differently, like English k + v in rapid succession, thus **quer, Quatsch, Qualität**.

s   [s],   [z]   Like the English s, it is pronounced in two different ways: like the s in 'sits' and 'its', and like the z sound in 'busy' and 'is'. However, distribution of the two types of **s** in German is exactly opposite to that in English. Whereas in English the s-sounding s occurs at the start of words (and syllables) and the z-sounding s is usually found at the end, German **s**

is always pronounced like z at the start of words (except in the combinations **sp** and **st**, see below), and like s at the end of words and syllables:

like z:
sein, Symbol, Absicht (Ab|sicht), Fürsorge (Für|sorge), Rose (Ro|se), Riese (Rie|se)

like s:
Gast, längst, Wespe (Wes|pe), Muster (Mus|ter), meins, meines (mei|nes)

Words containing both sounds:
süß, seins, seines (sei|nes), dieses (die|ses)

[sh]

s in the combinations **sp** and **st** at the start of words and syllables is pronounced like English 'sh':
Speck, spät, spülen, gespannt (ge|spannt), Stamm, sterben, Strecke, steigen, erstaunt (er|staunt), verstimmt (ver|stimmt), Anstand (An|stand).

th [t]

Is never like 'th' in 'this' or 'thing', but pronounced simply as t/**t**. Found only in words of foreign origin, for example:
Apotheke, Hypothek, Thymian, These.

tion [tsiohn]

Found only in the many 'imported' words ending in **-tion**, thus:
Station, Aktion, Funktion, Tradition.

v [f]

Is almost always like English f in 'from':
Vater, von, Verlag, bevor.

w [v]   Is like English v in 'very', for example: **was**, **Wein**, **Weg**, **Wirt**.

y [ue]   Is not like the English y in either 'yet' or 'very', but is pronounced like the German (short) vowel **ü** (see section 4), thus: **System**, **sympatisch**.

z [ts]   Is NEVER like the English z as in 'hazard', but like t + s spoken in rapid succession, almost simultaneously, often with no more than a trace of the t. Something similar is found in the usual English pronunciation of the name 'Mozart', though **z** can also start a word, where the sound seems very odd to speakers of English:
Zeit, zu, Zinsen, Zange, Zorn, zusammen, beizeiten, inzwischen (in|zwischen), Weizen (wei|zen), Schnauze (Schnau|ze), Konzert, Winzer, Geiz, Sitz, Franz, Holz, Harz, Lenz.

The appearance of consonants in unfamiliar groups, or in unfamiliar places in words, can make a written foreign language difficult for the eye to grasp. The following combinations contain only sounds that the English speaker can easily pronounce, so it is well worthwhile getting used to seeing the combinations as 'blocks' for which the right pronunciation is ready to hand.

dsch [dj]   Like the j in 'jump'. Quite rare and only used for some foreign words: **Dschungel, Dschihad, Dschunke.**

gd [kt]   Pronounced 'kt', like the end of 'flicked'. Rare, but the first example given is much used: **Jagd, Magd.**

hd, hl(t), hm(t), hn(t), hr(t), ht	Ignore the **h**, which merely shows that the preceding vowel is pronounced long (see section 4). Similarly ignore **h** between vowels, except in compounds: **Fehde, Mehl, wählt, lahm, rahmt, kühn, wohnt, wahr, lehrt, weht; sehen, ruhen** BUT **Seehafen (See|hafen), bleihaltig (blei|haltig).**
ng	There is no g sound in this combination when it occurs between vowels, so care is needed with words like **Anger, Finger, Hunger.**
pf	This can come at the beginning or end of words and syllables; p + f are spoken in rapid succession, almost simultaneously, often with no more than a trace of the p: **Pfeil, Pferd, Pfund, Dampfer, impfen, Kupfer, Sumpf, Krampf, glimpflich.**
sch, schl, schm, schn, schr, schw	**sch** is like 'sh' in 'shut', 'wish'. While **sch** can start or end words and syllables, combinations with the further consonant letter can only start them: **Schande, Rausch, Schlampe, schmelzen, Schnauze, Schraube, schwitzen.**
tsch [ch]	This is like '(t)ch' in 'chap', 'much', 'match'. It is found less at the start than in the middle or at the end of words: **tschüs, Tscheche, Matsch, futsch, Deutschland, Rutsch.**
tz [ts]	This only occurs in the middle or at the end of words. It is like the 'ts' in 'gets', or like German **z**: **plötzlich, platzen, sitzen, Fritz, Gesetz.**

zw [tsv] This is like t + s + v spoken in rapid succession and occurs only at the start of words and syllables:
Zwang, bezwingen (be|zwingen), Zwerg, zwei, inzwischen (in|zwischen), Zweck.

4 VOWELS AND VOWEL COMBINATIONS

Though there are only eight vowel letters in German (the five of the English alphabet, plus **ä, ö, ü**), there are potentially 16, in practice 15, vowel sounds, because each vowel letter has two pronunciations, a long and a short one. It is vital to note and produce this distinction, as the long–short contrast is accompanied by a difference in the nature of the sound. The spelling is sometimes an aid to knowing whether a vowel is long or short:

A vowel is long if:
- the vowel letter is doubled: **Beet, Saat, Boot**
- the vowel letter is followed by **h**:
  Bahn, Huhn, Lohn
- the vowel **i** is followed by **e**:
  fies, mies, Grieß
- the vowel letter is followed by **ß**:
  Maß, bloß, Muße, Füße, Blöße, Maße.

A vowel is short if:
- the vowel letter is followed by a doubled consonant letter or by **ck**:
  Hütte, Affe, Zweck
- the vowel letter is followed by **ss**:
  blass, Ross, muss
- the vowel letter is followed by **ng**:
  Rang, jung, ging.

All the following vowel descriptions in terms of English sounds are, of course, only approximations and no substitute for genuine models of pronunciation. One general, though impressionistic, guideline to help you to know what to aim at in the vowels is a greater tenseness and energy than with those of English.

Avoid at all costs substituting English vowel glides, where the nature of the vowel sound changes progressively (as in standard southern English 'lane' and 'home'), for any of the German single-sound vowels. It is for this reason that we use northern English vowels as benchmarks, especially for the German long vowels. Northern English vowels tend to have more of a single-sound quality than do those of standard southern English.

1 Vowels

long **a**   [ah]   Long **a** as the vowel in northern English 'father', 'barn'.

short **a**   [ah]   Short **a** as in northern English 'fat', 'track'.
**Bahn/Bann, Kahn/kann,
Wahn/wann, kam/Kamm,
mahn/Mann, Saat/satt**

long **e**   [eh]   Long **e** as the vowel in northern English 'lane', 'drape'.

short **e**   [e]   Short **e** as in standard southern English 'get', 'crept'.
**Beet/Bett, wen/wenn, den/denn,
hehl/hell, fehl/Fell, gehl/gell**

long **i(e)** [ee]   Long **i(e)** as the vowel in northern English 'keen', 'lean'.

short **i**   [i]   Short **i** as in standard southern English 'fit', 'clip'.
**ihm/im, schief/Schiff, Stil/still,
rief/Riff, siech/sich, mies/miss**

long **o**   [oh]   Long **o** as the vowel in northern English 'home', 'bone'.

short **o**	[o]	Short **o** as in standard southern English 'shot', 'crop'. **Hof/hoff, Ofen/offen, wohne/Wonne, Wohle/Wolle**
long **u**	[oo]	Long **u** as the vowel in northern English 'moon', 'doom'.
short **u**	[oo]	Short **u** as the vowel in standard southern English 'put', 'foot'. **Pute/Putte, Ruhm/Rum, Kruke/Krucke, Mus/muss**
long **ä**	[e]	Long **ä** similar to northern English vowel in 'lane', but more open in the direction of the vowel in standard southern English 'leg'.
short **ä**	[e]	Short **ä** exactly like short German **e**. **käme/Kämme, stähle/Ställe, Pfähle/Fälle, wähle/Wälle**
long **ö**	[oe]	For long **ö** say German long **e** while rounding and protruding the lips.
short **ö**	[oe]	For short **ö** say German short **e** while rounding and protruding the lips. Both are similar to the tight, pursed vowel of French 'oeuf'. **Höhle/Hölle, Flöße/flösse**
long **ü**	[ue]	For long **ü** say German long **i(e)** while rounding and protruding the lips.
short **ü**	[ue]	For short **ü** say German short **i** while rounding and protruding the lips. Both are similar to the tight, pursed vowel in French 'tu', 'une'. **Wüste/wüsste, Hüte/Hütte, fühlen/füllen, führst/Fürst**

2 Vowel combinations or glides

Vowel combinations are always pronounced long. All three glides resemble sounds from standard southern English, but they will sound much more German if you move your tongue (and jaw) more dramatically than for the matching English sounds.

ai/ei   [y]   Similar to the standard southern English glide in 'bribe', 'guide':
Hain, Mai, Kai, weiß, Kleid, weich.

au   [ow]   Similar to the standard southern English glide in 'cow', 'mouth':
Raum, Zaun, Maul, Haus, Haut, Raub.

äu/eu   [oy]   Similar to the standard southern English glide in 'void', 'annoy':
häuft, läuft, Säume, deutet, freut, neun.

(c)   Unstressed syllables containing **e** or **er**

[*e*]   Unstressed syllables containing the vowel letter **e** require a sound similar to that in English 'prop*er*ty', 'rel*a*tive', 'anem*o*ne', 'Sat*ur*day', but with a trace more of the short **e** described above:
Befund, Gericht, waagerecht, Hilferuf.

The same sound is required if the **e** ends a word; the final sound of English 'never', 'weather' is not quite right, because the jaw drops further, resulting in a sound closer to unstressed 'er':
Hilfe, welche, Menge, ihre.

Much the same sound is required if the **e** is followed by a consonant (other than **r**): **Hallenbad, Spiegelei, Dankesbrief, deutet.**

[*er*]   Unstressed syllables containing the letters **er** require a sound similar to that in standard southern English 'hut', 'clutch'; the **r** is NOT pronounced in this particular context: **Wiederkehr, Kinderwagen, Messerkante, besser, heller, ihrer.**

The same sound, only lengthened, is required if the **er** is followed by **n**. Again the **r** is not pronounced: **gestern, Brüdern, andernfalls, kentern.**

The distinction between **e** and **er**, between **en** and **ern**, is essential, since understanding correctly and being correctly understood depend on it. The following pairs show the contrast:
Ehe/eher, Feste/fester, Silbe/Silber, Güte/Güter, Lehren/Lehrern, wischen/Wischern, Wäschen/Wäschern.

5 CONSONANTS

You saw in section 3 that most of the consonants are straightforward for the English-speaking learner. The only three consonants that present any difficulty are: **ch**, **l**, and **r**.

ch   Although always using the same letters, this has two radically different versions, neither found in English:

(i)   [*h*]   After **e, ei, eu, i, ie, ä, äu, ü**, and after consonants: The best way to achieve the sound required is to whisper very forcefully words like 'Hugo', 'human', and then to use the initial sound of the h for German **ch**.

Blech, Reich, Seuche, mich, riechen, Bäche, Bäuche, Küche, Storch, Dolch, durch.

The same sound is used in three common words of foreign origin, **Chemie, China, Chirurg**, and at the start of the diminutive ending **-chen** ('little …'), no matter what precedes: **Mädchen, Riemchen, Häuschen, Küsschen, Gläschen, Frauchen.**

It is also a common pronunciation of the consonant letter **g**, either alone or with other consonants, when at the end of a word or syllable following any of the vowel and vowel-glide sounds listed above. It is thus an alternative to the pronunciation of such **g**'s as **k**'s (see section 3): **wichtig, grantig, Predigt, liegst, Zweig, gütig.**

(ii)   [k]   After **a, au, o, u**:
This is similar to the Scottish pronunciation of 'ch' in 'loch', 'Pitlochry', and is made by tensing the back of the throat while forcing plenty of breath through it: **auch, Bach, Suche, Loch, brauchen, Sucht, machen.**

The same sound is also a very common pronunciation of the consonant letter **g**, either alone or with other consonants, when at the end of a word or syllable following any of the vowel and

vowel-glide sounds listed above. It is thus another alternative to pronunciation of such **g**'s as **k**'s (see section 3):
Zug, wagt, mag, saugt, klug, flog, Sog, fragt.

l

Each English speaker has a range of pronunciations of l according to its position in a word and the sounds that surround it. German **l**, however, whatever its environment, is restricted to one type only. The closest parallels in standard southern English are the l sounds in 'clean', 'leek', 'language' (though even these are not totally right), whereas those in 'vault', 'feel', 'Oliver', 'culvert', 'apple' are very different from the German sound. Consequently it is the German **l** in such positions as these that needs the most care and practice:
lieb, leben, lang, laut, Leute; Klippe, Klang, Flamme, klug, Flucht; goldig, Walzer, älter, albern, ulkig; belebt, Brille, Rolle, völlig; fällig; Esel, fühl, voll, wohl, Stahl; wedelt, wählt, Silber, Felder, Helm.

r

The **r** sound, if pronounced at all, is best made at the back of the throat in the same place as **ch** (ii), but with much less breath force. No r sound found in standard southern English is really satisfactory.

r must be pronounced as a consonant:

- alone at the start of a word:
  Rand, rund, Rasen, Riese
- after another consonant at the start of a word:
  Frau, grün, Gras, Gruß

■ between vowels or vowel glides in the middle of words:
Beere, Fähre, Karre, mürrisch, waren.

r is not pronounced as a consonant but merely affects the preceding vowel sound, often lengthening it or turning it into a sort of vowel glide

■ alone at the end of a word or syllable:
besser, woher, war, klar, Herr, Meer, mehr, fror, gar, wurde, warte, würdig (Narr is an exception needing the consonant sound);
■ before another consonant at the end of a word or syllable:
Schwert, Wurst, Herz, warnte, horchte.

6 THE HIATUS OR STOP

Whereas in standard southern English the words in a phrase or sentence run into one another, so that a word beginning with a vowel appears to borrow the final consonant of the preceding word as a bridge, German does not allow this. Words beginning with a vowel have to start with the hiatus or 'stop'. This is not difficult to do – simply clear your throat gently in a whisper – but it is difficult to use. It is required even within a word, when the word is a compound of two or more words or contains a prefix before a vowel. The stop is also required to separate a vowel ending from a vowel beginning. For example:
mach * aus, im * Auge, hau * ab, Vor*arbeiter, miss*-achten, ge*einigt, im * Ofen, würde * ich * auch

Compare the pronunciation of **hau * ab** with the English 'How are you?', and **Vor*arbeiter** with 'for ages'.

Effective speech depends on copying the speech rhythms and tunes of the phrases and sentences of a language. However, as far as individual words are concerned, in German the stress usually falls on the first syllable, though there are many exceptions. One reliable rule is that whereas all English words starting with 'un-' are unstressed on that first syllable, such words in German have stress on the **un-:**
únglücklich, únerfahren, únfreundlich, úngeduldig

German creates many compound words out of smaller word-units. In these cases the stress is on the stressed syllable of the first word-unit:
kréideweiß, Pláttenspieler, Bríllenetui, Studéntenwohnheim (kreide|weiß, Platten|spieler, Brillen|etui, Studenten|wohn|heim)

Most of the exceptions to first-syllable stress are either words of foreign origin or words containing specifically unstressed first syllables or prefixes (see section 47B):

foreign words:
kontrollíeren, telefoníeren, Maschíne, Pakét, offiziéll

unstressed prefixes:
be|spréchen, miss|bráuchen, ver|ráten, ge|língen, er|röten

However, some short words in frequent use are also exceptions, while combinations with **da-** and **wo-** (see week 8, section 40 and week 11, section 63) are usually not stressed on the **da-** or **wo:**
jedóch, sogár, damít, dazú, danében, woráuf, inzwíschen

In our imitated pronunciation, the stressed syllable is always printed in bold type. Good dictionaries give reliable information about stress and also about the length of vowels.

8 PUNCTUATION

In some respects, German uses punctuation in a more formal way than English, so it is not possible to relate commas to speech pauses and meaning as in the following two examples:

My sister, who hates noise, was sent to a hotel next to a disco.
The girl who rang yesterday was a friend of my sister's.

In German, there would have to be commas following 'girl' and 'yesterday'.

The punctuation used for quoted speech is different from English usage (see week 13, section 80), and colons are used more often, to introduce short inserts into the middle of sentences, for example. Exclamation marks are also used more frequently than in English.

Week 2

- *greetings and useful everyday phrases*
- *word order in a German sentence*
- *how the word for 'the' ('der', 'die', 'das') varies according to the gender of the noun it refers to and whether it is singular or plural*
- *how to form the plurals of nouns*

9 WORD ENDINGS AND WORD ORDER

1 Words that in English never vary, like 'the' and 'a/an', and simple invariable suffixes, like adding 's' or 'es' for the plural ('dog/dogs', 'class/classes'), have no single equivalents in German but sets of equivalents.

2 The word order in a German sentence is often different from the word order in English. 'I can't find the key because it's too dark' would be 'I can the key not find because it too dark is' or 'The key can I not find because it too dark is' in German.

These two features mean that you have to think differently to speak, write, and understand German. To help you, we separate **1** and **2**, firmly establishing the principles behind **1** and then introducing **2** gradually from Week 7.

10 GREETINGS AND EVERYDAY PHRASES

All over Germany the most common greeting during the daytime is **Guten Tag!** (or, in the morning, **Guten Morgen!**). In the evening people say **Guten Abend!** In southern Germany and Austria **Grüß Gott!** is usual at any time of day. All these are often accompanied by a handshake, even within the family.

After the greeting, one person will often add **Wie geht's?** or **Wie geht's Ihnen?** ('How are you?'), to which the response is usually **Danke, gut**, or **Gut, danke**, or simply **Danke**.

2

IMITATED PRONUNCIATION

goo-ten t<u>a</u>hk; **goo**-ten **moer**-gen; **goo**-ten **ah**-bent; grues
got; v<u>ee</u> g<u>eh</u>ts <u>ee</u>-nen; **dahng**-ke g<u>oo</u>t

Exercise 1

Practise saying the sentences in this dialogue until you
know them by heart.

Two hard-up customers at a refreshment kiosk

KUNDE	Guten Tag!
BESITZERIN	Guten Tag! Bitte schön …?
KUNDE	Zwei Coca-Cola und eine Wurst mit Brot, bitte.
BESITZERIN	Was? Sie wollen zwei Cola aber nur eine Wurst?
KUNDE	Ja …, das heißt, ja und nein. Wie teuer ist eine Wurst?
BESITZERIN	Nur drei Euro.
KUNDE	Na gut, dann zwei Cola und zweimal Wurst mit Brot.
BESITZERIN	Bitte schön … Zehn Euro zusammen.
KUNDE	Danke schön. Auf Wiedersehen!
BESITZERIN	Auf Wiedersehen!

Translation

CUSTOMER	Hello!
PROPRIETRESS	Hello! Yes please …?
CUSTOMER	Two Coca-Colas and one sausage with bread, please.
PROPRIETRESS	What? You want two Colas but only one sausage?
CUSTOMER	Yes …, I mean yes and no. How much is a sausage?
PROPRIETRESS	Only three euros.
CUSTOMER	All right, then two Colas and two sausages with bread.
PROPRIETRESS	Here you are … Ten euros altogether.
CUSTOMER	Thank you. Goodbye!
PROPRIETRESS	Goodbye!

'THE' AND GENDER

German has a total of six words for 'the': **der, die, das, den, dem, des**, so it is best to think of the word as **d. .** plus a variable ending. The correct ending depends on three factors, one of which is gender.

All German nouns (naming words) are either masculine (m.), feminine (f.) or neuter (n.). Most nouns for male/female beings are masculine/feminine respectively, but this is not very useful as a guide. It is best to learn each noun with the appropriate **der, die**, or **das** in front of it, as shown in the following sentences:

der Junge (m.) ist krank (the boy is ill)
so **der Junge**
der Preis (m.) ist hoch (the price is high)
so **der Preis**
die Tante (f.) ist freundlich (the aunt is kind)
so **die Tante**
die Farbe (f.) ist dunkel (the colour is dark)
so **die Farbe**
das Kind (n.) ist nett (the child is nice)
so **das Kind**
das Haus (n.) ist alt (the house is old)
so **das Haus**

IMITATED PRONUNCIATION

de*er* **yoong**-*e* ist krahnk; de*er* prys; h*oh*k; d*ee* **tahn**-t*e*; **froynt**-li*h*; d*ee* **fah**-b*e*; **doong**-k*el*; dahs kint; net; dahs hows; ahlt

Exercise 2

Learn the lists of words in **A** about house and family, saying each word with 'der', 'die', or 'das' in front of it.

Then cover up the lists and say the jumbled sequence in **B** giving each word the correct 'der', 'die', 'das', and checking that you also know the meaning.

Finally cover up **B** as well and say the German words (preceded by 'der', 'die', or 'das') for the jumbled English list in **C**.

(NOTE: We shall not use this type of exercise again, but it is one that you will need to devise for yourself with each new set of words, week by week.)

A

m. (der)		f. (die)		n. (das)	
Mann	man/ husband	Frau	woman/ wife	Kind	child
				Mädchen	girl
Vater	father	Mutter	mother	Haus	house
Sohn	son	Tochter	daughter	Zimmer	room
Bruder	brother	Schwester	sister	Fenster	window
Wirt	landlord	Wirtin	landlady	Bett	bed
Tisch	table	Küche	kitchen	Wasser	water
Stuhl	chair	Tür	door	Auto	car
Schrank	cupboard	Zeitung	newspaper	Buch	book
Flur	hall	Uhr	clock	Messer	knife
Hund	dog	Katze	cat		

B

Auto, Fenster, Wirt, Uhr, Tochter, Haus, Flur, Messer, Tür, Hund, Küche, Katze, Bruder, Mann, Kind, Zeitung, Sohn, Schwester, Stuhl, Buch, Wirtin, Schrank, Frau, Bett, Vater, Zimmer, Mutter, Wasser, Mädchen, Tisch

C

book, knife, sister, door, newspaper, woman, room, landlord, car, table, water, clock, house, window, child, cupboard, girl, cat, kitchen, father, dog, brother, daughter, hall, mother, chair, son, man, landlady, bed

IMITATED PRONUNCIATION:

mahn; **fah**-ter; zohn; **broo**-der; viert; tish; shtool;
shrahnk; flooer; hoont; frow; **moo**-ter; **tok**ter; **shves**-ter;
vier-tin; **kue**-he; tueer; **tsy**-toong; ooer; **kaht**-se; kint;
met-hen; hows; **tsi**-mer; **fens**-ter; bet; **vah**-ser; **ow**-toh;
book; **me**-ser

12 PLURAL OF 'THE'

When the noun is in the plural (i.e. refers to more than
one), **die** is always used for 'the', regardless of gender:

die	**Preise sind hoch**	the	prices are high
	Farben sind dunkel		colours are dark
	Häuser sind alt		houses are old

Summary:

singular			plural
m.	f.	n.	m. f. n.
der	**die**	**das**	**die**

IMITATED PRONUNCIATION

deer; dee; dahs; dee

13 PLURAL OF NOUNS

You have seen in section 12 that though the plural **die** is
simple, the noun itself has no single way of showing the
plural. You must therefore learn each noun not only with
der, die, das, but also with its plural. There are a few
rough guidelines for emergency use:

1 Feminine nouns usually add **-n** or **-en** to the singular:

Küche→ Küchen	*but*	**Mutter→ Mütter**
Zeitung→ Zeitungen		**Tochter→ Töchter**
Frau→ Frauen		**Wirtin→ Wirtinnen**

2 Masculine and neuter nouns often add:

-e   **Hund→ Hunde**
-en   **Bett→ Betten**
-er   **Kind→ Kinder**

and any of these endings may be accompanied by a change in the sound of the following vowels:

-a-   **Mann→ Männer**
-o-   **Sohn→ Söhne**
-u-   **Stuhl→ Stühle**
-au- **Haus→ Häuser**

3 Some masculine and neuter nouns don't change at all:

Zimmer→ Zimmer
Messer→ Messer

4 With some masculine and neuter nouns the only change is in the vowel sound, which is changed by adding an umlaut:

Vater→ Väter
Bruder→ Brüder

5 Some words taken from other languages add **-s**:

Auto→ Autos

Exercise 3

A lists the words you learned in Exercise 2, but they are now shown first with the plural abbreviation used in dictionaries* and then in the full plural form. Learn these, then cover up **A** and try to say the plurals of all the jumbled singular words in **B**.

A			
Mann (¨er)	Männer	Frau (-en)	Frauen
Vater (¨)	Väter	Mutter (¨)	Mütter
Sohn (¨e)	Söhne	Tochter (¨)	Töchter
Bruder (¨)	Brüder	Schwester (-n)	Schwestern
Wirt (-e)	Wirte	Wirtin (-nen)	Wirtinnen
Tisch (-e)	Tische	Küche (-n)	Küchen
Stuhl (¨e)	Stühle	Tür (-en)	Türen
Schrank (¨e)	Schränke	Zeitung (-en)	Zeitungen
Flur (-e)	Flure	Uhr (-en)	Uhren
Hund (-e)	Hunde	Katze (-n)	Katzen
Kind (-er)	Kinder	Bett (-en)	Betten
Mädchen (-)	Mädchen	Wasser	No plural
Haus (¨er)	Häuser	Auto (-s)	Autos
Zimmer (-)	Zimmer	Buch (¨er)	Bücher
Fenster (-)	Fenster	Messer (-)	Messer

*In later word lists and in the Mini-dictionary at the back of this book, the plural of each noun is given by the appropriate abbreviation in brackets.

B Auto, Fenster, Wirt, Uhr, Tochter, Haus, Flur, Messer, Tür, Hund, Küche, Katze, Bruder, Mann, Kind, Zeitung, Sohn, Schwester, Stuhl, Buch, Wirtin, Schrank, Frau, Bett, Vater, Zimmer, Mutter, Mädchen, Tisch

IMITATED PRONUNCIATION

me-ner; **fe**-ter; **zoe**-ne; **brue**-der; **vier**-te; **ti**-she; **shtue**-le; **shreng**-ke; **floo**-re; **hoon**-de; **frow**-en; **mue**-ter; **toeh**-ter; **shves**-tern; **vier**-ti-nen; **kue**-hen; **tue**-ren **tsy**-toong-en; **oo**-ren; **kaht**-sen; **kin**-der; **met**-hen; **hoy**-zer; **tsi**-mer; **fens**-ter; **be**-ten; **ow**-tohs; **bue**-her; **me**-ser

Week 3

■ the important principle of 'case' in the German language
■ more about the German word for 'the'
■ the pronouns 'I' and 'me', 'we' and 'us', etc
■ the present tense of 'to be' ('sein') and 'to have' ('haben')
■ the present tense of verbs which follow a regular pattern

3

14 'THE' AND CASE

You have seen that the choice of **der**, **die**, or **das** is affected by:
1 gender (m./f./n.)
2 number (singular/plural)

The third factor determining the choice is case, which means the function of a noun in the sentence. Compare:

A **Der Hund ist harmlos.** The dog is harmless.
B **Der Junge liebt den Hund.** The boy loves the dog.

In A it is the dog that *is* or *does* something, while in B it is the boy that *is* or *does* something, and the dog has become the thing *affected* by this.

The 'be-er' or 'doer' is called the 'subject' of a sentence, and the thing directly affected is the 'direct object'. We shall need to use these terms often, so will use the abbreviations SU for subject and DO for direct object.

In A, **der Hund** is the subject (SU); in B, **der Junge** is the subject and **den Hund** is the direct object (DO) .

Note the change from **der** to **den**. This change, required when a m. noun is used as DO instead of SU, does not apply to singular f. and n. nouns or to plural nouns.

	singular			plural
	m.	f.	n.	m. f. n.
SU	**der**	**die**	**das**	**die**
DO	**den**	**die**	**das**	**die**

15 PRONOUNS: 'I, ME, WE, US, YOU,' ETC

	1st person		2nd pers.	3rd person			
case SU	**ich**	**wir**	**Sie***	**er**	**sie**	**es**	**sie**
	I	we	you	he	she	it	they
case DO	**mich**	**uns**	**Sie***	**ihn**	**sie**	**es**	**sie**
	me	us	you	him	her	it	them

*Except when addressing children, family, friends and animals (see sections 31 and 76).

IMITATED PRONUNCIATION

d_ehn_; i_h_; mi_h_; v_eee_r; oons; z_ee_; e_er_; _een_; z_ee_; es; z_ee_

16 USEFUL VERBS: 'TO BE', 'TO HAVE' AND 'TO MAKE'

In order to make sentences, we need verbs (process words) as well as nouns and pronouns. **Sein** ('to be') and **haben** ('to have') are irregular verbs, which means they do not follow a set pattern. However, **machen** ('to make') is a model for all standard German verbs. Here are the different verb forms needed to form the present tense (e.g. 'I work', 'I am working', 'I do work').

1 to be, **sein**

I am	**ich bin**
we are	**wir sind**
you are	**Sie sind**
they are	**sie sind**
he is	**er ist**
she is	**sie ist**
it is	**es ist**

2 to have, **haben**

I have	**ich habe**
we have	**wir haben**
you have	**Sie haben**
they have	**sie haben**
he has	**er hat**
she has	**sie hat**
it has	**es hat**

3 to make, **machen**

I make	**ich mache**
we make	**wir machen**
you make	**Sie machen**
they make	**sie machen**
he makes	**er macht**
she makes	**sie macht**
it makes	**es macht**

Verbs are found in a dictionary, and in the Mini-dictionary, in the form stem + **en**, e.g. **mach** + **en**→ **machen**. To make the present tense of most verbs, you simply take the stem and add these endings:

1st person	singular	(I ...)	**-e**
1st person	plural	(we ...)	**-en**
2nd person	singular	(you ...)	**-en**
2nd person	plural	(you ...)	**-en**
3rd person	plural	(they ...)	**-en**
3rd person	singular	(he, etc ...)	**-t**
			-et for stems ending in **-d** or **-t**

IMITATED PRONUNCIATION

zyn; bin; zint; ist; **h<u>ah</u>-**ben; **h<u>ah</u>-**be; haht; **mah-**_ke_n; **mah-**_ke_; mah_k_t; (Ex. 4) **lee**-ben; **kow-**fen; **mah-**_ke_n; **h<u>oh</u>-**len; **roo-**fen; ko-men; **bring-**en; **tring-**ken

Exercise 4

A Learn the following verbs and then translate the sentences in **B**:

lieben	to love
kaufen	to buy
machen	to make
holen	to fetch
rufen	to call
kommen	to come
bringen	to bring
trinken	to drink

B Translate into German:

1 The father loves the landlady.

2 It is harmless!

3 He buys the newspaper.

4 She makes the beds.

5 The daughter fetches the car.

6 She calls the cat and the dog.

7 The cat and the dog come.

8 The landlady brings water.

9 Father, landlady, daughter, dog and cat drink the water.

3

VOCABULARY

Practise all the sentences in the conversation that follows until you know them by heart. These are new words:

	Entschuldigung!	Excuse me!
	suchen	to look for
die	**Touristeninformation**	tourist information office
	liegen	to be (situated)
	am	in/on the
der	**Theaterplatz**	Theatre Square
	wie?	how?
	dahin	(to) there

	nicht	not
	leicht	easy
	Moment mal	just a moment
	gehen	to go
	über	over, across
die	**Kreuzung (-en)**	crossroads
	zweite	second
die	**Straße (-n)**	street
	rechts	on the right
der	**Marktplatz (¨e)**	marketplace
	sehen	to see
	dann	then
die	**Kirche (-n)**	church
das	**Gasthaus (¨er)**	inn
die	**Rose (-n)**	rose
	nehmen	to take
	zwischen	between
	eins	one
	zwei	two
	drei	three
	vierte	fourth
	immer geradeaus	straight ahead
	für	for
	etwa	about
	fünfhundert	five hundred
der	**Meter (-)**	metre
	finden	to find
	sofort	immediately
	furchtbar	terribly
	schwierig	difficult
	es macht nichts	it doesn't matter
	um	at (time of day)
	dieser	this
die	**Zeit (-en)**	time
	sowieso	anyway
	geschlossen	closed

IMITATED PRONUNCIATION

ent-**shool**-di-goonk; **zoo**-k*en*; d*ee* t*oo*-**ris**-t*en**in-fo*e*-mah-
tsi*oh*n; **lee**-g*en*; ahm; d*eer* t*eh*-**ah**-t*er*-plahts; v*ee*;
dah-**hin**; ni*h*t; ly*h*t; m*oh*-**ment** mahl; **geh**-*en*; **ue**-b*er*;
d*ee* **kroy**-tsung; **tsvy**-t*e*; d*ee* **shtrah**-s*e*, r*eh*ts; d*eer*
mahkt-plahts; **zeh**-*en*; dahn; d*ee* **kee***er*-*he*, dahs
gahst-hows; d*ee* **roh**-z*e*; **neh**-m*en*; **tsvi**-sh*en*; yns; tsvy;
dry; **fee***er*-t*e*; **i**-m*er* ge-**rah**-de***ows**; f*uee*r; **et**-vah;
fuenf-hoon-d*er*t; d*eer* **meh**-t*er*; **fin**-d*en*; z*oh*-**fo***er*t;
foo*er*ht-b*ah*; **shvee**-ri*h*; es mah*k*t ni*h*ts; oom; d*ee*-z*er*;
d*ee* tsyt; **zoh**-**vee**-z*oh*; ge-**shlo**-s*en*

3

CONVERSATION

An encounter in the street

TOURISTIN **Entschuldigung! ... ich suche die
Touristeninformation.**
PASSANT **Ja ... die liegt am Theaterplatz.**
TOURISTIN **Und wie komme ich dahin?**
PASSANT **Das ist nicht so leicht .... Moment mal ....
Sie gehen über die Kreuzung, zweite Straße
rechts, über den Marktplatz. Sie sehen
dann die Kirche und das Gasthaus Zur
Rose. Sie nehmen die Straße zwischen
Gasthaus und Kirche, dann ... eins ... zwei
... drei ... ja, dann die vierte Straße rechts,
dann immer geradeaus für etwa
fünfhundert Meter. Sie finden dann sofort
den Theaterplatz.**
TOURISTIN **O, das ist furchtbar schwierig!**
PASSANT **Es macht nichts, die Touristeninformation
ist um diese Zeit sowieso geschlossen.**

3

An encounter in the street

TOURIST   Excuse me … I'm looking for the tourist information office.

PASSER-BY   Oh … that's in Theatre Square.

TOURIST   And how do I get there?

PASSER-BY   That's not so easy …. Just a moment …. You go over the crossroads, second street on the right, across the marketplace. You'll then see the church and the Rose Inn. You take the street between (the) inn and (the) church, then … one … two … three … yes, then the fourth street on the right, then straight ahead for about five hundred metres. You'll then find (the) Theatre Square immediately.

TOURIST   Oh, that's terribly difficult!

PASSER-BY   It doesn't matter, the information office is closed at this time anyway.

Week 4

- *the German words for 'a/an' and 'not a/an', and how they vary with the gender and case of the noun*
- *numbers from zero to a million*
- *how to talk about years and prices*
- *the 'indirect object' case*
- *some verbs that are used with the indirect object case*

17 'A/AN'

German uses the same word for 'a/an' as it does for 'one': **ein**. When **ein** is used to mean 'a/an' (or 'one' before nouns, e.g. 'one cup'), it has the following endings:

	m.	f.	n.
SU	ein	eine	ein
DO	einen	eine	ein

Used like this, **ein** has no plural as its meaning is singular by definition. As in English, sometimes the plural noun is used alone. Other times the noun is preceded by words like **einige** ('some'), **mehrere** ('several'), or **ein paar** ('a few'). These words are always found in the same form, without changing endings.

Wir haben ⎡ **Freunde**
⎢ **einige Freunde** ⎤ **hier.**
⎢ **mehrere Freunde**
⎣ **ein paar Freunde** ⎦

ein has a parallel, **kein**, which means 'not a/not an' or 'no…'. This naturally does have a plural (cf. 'no friends').

	singular			plural
	m.	f.	n.	m. f. n.
SU	kein	keine	kein	keine
DO	keinen	keine	kein	keine

Whereas in English we say, for example, 'I haven't any friends', in German the expression is **Ich habe keine Freunde**. Therefore **kein** is in constant use, as the following examples show (the phrases in brackets give the literal meanings):

Wir trinken kein Bier.
We don't drink beer. (We drink no beer.)
Ich habe keine Ahnung.
I haven't a clue. (I have no clue/no idea.)
Kein Mensch glaubt so etwas.
Nobody would believe anything like that. (No person believes such a thing.)
Sie hat Angst, aber er hat keine Angst.
She is afraid but he is not. (She has fear but he has no fear.)
Er hat keinen Beruf.
He isn't trained for anything. (He has no profession/trade.)
Wir sind keine Anfänger.
We aren't beginners. (We are no beginners.)

Saying what someone's job is does not involve using **ein**. Stating what someone's job is *not* is usually done with **nicht** ('not'):

Die Mutter ist Lehrerin.
The mother is a teacher.
Er ist nicht Zahnarzt, er ist Kinderarzt.
He's not a dentist, he's a paediatrician.

Exercise 5

Translate the following sentences into German. You will need these new words:

	bauen	to build
die	Wohnung (-en)	flat
das	Problem (-e)	problem
	installieren	to install
das	Wassersystem (-e)	water system
die	Elektrizität	electricity
der	Elektriker (-)	electrician
die	Katastrophe (-n)	catastrophe

4

1 They are buying a house and making flats.

2 One flat hasn't got a kitchen.

3 That's a problem and they are building a kitchen.

4 One flat hasn't any water.

5 That's also a problem but the father is installing a water system.

6 One flat hasn't got electricity.

7 That's no problem. The son is an electrician.

8 One flat has a kitchen, water, electricity, and some cupboards, but no windows.

9 That's not a problem, it's a catastrophe.

IMITATED PRONUNCIATION

bow-*e*n; d<u>ee</u> **voh**-noong; dahs prob-**lehm**;
in-stah-**lee**-r*e*n; dahs **vah**-s*e*r-zues-t<u>ehm</u>;
d<u>ee</u>*e-lek-tri-tsi-**tet**; de*er**e-**lek**-tri-k*e*r,
d<u>ee</u> kah-tahs-**troh**-f*e*

First learn to count from 0 to 10. **Null** is needed mainly when citing decimals or reading out single digits (as sometimes in telephone numbers).

0	null	6	sechs
1	eins	7	sieben
2	zwei	8	acht
3	drei	9	neun
4	vier	10	zehn
5	fünf		

Now count up to 20. Always stress the first syllable.

11 elf
12 zwölf
13 dreizehn
14 vierzehn
15 fünfzehn
16 sechzehn (note that the **-s** of **sechs** disappears)
17 siebzehn (note that the **-en** of **sieben** vanishes)
18 achtzehn
19 neunzehn
20 zwanzig

Next count from 21 to 30. Be careful to stress the first syllable. Note that the units precede the tens and are joined to them by **und**.

21 einundzwanzig
22 zweiundzwanzig
23 dreiundzwanzig
24 vierundzwanzig
25 fünfundzwanzig
26 sechsundzwanzig (because this means 'six-and-twenty' the **-s** of **sechs** has returned!)
27 siebenundzwanzig (the **-en** is back)
28 achtundzwanzig
29 neunundzwanzig
30 dreißig

Now count from 10 to 100 in tens.

10	zehn
20	zwanzig
30	dreißig
40	vierzig
50	fünfzig
60	sechzig (note that the -s is lost again)
70	siebzig (the -en of sieben is again lopped off)
80	achtzig
90	neunzig
100	hundert

Then learn the following examples combining units and tens. Because you are saying isolated numbers, instead of counting in sequence, the stress is always on the second-to-last syllable.

31	einunddreißig
42	zweiundvierzig
53	dreiundfünfzig
64	vierundsechzig
66	sechsundsechzig
75	fünfundsiebzig
77	siebenundsiebzig
86	sechsundachtzig
97	siebenundneunzig

Beyond 100, any written number below the millions appears as one word. There is hardly ever an **und** after the hundreds in German and never in sequence counting. The units and tens appear in the reverse order to English, with **und** in between. However long the number, a number spoken in isolation has the stress on the normally stressed syllable of its final component (300 **dreihúndert**, 507 **fünfhundertsíeben**, 629 **sechshundertneunundzwánzig**).

Practise saying these examples:

101	**hunderteins,** (or, less usually) **einhunderteins**
212	**zweihundertzwölf**
323	**dreihundertdreiundzwanzig**
434	**vierhundertvierunddreißig**
545	**fünfhundertfünfundvierzig**
656	**sechshundertsechsundfünfzig**
666	**sechshundertsechsundsechzig**
767	**siebenhundertsiebenundsechzig**
777	**siebenhundertsiebenundsiebzig**
878	**achthundertachtundsiebzig**
989	**neunhundertneunundachtzig**

Now count in hundreds from 100 to 1000:

100	**(ein)hundert**
200	**zweihundert**
300	**dreihundert**
400	**vierhundert**
500	**fünfhundert**
600	**sechshundert**
700	**siebenhundert**
800	**achthundert**
900	**neunhundert**
1,000	**tausend**

A million is **eine Million (-en)**, so the figure 5,723,926 would be spoken: **fünf Millionen siebenhundertdrei- undzwanzigtausendneunhundertsechsundzwanzig.** A number of more than four figures is separated in thousands by thin spaces, not by commas (e.g. 2 344). Note also (section 19) that a comma is used for the decimal point in German (e.g. 3,06).

Years before 2000 are designated, as in English, using only hundreds, so 1992 is **neunzehnhundertzweiund- neunzig**. 2005, however, is **zweitausendfünf**. 'The 1920s' is **die zwanziger Jahre**, 'the 1980s' **die achtziger Jahre**, with the ending **-er** added on to the cardinal number. Unlike most endings this one never changes. All the numbers given here can be used both in counting (1, 2, 3, etc) and as single items in front of nouns ('fifty pages', **fünfzig Seiten**), without any change. The sole exceptions are any numbers ending in **-eins**, where the **-s** is dropped before a noun:

'The book has 201 pages' is either
A **Das Buch hat zweihundertundeine Seite.**
or
B **Das Buch hat zweihundert(und)ein Seiten.**

In A the **-ein** is given the f. singular ending **-e** and the noun is singular; in B the **-ein** is left without ending, the **und** can be dropped as in sequence counting, and the noun is plural.

Cardinal numbers are usually followed by a plural noun, but there are common exceptions, such as units of currency (see section 19) and of measurement (see section 36).

IMITATED PRONUNCIATION

nool, yns, tsvy, dry, feeer, fuenf, zeks, **zee**-ben, ah*k*t, noyn, tsehn; elf, tsvoelf, **dry**-tsehn, **fee**er-tsehn, **fuenf**-tsehn, **zeh**-tsehn, **zeep**-tsehn, **ah***k*t-tsehn, **noyn**-tsehn, **tsvahn**-tsi*h*; **yn***oont-tsvahn-tsi*h*, **tsvy***oont-tsvahn-tsi*h*, …; **dry**-si*h*, **fee**er-tsi*h*, **fuenf**-tsi*h*, **zeh**-tsi*h*, **zeep**-tsi*h*, **ah***k*t-tsi*h*, **noyn**-tsi*h*, **hoon**-d*e*rt; hoon-d*e*rt***yns**; **tow**-z*e*nt; **y**-n*e* mi-li-**yohn**

19 | PRICES

The basic unit of German currency is the **Euro** (m.), which is divided into 100 **Cent** (m.). Though often preceded by cardinal numbers, **Euro** and **Cent** are hardly ever found in the plural. Price tags are usually written, and the sums spoken, as follows:

written	spoken
€0,55 *or* **55 Cent**	**fünfundfünfzig Cent**
€1,20	**ein Euro zwanzig** **eins zwanzig** (equally common) **ein Euro und zwanzig Cent** (less common)
€4,85	**vier Euro fünfundachtzig** **vier fünfundachtzig** **vier Euro und fünfundachtzig** **Cent**

Price tags are sometimes more explicit, for example:

written	spoken and meaning
Kilo €4,80	**vier Euro achtzig das Kilo** €4,80 per kilo
Pfd €2,40	**zwei Euro vierzig das Pfund** €2.40 per pound (the German pound = 500 grams)
Stück €3,00 **Stck €3,00**	**das Stück drei Euro** *or* **drei Euro das Stück** €3.00 for one item or each

You ask how much things cost as follows:

Was kostet das?
or **Wie teuer ist das?**
How much is that?

Was kosten die Kartoffeln?
or **Wie teuer sind die Kartoffeln?**
How much are the potatoes?

IMITATED PRONUNCIATION

tsent; **yn**-oy-r<u>oh</u>; dahs keelo; dahs pfoont; dahs shtuek

Exercise 6

1 Ein Buch kostet €12,80 (zwölf Euro achtzig).
Zwei Bücher kosten €25,60 (fünfundzwanzig
Euro sechzig).

Now continue the pattern with the following, writing
out the missing sentences and giving the prices in
figures and words:

2 Ein Brot kostet €2,50 (zwei Euro fünfzig).
Zwei …

3 Eine Wurst kostet €1,50 (ein Euro fünfzig).
Zwei …

4 Eine Uhr kostet €85,00 (fünfundachtzig Euro).
Zwei …

5 Eine Zeitung kostet €1,75 (ein Euro
fünfundsiebzig).
Zwei …

6 Ein Bett kostet €344,00 (dreihundert
vierundvierzig Euro).
Zwei …

7 Ein Schrank kostet €505,00 (fünfhundertfünf
Euro).
Zwei …

8 Ein Messer kostet €3,60 (drei Euro sechzig).
Zwei …

9 Eine Rose kostet €2,15 (zwei Euro fünfzehn).
Zwei …

10 Ein Auto kostet €18 000,00 (achtzehntausend
Euro).
Zwei …

20 THE INDIRECT OBJECT CASE

The English sentence 'I am lending him it' has not one but two objects: 'it' denotes the item directly affected by the process 'am lending' and is the direct object, while 'him' denotes the recipient or beneficiary of the verb, so may be called the indirect object (IO). In English we are hardly aware of the IO as a case, since we either use words like 'to' or 'for' to indicate a recipient, or just let the noun stand alone.

I am lending him it.
I am lending it to my friend.
I am lending the book to my friend.
I am lending my friend the book.

German speakers, however, have a strong sense of case, and the indirect object (IO) has a distinctive set of words for 'the', '(not) a/an', and 'no', as well as a separate set of pronouns.

1 '(to/for) the, (not) a/an, no'

	singular			plural
	m.	f.	n.	m. f. n.
IO	dem	der	dem	den
IO	(k)einem	(k)einer	(k)einem	keinen

2 Indirect object pronouns

IO	mir	uns	Ihnen	ihm	ihr	ihm	ihnen
(to/for)	me	us	you	him/ it (m.)	her/ it (f.)	it (n.)	them

Summary of SU, DO, and IO cases for 'the', '(not) a/an', and 'no':

	singular			plural
	m.	f.	n.	——
SU	der	die	das	die
	(k)ein	(k)eine	(k)ein	keine

DO	den	die	das	die
	(k)einen	(k)eine	(k)ein	keine
IO	dem	der	dem	den
	(k)einem	(k)einer	(k)einem	keinen

Summary of SU, DO, and IO cases for pronouns:

	1st pers. sing.	plural	2nd pers.	3rd pers. singular m.	f.	n.	plural
SU	ich	wir	Sie	er	sie	es	sie
DO	mich	uns	Sie	ihn	sie	es	sie
IO	mir	uns	Ihnen	ihm	ihr	ihm	ihnen

It may help to note that, with **der, die, das,** etc, **(k)ein,** and the pronouns, the m. and n. singular IO case always ends with the letter **m**; that the f. singular IO case always ends with the letter **r**; and that the plural IO case of **der, die, das,** and **kein,** along with the 2nd person and the 3rd person plural pronouns, all end with the letters **en**.

IMITATED PRONUNCIATION

de*er*, yn, kyn; d<u>eh</u>n, **y**-n*en*, k**y**-nen; d<u>eh</u>m, **y**-n*em*, k**y**-nem; d<u>ee</u>, **y**-n*e*, k**y**-n*e*; de*er*, **y**-n*er*, k**y**-n*er*; dahs, yn, kyn; ... i*h*, mi*h*, m<u>ee</u>*er*; v<u>ee</u>*er*, oons; z<u>ee</u>, **ee**-nen; e*er*, <u>ee</u>n, <u>ee</u>m; z<u>ee</u>, <u>ee</u>*er*; es, <u>ee</u>m

21 VERBS USING THE IO CASE

Apart from verbs like:

bringen	to bring (someone something)
geben	to give (someone something)
schenken	to give (someone something) as a present
wünschen	to wish (someone something)

which may relate to both a direct object and an indirect object, German has some verbs which, if they have an object that is human, require this to be an indirect object.

For example:

begegnen	to meet (someone)
helfen	to help (someone)
gefallen	to please (someone)
glauben	to believe (someone)
verzeihen	to forgive (someone)
raten	to advise (someone)

IMITATED PRONUNCIATION

bring-en; **geh**-ben; **sheng**-ken; **vuen**-shen; be-**gehg**-nen; **hel**-fen; ge-**fah**-len; **glow**-ben; fer-**tsy**-en; **rah**-ten

Exercise 7

Rewrite the following sentences, substituting the nouns in brackets for those that precede them and making the other changes needed. The words that have to be changed are in *italic*.

Ich bringe *meiner Mutter* (Vater) *eine Zeitung* (Buch).

Ich gebe *sie ihr* in *der Küche* (Flur).

Ich schenke *meiner Schwester* (Bruder) *eine Katze* (Hund) und wünsche *ihr* einen guten Tag.

VOCABULARY

Study the conversation that follows until you know all the sentences (and their meaning) by heart. These are new words:

	heute Abend	this evening
	eingeladen	invited (out)
	man	one
	netten	nice
die	**Dame (-n)**	lady
	rote	red

	bestimmt	definitely
	gut	fine
	wieviele?	how many?
	sollen	shall, is to, are to
	ach!	oh!
	verheiratet	married
	vielleicht	perhaps
	nie	never
	wieso denn?	why is that?
	bedeuten	to mean
	gelbe	yellow
die	Nelke (-n)	carnation
	bitte schön!	there you are! you're welcome!
	viel Spaß!	(have) a nice time!

4

IMITATED PRONUNCIATION

hoy-*te****ah**-b*e*nt; **yn**-g*e*-**lah**-d*e*n; mahn; **ne**-t*e*n; d*ee*
dah-m*e*; **roh**-*te*; b*e*-**shtimt**; goot; v*ee*-**fee**-l*e*; **zo**-l*e*n;
ah*k*; f*e*r-**hy**-*r*ah-t*e*t, **fee**-ly*h*t; n*ee*; v*ee*-**zoh** d*e*n;
b*e*-**doy**-t*e*n; **gel**-b*e*; d*ee* **nel**-k*e*; **bi**-*te* sh*oe*n; f*ee*l
shp**ah**s

CONVERSATION

A problem of etiquette at the florist's

KUNDE **Ich bin heute Abend eingeladen. Was
schenkt man einer netten Dame?**
BESITZERIN **Moment bitte .... Ich helfe Ihnen sofort.
Rote Rosen gefallen ihr bestimmt.**
KUNDE **Wie teuer sind rote Rosen?**
BESITZERIN **Sie kosten ein Euro fünfzig das Stück.**
KUNDE **Gut, ich nehme Rosen.**
BESITZERIN **Wieviele sollen es sein? ... fünf ... sieben ...
neun ...?**

KUNDE	**Geben Sie mir fünf Stück bitte? ... Ach ja, bringe ich ihrem Mann auch etwas?**
BESITZERIN	**Was!? Die Dame ist verheiratet!!?? Rote Rosen gefallen ihr vielleicht, aber ihr Mann verzeiht Ihnen nie, glauben Sie mir.**
KUNDE	**Wieso denn?**
BESITZERIN	**Rote Rosen bedeuten Liebe. Ich rate Ihnen, schenken Sie ihr gelbe Nelken .... Bitte schön .... Ich wünsche Ihnen viel Spaß heute abend!**

TRANSLATION

CUSTOMER	I am invited out this evening. What does one give a nice lady?
PROPRIETRESS	Just a moment please ... I'll help you straight away. Red roses will definitely please her.
CUSTOMER	How much are red roses?
PROPRIETRESS	They cost one euro fifty each.
CUSTOMER	Fine, I'll take roses.
PROPRIETRESS	How many is it to be? ... five ... seven ... nine?
CUSTOMER	Will you give me five please? ... Oh yes, shall I take something for her husband too?
PROPRIETRESS	What!? The lady is married!!?? Red roses will perhaps please her, but her husband will never forgive you, believe me!
CUSTOMER	Why is that?
PROPRIETRESS	Red roses mean love. I advise you, give her yellow carnations .... There you are .... I wish you a pleasant time this evening!

Week 5

- *how to ask questions and give instructions*
- *question words such as 'who?', 'when?', and 'why?'*
- *using 'nicht' ('not') to make negative sentences*
- *word order in instructions and requests*
- *some common descriptive words (adjectives and adverbs)*
- *comparatives and superlatives (e.g. 'old, older, oldest')*

22 ASKING QUESTIONS

1 When the answer is expected to be **ja** ('yes') or
nein ('no')

To ask a question requiring a 'yes' or 'no' answer, simply
begin with the verb and follow immediately with the SU:

Ist er Elektriker?
Is he an electrician?
Kommt er heute?
Is he coming today?
Kommt er oft?
Does he come often?
Hat sie Geschwister?
Has she (got)(any) brothers and sisters?
Arbeiten sie?
Are they working?

2 When the answer is expected to be a piece of
information

To ask a question requiring particular information in the
answer, start with the appropriate question word:

was?	what?
wie?	how?
wo?	where?
wer?	who?
wen?	who(m)?
wem?	who(m) to/for?
wann?	when?
warum?	why?

Follow this with the verb, then with the SU, except when the SU is the question word itself, as is sometimes the case with **wer?** and **was?** (e.g. questions marked with an asterisk below):

Was kosten die Kartoffeln?
What do the potatoes cost?
Was macht das?
How much is that?
*Was kommt jetzt?
What is coming now?
Wie fahren Sie?
How are you travelling (i.e. by what means)?
Wie heißt der Sohn?
What is the son's name? (literally: How is the son called?)
Wo wohnt die Freundin?
Where does the girlfriend live?
*Wer wohnt hier?
Who lives here?
Wer ist der Besitzer?
Who is the proprietor?
Wen kennt der Junge?
Who(m.) does the boy know?
Wem bringt er die Blumen?
Who(m.) is he taking the flowers to?
Wann fahren wir?
When are we travelling (i.e. when do we leave)?

This list of question-words is not exhaustive.

IMITATED PRONUNCIATION

ist * e*er* * e-**lek**-tri-k*er*; komt * e*er* **hoy**-t*e*; komt * e*er* * oft; haht z*ee* ge-**shvis**-t*er*; **ah**-by-t*e*n z*ee*; vahs; v*ee*; v*oh*; v*eer*; v*e*hn; v*e*hm; vahn; vah-**room**; vahs **kos**-t*e*n d*ee* k*ah*-**to**-f*e*ln; vahs mah*k*t dahs; vahs komt yetst; v*ee* **fah**-r*e*n z*ee*; v*ee* hyst d*er* z*oh*n; v*oh* vohnt d*ee* **froyn**-din; v*eer* v*oh*nt he*eer*; v*eer* * ist d*er* be-**zit**-s*er*; v*e*hn kent d*er* **yoong**-*e*; v*e*hm bringt * e*er* d*ee* **bloo**-m*e*n; vahn **fah**-r*e*n v*eeer*

NOTES

1 If the person you are asking does not know the answer, a typical response might be:

Ich weiß (es) nicht.   I don't know.

The use of **nicht** is explained in section 23.

2 Questions in German are often used as a way of making polite requests. They may take the same form as the English 'Would you …?' (see section 69) or be more direct, in a form that would be considered rude in English:

Geben Sie mir bitte die Zeitung?
Will you give me the paper, please?
(literally: Are you giving me the paper, please?)
Reichen Sie bitte den Zucker?
Will you pass the sugar, please?

3 The phrase **was für (ein)?** means 'what sort of (a)?':

Was für ein Auto haben Sie?
What sort of (a) car do you have?
Was für Blumen bringt er?
What sort of flowers does he bring?
Was für einen Teppich sucht sie?
What sort of (a) carpet is she looking for?
Was für ein Mensch ist er?
What sort of a person is he?

In **was für ein?**, the **ein** has the same ending as in the hypothetical statement on which the question is based:

Sie haben ein Auto. Was für ein Auto haben Sie?
You have a car. What sort of a car do you have?
Sie sucht einen Teppich. Was für einen Teppich sucht sie?
She's looking for a carpet. What sort of a carpet is she looking for?

IMITATED PRONUNCIATION

i*h* vys * es ni*h*t; **geh**-ben z<u>ee</u> m<u>e</u>e*er* **bi**-*te* d<u>ee</u> **tsy**-toong;
ry-*he*n z<u>ee</u> **bi**-*te* d<u>eh</u>n **tsoo**-k*er*; vahs fue*er* * yn * **ow**-t<u>oh</u>
hah-ben z<u>ee</u>, vahs fue*er* **bloo**-men bringt * ee*r*, vahs
fue*er* * **y**-n*e*n **te**-pi*h* z<u>oo</u>kt z<u>ee</u>; vahs fue*er*
* yn mensh * ist * ee*r*; z<u>ee</u> **hah**-ben * yn * **ow**-t<u>oh</u>; vahs
fue*er* * yn * **ow**-t<u>oh</u> **hah**-ben z<u>ee</u>; z<u>ee</u> z<u>oo</u>kt * **y**-n*e*n
te-pi*h*; vahs fue*er* * **y**-n*e*n **te**-pi*h* z<u>oo</u>kt z<u>ee</u>

Exercise 8

Insert the correct question-word from the column on
the right in the following questions:

1	… für ein Auto hat er?	Wen
2	… kommt er?	Wer
3	… besucht er?	Was
4	… wohnt die Freundin?	Wie
5	… ist sie?	Warum
6	… heißt sie?	Wann
7	… liebt er sie?	Wo

23 NEGATIVE SENTENCES

Section 17 showed the wide use of **kein** to make negative sentences. But **kein** can only be used before nouns and can only mean 'not a/an' or 'no', never 'not the'. Where **kein** is not possible, **nicht** ('not') is used.

nicht often comes late in the sentence, or even last. It never comes between the SU and the verb, and it has no effect on the verb:

Er schwimmt nicht immer. He doesn't always swim.
Wir kennen sie noch nicht. We don't know her yet.
Es funktioniert nicht gut. It isn't working well.

The same principle applies to questions:

Ist er nicht Elektriker? Isn't he an electrician?
Kommt er nicht heute? Isn't he coming today?
Kommt er nicht oft? Doesn't he come often?
Warum arbeiten sie nicht? Why aren't they working?
but
Hat sie keine Geschwister?
Has she no brothers or sisters? *or* Hasn't she any brothers or sisters?

5

24 INSTRUCTIONS AND REQUESTS

To give an order or instruction, say the basic form of the verb, with its **-en** ending, and follow it directly with **Sie**:

Kommen Sie sofort! Come at once!

This is less abrupt than the English equivalent and can be toned down further by adding **bitte** ('please'):

Geben Sie mir bitte die Zeitung!
Give me the paper please!

Note the distinction between this sentence and the apparently identical question sentence in section 22. They look the same but are spoken differently.

The only irregular instruction form is that for the verb 'to be' (**sein**): **seien Sie!** For example:

Seien Sie so nett und bringen Sie mir die Zeitung!
Be so kind and bring me the paper!

VOCABULARY

	bitte schön ...?	yes please ...?
der	**Führer (-)**	guide
der	**Stadtführer (-)**	town guide
	fragen	to ask
der	**Chef (-s)**	boss, manager
	suchen	to look for
	so etwas	such a thing
	sicher	certainly
	drüben	over there
	gucken	to have a look
	(pronounced **kucken**)	
	dort	there
	verrückt	crazy
	von	of
	natürlich	of course
	brauchen	to need
	hier	here
	kennen	to know
die	**Stadt (ⸯe)**	town

IMITATED PRONUNCIATION

bi-t*e* sh<u>oe</u>n; de*er* **fue**-r*er*; de*er* shtaht-f<u>ue</u>-r*er*, fr<u>ah</u>-gen; de*er* shef; z<u>oo</u>-*ke*n; <u>zoh</u> * et-vahs; **zi**-h*er*, **dr<u>ue</u>**-b*en*; **koo**-*ke*n; do*er*t; f*er*-**ruekt**; fon; na-t**ue***er*-li*h*; **brow**-*ke*n; h<u>ee</u>*er*, **ke**-nen; d<u>ee</u> shtaht

Exercise 9

Translate this encounter into German. Only translate what the speakers say. You will need the new words in the vocabulary opposite. Correct your translation with the help of the Key, then learn the dialogue by heart.

A stranger (Fremde) tries to buy a town guide in a bookshop in Bunsenheim

ASSISTANT   Yes please ...?
STRANGER   Hello. Have you got a guide?
ASSISTANT   What sort of a guide?
STRANGER   A town guide.
ASSISTANT   I don't know. Please ask the boss.
STRANGER   (to Manager) Hello. I'm looking for a town guide. Have you got such a thing?
MANAGER   Yes, certainly. The town guides are over there. Have a look there.

Ten minutes later

STRANGER   It's crazy. I find town guides of Frankfurt, Gießen, Marburg, and Kassel but I don't find a town guide of Bunsenheim.
MANAGER   Of course not. Why do we need town guides of Bunsenheim? We live here and know the town!

25   ADJECTIVES AND ADVERBS

Adjectives and adverbs are descriptive words. Adjectives either precede nouns directly ('*fine* weather') or follow them and refer to them by having the verb 'to be' (**sein** in German) sandwiched in between ('the weather was *fine*'). Adverbs are used more loosely and describe the process indicated by the verb ('he stumbled *badly*') or by the sentence as a whole ('she thumped the table *violently*'). In German the same word can be used as either adjective or adverb:

Das Wetter ist schlecht.   The weather is bad.
Das Kind singt schlecht.   The child sings badly.

We shall look at adjectives preceding nouns in section 29.

Adjectives and adverbs are often preceded by words that qualify them:

sehr	very
zu	too
so	so
ziemlich	fairly, rather, pretty
etwas	rather, somewhat
nicht	not
nicht so	not so
gar nicht	not at all

Der Chef ist gar nicht höflich.
The boss isn't at all polite.
Das Kind trinkt die Milch ziemlich schnell.
The child drinks the milk pretty quickly.

IMITATED PRONUNCIATION

z<u>eh</u>er; ts<u>oo</u>; z<u>oh</u>; **tseem**-li*h*; **et**-vahs; ni*h*t; ni*h*t z<u>oh</u>; g<u>ah</u> ni*h*t

Adjectives and adverbs share the same methods of making comparisons.

1 Comparatives ('more', 'less', etc)

To make comparatives add **-er** to the basic adjective or adverb and, if you need 'than', use **als**:

Das Wetter ist heute schlechter als gestern.
The weather is worse today than yesterday.
Das Kind singt schlecht, aber die Mutter singt schlechter.
The child sings badly, but the mother sings worse.

With some adjectives and adverbs you also have to change the sound of the vowel:

alt	old	**älter**	older
arm	poor	**ärmer**	poorer

groß	big	**größer**	bigger
hart	hard	**härter**	harder
jung	young	**jünger**	younger
kalt	cold	**kälter**	colder
klug	clever	**klüger**	cleverer
krank	ill	**kränker**	more ill
kurz	short	**kürzer**	shorter
lang	long	**länger**	longer
oft	often	**öfter**	more often
schwach	weak	**schwächer**	weaker
stark	strong	**stärker**	stronger
warm	warm	**wärmer**	warmer

These vowel changes are carried over into the superlative.

2 Superlatives ('most', 'least', etc)

To make superlatives, put **am** before the adjective or adverb and add **-(e)sten** to the word itself:

Das Wetter war vorgestern am schlechtesten.
The weather was worst (of all) the day before yesterday.
Der Vater singt am schlechtesten.
The father sings worst (of all).
Das Wetter war vorvorgestern am schönsten.
The weather was nicest (of all) three days ago (literally:
the day before the day before yesterday).
Die Kusine singt am schönsten.
The (female) cousin sings the most beautifully (of all).

The **-(e)** is generally used when the word (i.e. the stem) ends in **-s**, **ss**, **-ß** (but not **groß**→ **am größten**), **-d**, **-t**, and **-z**.

fies	nasty	**am fiesesten**	nastiest
blass	pale	**am blässesten**	palest
heiß	hot	**am heißesten**	hottest
gesund	healthy	**am gesundesten**	healthiest
hart	hard	**am härtesten**	hardest
schwarz	black	**am schwärzesten**	blackest

However, when a superlative adjective precedes the noun (as in English 'the finest weather'), **am** is not used and the ending may be other than **-en** (see section 29).

IMITATED PRONUNCIATION

ahlt, **el**-t*er*; *ah*m, **eer**-m*er*; gr<u>o</u>hs, **groe**-s*er*; hah*er*t, **hee**r-t*er*; yoong, **yueng**-*er*; kahlt, **kel**-t*er*; kl<u>oo</u>k, **kl<u>ue</u>**-g*er*; **krahnk**, kreng-k*er*; koo*er*ts, **kueer**t-s*er*; **lahng**, leng-*er*; oft, **oef**-t*er*; shvah*k*, **shve**-*her*; sht*ah*k, **stee**r-k*er*; v<u>ah</u>m, **vee**r-m*er*

3 Like English, German has a few adjectives that don't follow the usual pattern:

gut	good	**besser**	better	**am besten**	best
viel	much	**mehr**	more	**am meisten**	most
hoch	high	**höher**	higher	**am höchsten**	highest
nahe	near	**näher**	nearer	**am nächsten**	nearest

4 To say 'as … as', German uses **so … wie**:

Das Haus ist so klein wie ein Schuppen.
The house is as small as a shed.
Ich komme so schnell wie möglich.
I'll come as quickly as possible.

'just as … as' is **ebenso … wie**:

Das Schlafzimmer ist ebenso groß wie das Wohnzimmer.
The bedroom is just as big as the living room.
Der Vetter singt ebenso schön wie die Kusine.
The (male) cousin sings just as beautifully as the (female) cousin.

IMITATED PRONUNCIATION

g<u>oo</u>t, **be**-ser, ahm **bes**-ten; f<u>ee</u>l, m<u>eh</u>er, **ahm** mys-ten; h<u>oh</u>k, **hoe**-er, ahm **hoe**hs-ten; **nah**-e, **ne**-er, ahm **neh**s-ten; z<u>oh</u> ... v<u>ee</u>; **eh**-ben-z<u>oh</u> ... v<u>ee</u>

Exercise 10

1 Meine Mutter ist alt, aber mein Vater ist älter.

Now complete the following sentences in the same way:

2 Mein Bruder ist groß, aber meine Schwester ist ...

3 Die Frau ist jung, aber die Wirtin ist ...

4 Der Sohn ist klug, aber die Tochter ist ...

5 Das Zimmer ist warm, aber das Bett ist ...

6 Die gelbe Nelke ist lang, aber die rote Rose ist ...

7 Die Frau ist nett, aber der Mann ist ...

5

VOCABULARY

You will need these new words to translate the conversations on page 65 into English:

die	**Hausbesitzerin (-nen)**	house owner
	dies. .	this
das	**Wohnzimmer (-)**	living room
das	**Schlafzimmer (-)**	bedroom
der	**Mieter (-)**	tenant
der	**Flur (-e)**	hall
	dunk(e)l*	dark
die	**Straße (-n)**	street
	laut	noisy
	eigentlich	really, actually
	oben	upstairs
	hell	light, bright
der	**Raum (¨e)**	room, space
	bestimmt	definitely
	breit	wide
	unten	downstairs
die	**Decke (-n)**	ceiling

	niedrig	low
	winzig	tiny
	gegenüber	opposite
die	**Aussicht (en)**	view
	wunderschön	glorious, splendid
der	**Garten (⸚)**	garden
	liegen	to lie
	nämlich	you see (in explanation)
	hinten	at the back, rear
	ruhig	quiet
	vorn	at the front
	nehmen	to take
	übrigens	by the way
der	**Monat (-e)**	month
	teu(e)r*	dear, expensive
	jetzt	now, at present
	zahlen	to pay

* The bracketed letter disappears when another syllable, like **-er**, is added to the adjective/adverb.

IMITATED PRONUNCIATION

d<u>ee</u> **hows**-be-zit-se-rin; d<u>ee</u>s; dahs **vohn**-tsi-mer; dahs **shlahf**-tsi-mer; deer **mee**-ter; deer fl<u>oo</u>er; **doong**-kel; d<u>ee</u> **shtrah**-se; lowt; **y**-gent-li*h*; **oh**-ben; hel; deer rowm; be-**shtimt**; bryt; **oon**-ten; d<u>ee</u> **de**-ke; **n<u>ee</u>**-dri*h*; **win**-tsi*h*; <u>geh</u>-gen***ue**-ber; d<u>ee</u> **ows**-zi*h*t; **voon**-der-shoen; deer **gah**-ten; **l<u>ee</u>**-gen; **n<u>e</u>m**-li*h*; **hin**-ten; **r<u>oo</u>**-i*h*; foern; **neh**-men; **<u>ueb</u>**-ri-gens; deer **moh**-na*h*t; **toy**-er; yetst; **tsah**-len

A house owner shows three vacant flats to a prospective tenant

In the ground floor flat:

HAUSBESITZERIN	**Diese Wohnung ist schön groß, zwei Wohnzimmer, vier Schlafzimmer, zwei Toiletten ....**
MIETER	**Der Flur ist zu dunkel, und die Straße ist ziemlich laut. Diese Wohnung ist mir eigentlich zu groß. Ich brauche keine vier Schlafzimmer, eigentlich nur zwei .... Sind die Wohnungen oben kleiner?**
HAUSBESITZERIN	**Ja. Sie sind auch etwas heller als diese.**

In the first floor flat at the front:

HAUSBESITZERIN	**Diese Räume gefallen Ihnen bestimmt ... nur ein Wohnzimmer, aber breiter und länger als das Wohnzimmer unten.**
MIETER	**Ja, schön, aber die Decke ist niedriger als unten. Die drei Schlafzimmer sind mir zu winzig, und es ist ebenso laut hier wie unten.**

In the first floor flat at the rear:

HAUSBESITZERIN	**Diese Wohnung ist am schönsten. Hier sind nur zwei Schlafzimmer. Sie sind aber etwas größer als die Schlafzimmer gegenüber. Die Aussicht ist wunderschön, der Garten liegt nämlich hinten.**
MIETER	**Ja, und diese Wohnung ist auch viel ruhiger als die Wohnungen vorn. Ja, ich nehme sie .... Wie hoch ist übrigens die Miete?**

HAUSBESITZERIN	**Siebenhundertfünfzig Euro pro Monat.**
MIETER	**Was!!?? Nein, das ist mir zu teuer. Das ist viel mehr, als ich jetzt zahle.**

TRANSLATION

In the ground floor flat:

HOUSE OWNER	This flat is beautifully spacious, two living rooms, four bedrooms, two toilets ....
TENANT	The hall is too dark, and the street is rather noisy. This flat is really too large for me. I don't need four bedrooms, only two really .... Are the flats upstairs smaller?
HOUSE OWNER	Yes. They're somewhat lighter than this one, too.

In the first floor flat at the front:

HOUSE OWNER	You'll definitely like these rooms ... only one living room, but wider and longer than the living room downstairs.
TENANT	Yes, fine, but the ceiling is lower than downstairs. The three bedrooms are too tiny for me, and it's just as noisy here as downstairs.

In the first floor flat at the rear:

HOUSE OWNER	This flat is the nicest of all. Here there are only two bedrooms. But they're somewhat larger than the bedrooms opposite. The view is glorious. The garden's at the back, you see.
TENANT	Yes, and this flat is quieter than the flats at the front, too. Yes, I'll take it .... By the way, how much is the rent?
HOUSE OWNER	Seven hundred and fifty euros a month.
TENANT	What!!?? No, that's too dear for me. That's much more than I'm paying now.

Week 6

- *prepositions ('in', 'by', 'of', etc)*
- *how prepositions affect the case of the following noun or pronoun*
- *using the expression 'es gibt' ('there is/there are').*

26 PREPOSITIONS

Prepositions are short words which are used to link together nouns, adjectives, and verbs to construct more complex sentences. They are called prepositions because they usually precede nouns or pronouns:

going *into* the house
stolen *by* a thief
a letter *from* you
fond *of* her mother
insist *on* payment

In English we can simply place a preposition in front of any noun or the pronouns 'me', 'us', 'you', 'him', 'her', 'it', and 'them', without further complication. In German, however, each preposition alters the case of the noun or pronoun following it. Some prepositions take the DO case, some the IO case, and some take either the DO or IO case, depending on the sense or meaning.

Here are the most important German prepositions, grouped according to the cases they take, together with their most common English equivalents. Note, though, that it is not really possible to translate prepositions out of context. You must learn them by observing how they are employed, noting any idiomatic or unusual usage.

1 Prepositions followed by the DO case

durch	through, by, by means of
für	for
gegen	against, towards
ohne	without
um	round, at (time of day)

Note three contracted forms frequently found when **das** follows:

durchs (= durch das) Fenster   through the window
fürs (= für das) Theater   for the theatre
ums (= um das) Feuer   round the fire

2 Prepositions followed by the IO case

aus   out of, from

bei   with, at (so-and-so's house), near, in (such-and-such conditions or weather), during, in the process/course of

mit   with

nach   to (certain locations, including one's own house: **nach Hause**), after (time), according to

seit   since, for (period of time up to now)

von   from (place and time), by (indicating agency or authorship), of (possession)

zu   to (certain locations), at (e.g. at home: **zu Hause**)

Note these contracted forms when **dem** follows:

beim (= bei dem) Gewitter   in/during the thunderstorm
vom (= von dem) Dach   from the roof
zum (= zu dem) Arzt   to the doctor

and when **der** (f. IO case) follows:

zur (= zu der) Seite   to the side, aside

3 Prepositions followed by either the DO or IO case

If the context indicates a change of location or condition, these prepositions are followed by the DO case; otherwise they are followed by the IO case.

	DO	IO
an	on to (the side of); up to (the edge of)	at, by, on (the side of a non-horizontal surface); on (with days and dates)
auf	on to (the top of a horizontal surface)	on (the top of a horizontal surface)
hinter	(to) behind	behind
in	into	in (spatial, and temporal, though year numbers need **im Jahre**, e.g. **im Jahre 2003**); inside, within
neben	(to) next to, (to) alongside	next to, alongside, along with
über	across, over (i.e. from one side to the other), via	above, over (i.e. on top of)
unter	(to) underneath, (to) below, under (from one side to the other)	below, underneath, under
vor	(to) in front of, (to) before	in front of, before; (in past time contexts) ago
zwischen	(to) in between	between

Note these contracted forms when **das** follows:

ans (= an das) **Feuer**	up to the fire
aufs (= auf das) **Wasser**	on to the water
ins (= in das) **Netz**	into the net
vors (= vor das) **Auto**	in front of the car

and when **dem** follows:

am (= an dem) **Montag**	on Monday
im (= in dem) **Schnee**	in the snow

The following sentences illustrate the principle underlying the selection of DO or IO:

Fritz geht an den Schrank, Liese steht am Schrank.
Fritz goes to the wardrobe. Liese stands by the wardrobe.
Er legt die Zeitung auf den Schrank, sie liegt jetzt auf dem Schrank.
He puts (lays) the newspaper on the wardrobe. It's now (now lies) on the wardrobe.
Fritz springt hinter den Schrank, Liese ist schon hinter dem Schrank.
Fritz jumps behind the wardrobe. Liese is already behind the wardrobe.
Fritz geht jetzt in den Schrank, Liese singt im Schrank.
Fritz now goes into the wardrobe. Liese is singing in the wardrobe.
Die Katze geht neben den Stuhl, der Hund liegt schon neben dem Stuhl.
The cat goes next to the chair. The dog is already lying next to the chair.
Die Katze springt über den Tisch, die Uhr hängt über dem Tisch.
The cat jumps over the table. The clock is hanging above the table.
Fritz kriecht unter den Tisch, die Zeitung liegt unter dem Tisch.
Fritz creeps under the table. The newspaper is (lies) under the table.

6

4 The preposition **bis** can be used in two ways

When expressing time/numbers, it means 'until', 'up to', 'by'. The DO case follows:

bis nächstes Jahr till next year
bis nächsten Montag till next Monday

In other expressions, it means 'up to', 'as far as'. In this usage **bis** cannot stand alone, except before place names. It must be followed by another preposition such as **an**, **auf**, or **in**. The case of the noun or pronoun is determined by this second preposition.

The following example shows both usages:

Fritz kommt nur bis Bunsenheim, findet ein Gasthaus, geht bis an die Tür, wartet bis fünf Uhr, zählt bis fünfzig, kommt dann bis in die Gaststube, aber: keiner ist da!
Fritz only gets as far as Bunsenheim, finds an inn, goes up to the door, waits until five o'clock, counts up to fifty, then gets as far as the lounge, but – no one is there!

6

5 The preposition **gegenüber** means 'opposite', 'towards', 'compared to'

Usually **gegenüber** follows the (pro)noun to which it relates, and takes the IO case:

Die Kirche steht am Marktplatz dem Gasthaus Zur Rose gegenüber, und Sie finden das Theater am Theaterplatz der Touristeninformation gegenüber.
The church is on the marketplace opposite the Rose Inn, and you'll find the theatre on Theatre Square opposite the tourist information office.

VOCABULARY

You will need the following new words to complete exercises 11 and 12.

der	**Verbrecher (-)**	criminal
der	**Pinsel (-)**	paintbrush
die	**Palette (-n)**	palette
die	**Hand (¨e)**	hand
das	**Bild (-er)**	picture
die	**Sache (-n)**	thing
die	**Tischdecke (-n)**	tablecloth
das	**Brot (-e)**	loaf
das	**Glas (¨er)**	glass
die	**Flasche (-n)**	bottle
der	**Korken (-)**	cork
das	**Etikett (-en)**	label
	wichtig	important
die	**Feile (-n)**	file

der	**Einbrecher (-)**	burglar/intruder
die	**Haustür (-en)**	front door
	klopfen	to knock
	niemand, keiner	no one
	gucken	to peep
	finden	to find
das	**Nummernschild (-er)**	number plate
die	**Garage (-n)**	garage
	zurück	back
	stecken	to put (inside or between)
der	**Rahmen (-)**	frame
	öffnen	to open
die	**Treppe (-n)**	stairs (i.e. staircase)
	sitzen	to sit
das	**Skelett (-e)**	skeleton
die	**Axt (¨e)**	axe

6

Exercise 11

The story that follows describes a prisoner painting a picture of objects on a table. On the tablecloth is a loaf of bread cut open to reveal a file, which has been inserted into it. Next to the loaf is a glass of wine and behind it, a wine bottle. Complete the story by inserting prepositions in the gaps marked (P) and putting the right case-endings on 'd. .' and 'ein'. The prepositions, listed in the order in which they are required, are:

mit, in, vor, auf, auf, neben, hinter, mit, auf, für, in

Der Verbrecher steht   (P)   ein. . Pinsel und ein. . Palette   (P)   d. . Hand   (P)   ein. . Bild.   (P)   d. . Bild sind mehrere Sachen.   (P)   ein. . Tischdecke liegt ein Brot.   (P)   d. . Brot ist ein Glas, und   (P)   d. . Brot ist eine Flasche   (P)   ein. . Korken.   (P)   d. . Flasche ist ein Etikett. Was ist aber   (P)   d. . Verbrecher am wichtigsten? Die Feile   (P)   d. . Brot natürlich!

Exercise 12

Translate the following sentences into German. You will need the words given in the vocabulary list on the opposite page. The appropriate prepositions are indicated at the end of each English sentence. The English words in brackets are just there to help with the sense of the sentences. You do not have to translate them.

The intruder goes (right) up to the front door. (**bis an**)

He knocks on the door. (**an**)

No one comes to the door. (**zu**)

He goes round the house and peeps through the windows. (**um**, **durch**)

He finds a car without (a) number plate between the house and the garage. (**ohne**, **zwischen**)

He goes back to the front door. (**an**)

He pushes a file between the door and the frame. (**zwischen**)

He opens the door with the file and goes into the hall. (**mit**, **in**)

Opposite him on the stairs sits a skeleton with an axe in the (its) hand. (**gegenüber**, **auf**, **mit**, **in**)

27 THE EXPRESSION 'ES GIBT' ('THERE IS', 'THERE ARE')

In any language there is a way to express the idea that something exists or doesn't exist, is available or not available. This is done in English with the expression 'there is/are'. In the following English examples, note how the verb changes, not only according to time but also to match the thing it is referring to, showing whether it is singular or plural:

There's a mouse in the larder.
There are rats by the river.
There was cake for tea.
There were hamburgers for supper.

German has **es gibt** (from **geben**, 'to give') as its equivalent of 'there is/are' in sentences saying whether something exists or is available. In this expression **es** is the SU, so the item(s) being talked about must be in the DO case:

Es gibt heute einen Film im Fernsehen.
There's a film on television today.
Gibt es keinen Kuchen mehr?
Is there no more cake?
Es gibt mehrere Fehler in dem Brief.
There are several mistakes in the letter.
Es gibt einige Ausländer im Hotel.
There are some foreigners in the hotel.
Es gibt jetzt Abendbrot!
Now we're going to have supper! (There is supper now.)

You will see from these examples that **es gibt** does not change for the plural.

The question **Was gibt es?** (usually spoken **Was gibt's?**) means 'What is there?' (e.g. for a meal, available in a shop, on television, etc).

VOCABULARY

der	Hotelgast (¨e)	hotel guest
das	Fernsehen	television
	im Fernsehen	on television
	heute Abend	this evening
der	Kellner (-)	waiter
die	Fernsehzeitung (-en)	TV magazine
die	Woche (-n)	week
	diese Woche	this week
die	Tageszeitung (-en)	daily paper
	hier	here
	leider	unfortunately
	gestern	yesterday

Exercise 13

6

Translate the following short conversation into German. You will need the words in the vocabulary list above.

In the television lounge of a hotel

HOTEL GUEST What is there on television this evening?
WAITER I don't know.
HOTEL GUEST Look in the TV magazine please. (**in** + DO)
WAITER There is no TV magazine this week.
HOTEL GUEST Is there a daily paper?
WAITER Yes, here is a daily paper ... but it is unfortunately from yesterday. (**von**)

Week 7

- *words which follow the same pattern as 'der', 'die', 'das', including the words for 'this' and 'that'*
- *words which follow the same pattern as 'ein' – the possessive words 'my', 'your', etc*
- *endings that are added to adjectives when they precede a noun*
- *ordinal numbers ('first', 'second', etc) and fractions*
- *the 'familiar' forms used when talking to friends or children*
- *the order of words in a simple German sentence*

28 WORDS FOLLOWING THE SAME PATTERN AS 'DER', 'DIE', 'DAS'

There are six other words that are like the **d. .** words (**der**, **die**, **das**, etc) in that they appear in the same position before the noun and have the **d. .** endings. These words are:

dies. .	this, these, *sometimes* that, those
jed. .	each, every, any
welch. . ?/!	which? what? what (a)!
jen. .	that, those
solch. .	such
manch. .	quite a few, a fair number of

NOTES
1 The usual way to say 'that' is **der**, **die**, or **das** spoken with stress, or **dies. .**

jen. . is not used often, unless paired with **dies. .** in the expression **jen. ., dies. .** 'the former, the latter'.

2 solch. . and **manch. .** in the singular have the alternatives **solch ein** and **manch ein**, where only the **ein** takes endings. To convey the meaning of **solch ein** there are the further alternatives **ein solch. .** (endings as in section 29) and the frequently used **so ein**.

3 manch. . has no exact equivalent in English. It means more than 'some' and fewer than 'many'. Whether singular or plural in form it is plural in meaning.

Here is a summary of **d. .** type endings, using **dies. .** as a model:

	singular			plural
	m.	f.	n.	m. f. n.
SU	dieser	diese	dieses*	diese
DO	diesen	diese	dieses*	diese
IO	diesem	dieser	diesem	diesen

*The neuter ending **-as** is replaced by **-es** in all six of these **d. .**-type words.

Examples:

dies. .	**Kennen Sie dieses Buch aus der Hugo-Reihe?** Do you know this book from the Hugo series?
jed. .	**Jedes Kind bekommt ein Ei.** Each (or Every) child will get an egg. **Ich bin für jeden Vorschlag offen.** I am open to any suggestion.
welch. . ?/!	**Auf welchen Bus warten Sie?** Which bus are you waiting for? **Welchen Druck hat der Reifen?** What pressure does the tyre have?
jen. .	**Der Film stammt aus jener Zeit vor dem 1. Weltkrieg.** The film comes from that period before World War I. **Wir sprechen oft über dieses und jenes.** We often talk about this and that.

7

solch. .	**Er hat solche Schwierigkeiten mit seinem Vater.**
	He has such difficulties with his father.
	Wir haben solches Glück mit dem Wetter.
	We're having such luck with the weather.
manch. .	**Mancher Polizist trinkt selbst zu viel.**
	Quite a few policemen drink too much themselves.

All this group of words can be used not only before nouns but on their own, with a noun being understood from the context:

Ich trinke aus diesem Glas. Trinken Sie aus diesem?
I'll drink from this glass. (Indicating) Will you drink from this one?

jeder (DO **jeden**, IO **jedem**) on its own means 'everybody', just as **keiner** (DO **keinen**, IO **keinem**) on its own means 'no one', 'nobody'.

28A WORDS TAKING THE SAME ENDINGS AS EIN

As well as words that are like the **d. .** words, there are others that are parallel to **ein**. The **ein** endings are exclusive to words indicating possession.

1st person		2nd pers.	3rd person			
singular	plural		singular			plural
_____	____	_____	m.	f.	n.	____
mein	**unser**	**Ihr**	**sein**	**ihr**	**sein**	**ihr**
my	our	your	his	her	its	their

Here is a summary of **ein**-type endings, using **unser** and **Ihr** as examples:

	singular			plural
	m.	f.	n.	m. f. n.
SU	unser	unsere	unser	unsere
DO	unseren	unsere	unser	unsere
IO	unserem	unserer	unserem	unseren

It is important not to mistake **unser**, in which the **-er** belongs to the stem, for a **d. .**-type word, in which the **-er** occurs only as an ending.

	singular			plural
	m.	f.	n.	m. f. n.
SU	**Ihr**	**Ihre**	**Ihr**	**Ihre**
DO	**Ihren**	**Ihre**	**Ihr**	**Ihre**
IO	**Ihrem**	**Ihrer**	**Ihrem**	**Ihren**

All the words in this group, which indicate possession, can be used not only before nouns but on their own, to mean 'mine, ours, yours, his, hers, its, theirs'. The endings are the same as above, except that the m. singular SU adds **-er** and the n. singular SU and DO add **-s**:

Leihen Sie mir bitte Ihren Bleistift. Meiner ist weg.
Lend me your pencil please. Mine has vanished (literally: is away).
Mein Fahrrad ist fünf Jahre alt. Wie alt ist Ihrs?
My bicycle is five years old. How old is yours?

Exercise 14

1 Geht er ohne seine Freundin ins Theater?
   Nein, er geht mit seiner Freundin ins Theater.

Complete the following sentences in the same way.

2 Ist sie ohne ihre Schwester bei Müllers
   eingeladen?
   Nein, …

3 Kommt der Vater mit unserem Geschenk für
   die Mutter?
   Nein, …

4 Esse ich den Kuchen ohne eine Tasse Kaffee?
   Nein, …

5 Geht er ohne seinen Stadtführer durch Frankfurt?
   Nein, …

6 Mache ich das Abendbrot mit meiner Tochter?
   Nein, …

7 Geht sie mit ihrem Bruder zur Tante?
   Nein, …

8 Kaufen wir die Wurst mit einer Cola?
   Nein, …

7

29 ADJECTIVES BEFORE NOUNS

When adjectives are not used in isolation after the noun (see section 25), but become part of the group of words directly preceding the noun, they require sets of endings similar to – but not identical with – those of **d. .** and **ein**.

There are three sets to learn, depending on whether (a) a **d. .**-type word is also present, (b) an **ein**-type word is also present, or (c) neither a **d. .** type nor an **ein**-type word is present.

1 Adjectives after **d. .**-type words

These adjectives have **-en** in all positions except for five positions with **-e**:

	singular			plural
	m.	f.	n.	m. f. n.
SU	der arme Mann	die arme Frau	das arme Kind	die armen Leute
DO	den armen Mann	die arme Frau	das arme Kind	die armen Leute
IO	dem armen Mann	der armen Frau	dem armen Kind	den armen Leuten*

*Plural nouns in the IO case always have **-n** added to the plural form unless the plural already ends in **-n** or is a foreign plural like **Autos**.

Summary of endings after **d. .**-type words:

	singular			plural
	m.	f.	n.	m. f. n.
SU	-e	-e	-e	-en
DO	-en	-e	-e	-en
IO	-en	-en	-en	-en

2 Adjectives after **ein**-type words

These also have -**en** in all positions except five, but three of these undergo change compared with 1:

	singular			plural
	m.	f.	n.	m. f. n.
SU	ihr armer Mann	seine arme Frau	ihr armes Kind	ihre armen Kinder
DO	ihren armen Mann	seine arme Frau	ihr armes Kind	ihre armen Kinder
IO	ihrem armen Mann	seiner armen Frau	ihrem armen Kind	ihren armen Kindern

Summary of adjective endings after **ein**-type words:

	singular			plural
	m.	f.	n.	m. f. n.
SU	-er	-e	-es	-en
DO	-en	-e	-es	-en
IO	-en	-en	-en	-en

3 Adjectives preceded by neither **d. .**-type nor **ein**–type words

These endings are easy to learn if you remember where they come from – see below:

	singular			plural
	m.	f.	n.	m. f. n.
SU	**kalter**	**kalte**	**kaltes**	**kalte**
	Wein	**Limonade**	**Bier**	**Getränke**
DO	**kalten**	**kalte**	**kaltes**	**kalte**
	Wein	**Limonade**	**Bier**	**Getränke**
IO	**kaltem**	**kalter**	**kaltem**	**kalten**
	Wein	**Limonade**	**Bier**	**Getränken**

Summary of adjective endings without **d. .**- or **ein**-type words:

	singular			plural
	m.	f.	n.	m. f. n.
SU	-er	-e	-es	-e
DO	-en	-e	-es	-e
IO	-em	-er	-em	-en

The principle behind the adjective endings for 2 and 3 above is that any letters in the endings of **d. .** which have been lost must appear in the adjective ending. So with **ein, -r** is lost in the m. singular SU case and **-s** is lost in the n. singular SU/DO cases. They are therefore transferred to the adjective. In 3, all the **d. .** endings are lost, so they are transferred to the adjective, except that the n. singular SU/DO **d + as** becomes **-es** when transferred (as with the **d. .**-type words in section 28).

30 ORDINAL NUMBERS AND FRACTIONS

1 The ordinal numbers ('first', 'second', 'third', etc) are as follows:

first: **erst**

second to nineteenth:
add **-t** to the cardinal number (section 18), so 'second' is **zweit**; 'ninth', **neunt**; and 'eighteenth', **achtzehnt**.

Exceptions:
third   **dritt**   (**-ei-** becomes **-i-**)
seventh   **siebt**   (**sieben** loses the **-en**)
eighth   **acht**   (**acht** does not get the additional **-t**)

twentieth onwards:
add **-st** to the cardinal number, so 'thirty fifth' is **fünfunddreißigst**; 'hundredth', **hundertst**; and 'thousandth', **tausendst**.

Ordinal numbers are mostly used as adjectives before nouns, so they take the endings described in section 29:

Die fünfte Person von rechts ist mein Vater.
The fifth person from the right is my father.
Ich nehme gern ein drittes Glas von dem herrlichen Wein.
I'd enjoy a third glass of that splendid wine.

The following examples use the same endings as in section 29 (**3**):
Sie benutzen als Erster (or **Erste** if person spoken to is female) **unsere neue Maschine.**
You're the first to use our new machine.
Ich bin als Siebter mit der Prüfung fertig.
I'm the seventh to finish the test.

2 Apart from 'half', **die Hälfte (-n)**, fractions are formed by adding **-el** to the ordinal number, which then becomes a n. noun: for example, 'quarter', **das Viertel (-)**; 'tenth',

7

das Zehntel (-). So 'two-thirds' is **zwei Drittel**; 'three-eighths', **drei Achtel**.

'Half (of) the …' is often die **Hälfte von** … (or, instead of **von**, the possessor case, section 50):

Die Hälfte von dem Geld gehört mir.
Half (of) the money belongs to me.

However, when 'half' is followed not by 'the' but by 'a/an', you must use the adjective **halb**. Thus 'half an hour' is **eine halbe Stunde** and 'half a loaf' is **ein halbes Brot**.

Viertel forms a lot of compounds, such as 'a quarter of an hour', **eine Viertelstunde**; 'a quarter of a litre', **ein Viertelliter** (m. or n., no change in the plural).

'One and a half' is **anderthalb, eineinhalb**, or even **einundeinhalb**, and 'five and a half' is **fünfeinhalb** or **fünfundeinhalb**. These do not take any adjective endings even when they precede nouns.

31 CONVERSATION BETWEEN FRIENDS

For conversation within the family, or between children, students, etc, you use the *familiar* 2nd person pronouns ('you/your') and verb forms. For now we shall just look at how these are formed in the singular:

pronouns	ein-type word (possession)	verbs present tense	instructions/ requests
SU **du**	**dein** (your)	of **sein: bist**	using **sein: sei**
DO **dich**		of **haben: hast**	other verbs:
IO **dir**		of other verbs:	stem only,
		stem + **(e)st***	no pronoun
			following
			(see section 24)

*The (**e**) is added after stems ending in -**t** or -**d**.

German word order was mentioned in week 2, section 9. You already began to practise it in week 6 :

location	verb	SU
Auf dem Bild	sind	mehrere Sachen.
Auf einer Tischdecke	liegt	ein Brot.
Neben dem Brot	ist	ein Glas.
Hinter dem Brot	ist	eine Flasche mit einem Korken.
Auf der Flasche	ist	ein Etikett.

In simple statements of this sort the 'natural' word order in German can easily be translated into 'natural' English, with information about time or place followed by the verb and then the subject.

In German, however, starting statements with something other than the standard SU can be taken much further, with, for example, a DO or IO at the beginning of the statement. This is because whatever comes first, the verb must come second.

Whatever comes first must be, or refer to, something already mentioned. Here are some examples:

DO	verb	subject	rest
zwei Cola	wollen	Sie	aber nur eine Wurst
den Theaterplatz	finden	Sie	dann sofort
so etwas	glaubt	kein Mensch	
viel Spaß	wünsche	ich	Ihnen heute Abend
einen Stadtführer	suche	ich	

IO	verb	subject	rest
ihr	gefallen	rote Rosen	bestimmt
Ihnen	wünsche	ich	viel Spaß heute Abend

Exercise 15

Put the correct word from the column on the right into the following sentences. There may be more than one grammatical possibility, but you will see that they do not all make sense.

1 ... glaubt einem Verbrecher.	Solches
2 ... Blumen sind für die Freundin?	Keiner
3 ... Kuchen haben sie für das Kind.	Welches?/!
4 ... Mann finde ich nett.	Jeder
5 ... Wein schmeckt wunderbar.	Dieser
6 ... Glück haben wir mit dem Wetter.	Welche?/!
7 ... Buch aus der Hugo-Reihe kennen Sie?	Jede
8 ... Hausbesitzer hat Schwierigkeiten.	Keinen
9 ... Katze kommt ins Haus./?	Diesen

7

VOCABULARY

	einkaufen	to do the shopping
	jawohl!	(yes) certainly!
die	Einkaufsliste (-n)	shopping list
	alles	everything
	erst	first (of all)
	holen	to fetch, bring
der	Bäcker (-)	baker
das	Weißbrot (-e)	white loaf
	frisch	fresh
das	Brötchen (-)	roll
	billig	cheap
(der)	Marktkauf	(typical hypermarket name)
	fahren	to go (other than on foot)
	heute Nachmittag	this afternoon
	dorthin	(to) there
	na gut!	all right (then)!
der	Metzger (-)	butcher
	halb	half
das	Pfund (-e)	pound
	(-) after numbers	

das	**Hackfleisch**	mince
	gekocht	boiled
der	**Schinken**	ham
	bedienen	to serve
	man	one/they/people
	immer	always
das	**Fleisch**	meat
	lieber	rather
die	**Altstadt**	old town
	müssen	to have to
	dahin	(to) there
das	**Gemüsegeschäft**	greengrocer's
der	**Kopfsalat (-e)**	lettuce
	fest	firm
die	**Gurke (-n)**	cucumber
die	**Bohne (-n)**	bean
	grüne Bohnen	French beans
die	**Sache (-n)**	thing, item
der	**Salat (-e)**	salad
	ander. .	other
das	**Gemüse**	vegetables
	eilen	to be urgent
	doch	after all
der	**Markt (¨e)**	market
	unbedingt	definitely
das	**Ei (-er)**	egg
	Edeka	(chain of small supermarkets)
	noch	still
	viele	many/a lot
	kriegen	to get

7

Translate this conversation into English. You will find the vocabulary you need on pages 86–87.

'She' tries to organise 'him' to do the shopping

SIE Gehst du bitte jetzt einkaufen?

ER Jawohl! Hast du eine Einkaufsliste für mich?

SIE Nein, ich sage dir alles .... Erst hol bitte vom Bäcker ein kleines Weißbrot und zehn frische Brötchen.

ER Sie sind billiger bei Marktkauf, und wir fahren heute Nachmittag dorthin.

SIE Na gut! Dann kauf beim Metzger ein halbes Pfund Hackfleisch und zweihundertfünfzig Gramm gekochten Schinken.

ER Beim Metzger bedient man mich immer schlecht. Ich kaufe Fleisch lieber in der Altstadt, und heute Nachmittag müssen wir auch dahin.

ER Na gut! Vom Gemüsegeschäft brauche ich dann einen Kopfsalat, anderthalb Pfund kleine feste Tomaten, eine schöne Gurke, zehn Pfund Kartoffeln und ein Pfund grüne Bohnen.

ER Die Sachen für den Salat und das andere Gemüse eilen nicht, und morgen ist doch Markt.

SIE Na gut, aber ich brauche unbedingt Eier von Edeka.

ER Nein, brauchst du nicht. Wir haben noch viele. Eier kriegen wir dann auch vom Markt.

SIE Na gut, dann brauchst du nicht einkaufen gehen.

Exercise 16

Practise repeating the conversation from memory, using the following key words as a guide.

SIE einkaufen?
ER Einkaufsliste?
SIE sage alles ... Bäcker ...Weißbrot ... Brötchen
ER Marktkauf fahren
SIE Metzger ... Hackfleisch ... Schinken
ER schlecht ... Altstadt ... Nachmittag
SIE Gemüsegeschäft ... Kopfsalat ... Tomaten ... Gurke ... Kartoffeln ... Bohnen
ER eilen nicht ... Markt
SIE Eier
ER brauchst nicht ... noch viele ... Markt
SIE nicht einkaufen

Exercise 17

Construct a dialogue in which each pair of sentences is based on a pair of items/locations listed. The first sentence should be an instruction to buy the item(s) somewhere; the second a response preferring ('lieber') to buy the item(s) elsewhere. The first pair is done for you.

1 anderthalb Pfund kleine feste Tomaten   auf dem Markt

Hol bitte anderthalb Pfund kleine feste Tomaten vom Gemüsegeschäft.

Die Tomaten kaufe ich lieber auf dem Markt.

2	ein kleines Weißbrot	bei Marktauf
3	250 Gramm gekochter Schinken	in der Altstadt
4	ein Kopfsalat	auf dem Markt
5	zwanzig Eier	auf dem Markt
6	eine schöne Gurke	auf dem Markt
7	zehn frische Brötchen	bei Marktkauf
8	ein halbes Pfund Hackfleisch	in der Altstadt
9	zehn Pfund Kartoffeln	auf dem Markt
10	ein Pfund grüne Bohnen	auf dem Markt

Week 8

- *word order in sentences with more than one verb*
- *auxiliary verbs – 'can', 'must', 'will', etc – and how they are used with a main verb*
- *quantities and measurements*
- *ways of saying where something 'is' and where something is 'put'*
- *the use of 'da-' or 'dar-' with prepositions to express 'on it', 'about them', etc*

33 MORE ON WORD ORDER

So far we have concentrated on sentences containing only one verb. But look at the first sentence of the conversation in week 7, page 88:

Gehst du jetzt bitte einkaufen?

This simple sentence contains two verbs: **gehst** and **einkaufen**. The verb **gehst** is matched up with the familiar 2nd person singular **du** and might be thought of as 'personalised'. This type of verb is often called 'finite' because it is *restricted* to a particular person (1st or 2nd or 3rd person, singular or plural).

The verb **einkaufen** is not matched up with anything or anybody but completes the sense of **gehst**. It is a non-personalised, non-finite form of the verb, often known as the 'infinitive'. We shall call it the '**-en** form'.

The important point to note is that if a simple sentence contains a finite verb and a non-finite verb, the non-finite verb always stands at the end of the sentence.

gehen can be combined with other verbs:

Ich gehe zweimal in der Woche schwimmen.
I go twice in the week swimming (i.e. for a swim).
Gehen wir morgen Abend mit der Gruppe essen?
Shall we go tomorrow evening with the group eating (i.e. out for a meal)?

Meine Mutter geht immer früh schlafen.
My mother goes always early sleeping (i.e. to bed).
Manchmal gehen wir stundenlang im Wald spazieren.
Sometimes we go for hours in the forest walking (i.e. for a walk).

34 AUXILIARY VERBS: WILL, CAN, MUST, ETC.

The same pattern is followed when the finite verb is one of the verbs similar to English 'will', 'can', 'must', 'may', 'shall'. These have little meaning of their own, but modify the way in which the main verb is understood. They are therefore called auxiliary verbs.

In German auxiliaries include a verb for expressing the future (**werden**) and another for expressing the idea of causing or permitting something to happen (**lassen**). Here is the complete set of eight auxiliary verbs, with all the forms of the present tense. They are all irregular.

	dürfen	**können**
	may, can	may, can
	(permission)	(possibility)
ich/er/sie(she)**/es**	**darf**	**kann**
wir/Sie/sie(they)	**dürfen**	**können**
du	**darfst**	**kannst**

	mögen	**müssen**
	may, can (poss.),	must,
	to like to	to have to
ich/er/sie(she)**/es**	**mag**	**muss**
wir/Sie/sie(they)	**mögen**	**müssen**
du	**magst**	**musst**

8

	sollen must, to be to, to be said to	wollen to want to, to intend to
ich/er/sie(she)/es	soll	will
wir/Sie/sie(they)	sollen	wollen
du	sollst	willst

	lassen to get/allow to, to have done	werden will (future)
ich	lasse	werde
wir/sie/sie(they)	lassen	werden
du	lässt	wirst
er/sie(she)/es	lässt	wird

35 USING AUXILIARY VERBS

1 dürfen: may/can (permission), mustn't

Darf ich hier rauchen?
Can I smoke here?
Darf ich meinen Freund vorstellen?
May I introduce my friend?
In der Kirche darf man nicht laut reden.
One mustn't talk loudly in church.

2 können: may/can (possibility), be able to

Für seine sechs Jahre kann er sehr gut schwimmen.
He can swim very well considering he's only six.
Seine Rede kann noch lange dauern.
His speech may go on for a long time yet.
Wir können seine Experimente nicht finanzieren.
We aren't able to finance his experiments.

3 mögen: may (possibility), to like to

Er mag wohl reich sein, er kommt trotzdem nicht in den Club.
He may have a lot of money, but he's still not going to get into the club.
Ich mag nicht über alles klagen, aber ....
I don't like complaining about everything, but ....

4 müssen: must, to have to, needn't, don't have to

Ich muss um zwölf zu Hause sein, sonst kommt das Mittagessen zu spät auf den Tisch.
I must be home at twelve, or else I shall be late with lunch.
Dieser Brief ist an dich. Du musst nicht unbedingt antworten.
This letter is (addressed) to you. You aren't absolutely obliged to reply.

5 sollen: must, to be supposed/expected to, to be to, to be said to

Du sollst erst essen und dann ins Kino gehen.
You're to eat first and then go to the cinema.
Ich kann nicht länger auf ihn warten, er soll sofort kommen.
I can't wait for him any longer, he's to come at once.
Ich kann ihn empfehlen, er soll ein sehr guter Klavierlehrer sein.
I can recommend him. He's said to be a very good piano teacher.

6 wollen: to want to, to be determined to, to intend to

Er ist vollkommen satt, er will nichts mehr essen.
He's completely full. He doesn't want to eat another thing.

8

Er will gar nichts mehr von der Sache hören.
He doesn't want to hear anything more at all about the
matter.
Er will seine Ferien in den Bergen verbringen.
He intends to spend his holidays in the mountains.

7 lassen: to get someone to, to make/have someone do,
to have something done, to let/allow someone (to) do

**Der Chef lässt seine Sekretärin unwichtige Briefe
unterschreiben.**
The boss gets his secretary to sign unimportant letters.
Er lässt seinen Wagen alle zwei Tage waschen.
He has his car washed every other day.
Mein Vater lässt grüßen.
My father sends his regards.
**Wir lassen unsere Tochter nicht alleine zur Schule
gehen.**
We don't let our daughter walk to school on her own.

8 werden: shall/will (future), to be going to

**Ich mache es jetzt, ich werde in den nächsten
Tagen keine Zeit haben.**
I'll do it now. I shan't have any time in the next few
days.
**Es ist schrecklich dunkel, es wird bestimmt
regnen.**
It's terribly dark. It's going to rain for sure.

VOCABULARY

Study the conversation on the next page until you know all the sentences (and their meaning) by heart. You will need these new words:

	etwas	somewhat
das	Übergewicht	surplus weight
	abnehmen	to slim, lose weight
der	Urlaub (-e)	holiday(s)
	anziehen	to wear, put on
der	Sportler (-)	sportsman
	unbedingt	absolutely
	Recht haben	to be right
	schwer	heavy
	hoffentlich	hopefully
	richtig	right, correct
	vorsichtig	careful, cautious
der	Arzt (¨e)	doctor
	mager	lean
der	Reis	rice
	passen	to fit
	vorig	last, previous
das	Jahr (-e)	year
	vernünftig	sensible
	weiß (from wissen)	(to) know
	schneiden	to cut
	lecker	delicious
die	Sahnesoße	cream sauce
	allein	on their own
	schmecken	to taste (good)
	achten (auf)	to pay attention (to), keep an eye (on)
der	Semmelknödel (-)	bread dumpling
das	Essen (-)	meal
das	Bierchen (-)	(nice) little beer
	Moment mal!	hold on!
	zunehmen	to put on weight

8

At Monday breakfast: discussing the menu for the day's main meal

MUTTER Was sollen wir denn heute essen?

TOCHTER Nach dem Wochenende habe ich bestimmt etwas Übergewicht. Von heute an muss ich abnehmen. In vier Wochen fahren wir in den Urlaub, da will ich meine Bikinis anziehen können. [Zu ihrem Bruder] Rudi, du bist Sportler, du musst auch unbedingt abnehmen.

SOHN Ich soll bei meiner Figur Sportler sein!? Aber du hast Recht, ich bin zu schwer. Ich darf in den nächsten Wochen keine Kartoffeln mehr essen. Und hoffentlich lassen wir kein Bier mehr ins Haus bringen!

VATER Ganz richtig. Mit fünfzig muss ich auch vorsichtiger sein. Der Arzt sagt, ich soll nur Fisch oder mageres Fleisch essen, dazu nur frisches Gemüse, keine Kartoffeln, keinen Reis.

MUTTER Was soll es denn geben? Ich passe nicht mehr in meine Sommerkleidung vom vorigen Jahr. Wir müssen vernünftig sein. Ich weiß was, ich lasse beim Metzger vier extra magere Steaks schneiden.

TOCHTER Ja, und dann brauchen wir dazu nur eine leckere Sahnesoße.

SOHN Fleisch und Sahnesoße allein schmecken nicht.

VATER Das mag sein, aber wir müssen auf die Kalorien achten.

SOHN Vielleicht können wir dann ein paar Semmelknödel und Karotten in Buttersoße dazu essen.

VATER Zu so einem Essen muss man ein kaltes Bierchen trinken, nicht?

MUTTER Moment mal, werden wir nicht auch von diesem Essen zunehmen?

MOTHER Well, what shall we eat today?

DAUGHTER I'm definitely somewhat overweight after the weekend. I must lose weight from today onwards. We're going on holiday in four weeks, and I want to be able to wear my bikinis. [To her brother] Rudi, you're a sportsman, you've absolutely got to lose weight too.

SON What, I'm supposed to be a sportsman with a figure like mine!? But you're right, I'm too heavy. I mustn't eat any potatoes in the next few weeks. And hopefully we won't be having any more beer brought into the house!

FATHER Quite right. At fifty I've got to be more careful too. The doctor says I must only eat fish or lean meat, and with it only fresh vegetables; no potatoes and no rice.

MOTHER Well, what is it to be? I don't fit into my summer clothes from last year any more. We've got to be sensible. I know, I'll get four particularly lean steaks cut at the butcher's.

DAUGHTER Yes, and then we only need a delicious cream sauce with them.

SON Meat and cream sauce don't taste good on their own.

FATHER That may be so, but we've got to keep an eye on the calories.

SON Perhaps we can also have a few dumplings and some carrots in butter sauce with them.

FATHER You have to drink a nice cold beer with a meal like that, don't you?

MOTHER Hold on, aren't we going to put on weight from this meal too?

8

Exercise 18

Insert the correct form of 'dürfen', 'können', or 'müssen' in the following sentences, choosing the auxiliary verb that best fits the sense:

1 Sie ... gut Englisch sprechen, ihre Lehrerin ist gut.
2 Wir ... den Wein trinken, sonst wird er schlecht.
3 Er ist sechzehn Jahre alt, er ... nicht Auto fahren.
4 Ich ... ins Geschäft gehen und einkaufen, wir haben heute Abend Freunde.
5 Er ... kein Bier trinken, er will abnehmen.
6 Die kleine Tochter ... den Film sehen, es ist Sonntag.
7 Das Mittagessen ... warten, sie will erst den Sherry trinken.

8

36 MEASUREMENTS AND QUANTITIES

Whereas English requires 'of' in expressions such as

two metres of string   (measurements)
a big pile of rubbish   (quantities)
some cans of beans   (other units)

the corresponding expressions in German place the two nouns together:

zwei Meter Bindfaden
ein großer Haufen Abfall
einige Dosen Bohnen

If the first noun is m. or n. it is always in the singular, even when the meaning is plural:

Ich brauche für dieses Rezept zwei Pfund Mehl.
I need two pounds of flour for this recipe.
Ich trinke jeden Abend drei Glas Rotwein.
I drink three glasses of red wine every evening.

37 THE EXPRESSIONS 'ES IST' AND 'ES SIND' ('THERE IS/ARE')

In section 27 we talked about using **es gibt** to mean 'there is/are'. When you know that something exists or is available and the dominant idea is its quantity or number and its location, 'there is/are' is conveyed by **es ist/sind**:

Es ist ein Brief für dich da.
There's a letter for you (here).
Es sind zwei Zeitungen für meine Mutter da.
There are two newspapers (here) for my mother.

The **es** in these sentences is not like the **es** of **es gibt**. You will remember that **gibt** remains singular in all cases, with the noun to which it relates in the DO case. With **es ist/sind** the choice of **ist** or **sind** is made according to whether the real subject of the sentence (here **Brief** and **Zeitungen**) is singular or plural. This real subject is, of course, in the SU case.

38 EXPRESSING SPECIFIC LOCATION

In the examples in section 37 the idea of location was rather weak (**da**) and could be omitted in translation. When the idea of location is more dominant and the information more precise, German has three verbs, in addition to **sein** ('to be'), to express 'is/are', which are all in common use.

1 When something is upright: **stehen**

Auf dem Tisch steht eine alte Vase.
or **Eine alte Vase steht auf dem Tisch.**
or **Es steht eine alte Vase auf dem Tisch.**
There's an old vase on the table.
Der Fernsehapparat steht in der Ecke.
The television set is in the corner.

2 When something is flat: **liegen**

Auf dem Boden liegt ein schmutziger Teppich.
or **Ein schmutziger Teppich liegt auf dem Boden.**
or **Es liegt ein schmutziger Teppich auf dem Boden.**
There's a dirty carpet on the floor.
Die Zeitung liegt auf dem Wohnzimmertisch.
The newspaper is on the living-room table.

3 When something is inserted into/between or concealed: **stecken**

Im Schloss steckt ein rostiger Schlüssel.
or **Ein rostiger Schlüssel steckt im Schloss.**
or **Es steckt ein rostiger Schlüssel im Schloss.**
There's a rusty key in the lock.

Was steckt hinter dem Vorhang?
What's behind the curtain?

Sentences like this beginning with **es** are only possible when the subject is a noun preceded either by **(k)ein** or by another indefinite word (e.g. **einige**), or by nothing.

39 HOW TO SAY 'PUT'

Just as 'to be' in a location can be indicated in a general way with **sein** or more precisely with **stehen**, **liegen**, and **stecken**, you can express 'put' in a general way with **tun** or more precisely with **stellen**, **legen**, and **stecken**:

	being in a location	putting in a location
generalised	**sein**	**tun**
upright	**stehen**	**stellen**
flat	**liegen**	**legen**
inserted	**stecken**	**stecken**

1 Generalised 'put': **tun** (to do, put)

ich	tue
wir/Sie/sie (they)	**tun**
du	**tust**
er/sie (she)/**es**	**tut**

Er tut seine Bücher immer auf das falsche Regal.
He always puts his books on the wrong shelf.
Sie tut etwas Milch in die Milchkanne.
She's putting a little milk in the milk jug.

2 'put' so that something stands: **stellen**

Wir stellen den Nachttisch neben das Bett.
We'll put the bedside table next to the bed.

8

Er stellt die leeren Flaschen vor die Tür.
He puts the empty bottles outside the door.

3 'put' so that something lies flat: **legen**

Sie legt einen Fünfzigeuroschein auf die Theke.
She's putting a fifty-euro note on the counter.

4 'put' so that something is inserted into/between or concealed: **stecken**

Er steckt gerade einen Zehneuroschein in deine Manteltasche!
He's just putting a ten-euro note in your coat pocket!

40 MORE ABOUT PREPOSITIONS

When any of the prepositions you learnt in week 6, section 26 **1–3**, except **ohne** and **seit**, is applied to a 3rd-person pronoun standing for something other than a living being, the pronoun is not used but is represented by **da(r)-** followed by the preposition.

The two bits form one word (e.g. **darüber**, **damit**) with the stress on the preposition. The -**(r)**- is used when the preposition begins with a vowel.

Compare:
Ich lache über sie.
I'm laughing at them (e.g. my children, **meine Kinder**).
Ich lache darüber.
I'm laughing at them (e.g. my mistakes, **meine Fehler**).

The case (DO or IO) that normally follows the preposition does not affect the **da(r)-** construction, which may also stand for a singular or a plural. It may even stand for no noun at all, but for a fact or an idea:

A: Ich höre, er ist arbeitslos.
B: Ja, aber er redet nie darüber.
A: I hear he's unemployed.
B: Yes, but he never talks about it
(i.e. about being unemployed).

Some combinations of **da(r)-** + preposition have
acquired permanent meanings of their own:

dafür	instead, on the other hand
dagegen	by contrast, on the other hand
daher	therefore
damit	so that (purpose), in order that
darum	therefore

ohne ('without') is simply followed by the standard
pronouns (see week 3, section 15).

To say 'since that', 'since it', or 'since then' using **seit**
there is a standard word: **seitdem**.

8

Insert the most appropriate word from the column
on the right into the gap in each of the following
sentences. You may need to juggle with the 'da(r)-'
words so you only use each one once.

1 Er hat eine Feile in der Hand,   dazwischen
   … öffnet er die Tür.

2 Vor dem Einbrecher ist eine Treppe,   danach
   … sitzt ein Skelett.

3 Wir trinken ein Glas Wein, …   darauf
   gehen wir schlafen.

4 Ich esse eine Wurst, … trinke   daneben
   ich eine Cola.

5 Ich nehme fünf Rosen, … muss   dahinter
   ich €10,75 bezahlen.

6 Auf der Tischdecke liegt ein Brot,   dazu
   … steht ein Glas.

7 Der junge Mann ist zu schwer, …   damit
   muss er etwas tun.

8 Sie sehen die Kirche und das   dagegen
   Gasthaus, Sie nehmen die
   Straße ….

9 Das Haus steht direkt an der Straße,   davor
   der Garten liegt ….

10 Wir wollen einkaufen gehen, …   dafür
    müssen wir noch essen.

VOCABULARY

	pass auf!	now look!
der	**Kühlschrank (¨e)**	refrigerator
	möglichst	as (far/much) as possible
	freihalten	to keep clear
das	**Hähnchen (-)**	chicken
die	**Himbeertorte (-n)**	raspberry flan
das	**Fertigessen (-)**	oven-ready meal
das	**Eisfach (¨er)**	freezer compartment
	morgen	tomorrow
	übermorgen	the day after tomorrow
der	**Pflaumenkuchen (-)**	plum tart
die	**Schüssel (-n)**	dish
die	**Schlagsahne**	(here) whipped cream, (but also) whipping cream
der	**Becher (-)**	(here) carton, (but also) beaker, mug
die	**Packung (-en)**	pack, packet
die	**Leberwurst (¨c)**	liver sausage
	einzeln	singly, separately
das	**Stück**	piece (but with number sometimes omitted in translation)
	zum Weichwerden	to get soft
	flach	flat
der	**Behälter (-)**	container
der	**Scheibenkäse**	cheese in slices
der	**Salat**	(here) lettuce
die	**Weintraube (-n)**	grape
der	**Beutel (-)**	bag
die	**Apfelsine (-n)**	orange
der	**Blumenkohl**	cauliflower
der	**Rosenkohl**	brussels sprouts
das	**Gemüsefach (¨er)**	vegetable compartment
das	**Glas (¨er)**	jar
der	**Honig**	honey
die	**Erdbeermarmelade**	strawberry jam
	meine Güte!	my goodness!
das	**Obst**	fruit

8

Exercise 20

Complete the monologue by filling the spaces with the appropriate words for 'be' and 'put'. Do this exercise twice, first using 'sein' and 'tun', and then using the more precise verbs from sections 38 and 39. The vocabulary you need is on page 105.

A mother is about to leave her teenage son on his own for a few days and tells him what she has left in the refrigerator for him.

Pass auf! Ich werde den Kühlschrank möglichst frei-
halten. Dann kannst du alles ganz leicht finden. Das
Hähnchen für Sonntag, die gefrorene Himbeertorte und
die beiden Fertigessen (1) … / … ich ins Eisfach. Die
Fertigessen kannst du morgen und übermorgen essen.
Der Pflaumenkuchen und die Schüssel mit Schlagsahne
(2) … / … oben. Da (3) … / … ich auch die beiden
Flaschen Wein hin … Ach, da ist gerade noch etwas
Platz, den Becher Yoghurt kann ich dazwischen (4) …
/ … Die vier Flaschen Bier (5) … / … ich unten in die
Tür, und zwei Packungen Milch (6) … / … daneben.
Ich (7) … / … die Packung gekochten Schinken, die
Salami und die Leberwurst in die Mitte. Sie sind natür-
lich für abends … Eier? … Die Eier (8) … / … ich
natürlich einzeln oben in die Tür, zwölf Stück. Zwei
Stück Butter (9) … / … ich in das obere Fach in der
Tür, das Dritte lasse ich draußen zum Weichwerden.
Der flache Behälter mit drei Sorten Käse (10) … / … in
der Mitte, und dahinter liegen eine Tube Mayonnaise
und der Scheibenkäse. Die Gurke, der Salat, die
Weintrauben und die Tomaten (11) … / … unten, und
den Beutel Apfelsinen, einen Kopf Blumenkohl und
den Rosenkohl (12) … / … ich ins Gemüsefach ganz
unten. Ein kleines Glas Honig und ein Glas
Erdbeermarmelade (13) … / … ich weiter oben in die
Tür … Meine Güte, ist der Kühlschrank wieder voll!

Exercise 21

Translate the monologue from Exercise 20

Week 9

- *further meanings and uses of 'der', 'die', 'das'*
- *more about the use of the present tense*
- *irregular present-tense forms of common verbs*
- *the pre-present tense and how it is formed*
- *time expressions, including months, days and dates, and times of day*

41 MORE ABOUT 'DER', 'DIE', 'DAS'

1 das not only means 'the' before n. nouns, but can stand alone without a noun to mean 'that':

(i) **A: Du sollst heute bezahlen** You've got to pay today.
B: Das weiß ich. I know (that).

(ii) **A: Zehn Brötchen kosten vier Euro.**
    Ten rolls cost four euros.
B: Das ist zu teuer. That's too much.

In the above, **das** – direct object in (i) and subject in (ii) – stands for facts or ideas rather than identifiable nouns.

2 der (m.), **die** (f.), and **die** (plural) can stand alone without a noun to mean **er** (m.), **sie** (f.), and **sie** (plural):

(i) **A: Der Kellner hat unsere Bestellung seit einer Stunde.**
    The waiter has had our order for an hour.
B: Der ist aber langsam! My goodness, he's slow!

(ii) **A: Ich warte auf die Schwester.**
    I'm waiting for the nurse.
B: Die kommt heute nicht. She's not coming today.

(iii) **A: Was kosten Bananen?**
    What's the price of bananas?
B: Die sind diese Woche billig.
    They're cheap this week.

This use of **der** and **die** so dominates the speech of some Germans as almost to replace **er** and **sie**. When employed in this way, they tend to be used to start sentences, and so are less common in questions, where this is not possible. They always have some degree of stress when spoken with this meaning, unlike when they are used to mean 'the'.

3 The uses described in 1 and 2 also apply to the DO and IO cases, producing the following scheme:

	singular			plural
	m.	f.	n.	
DO	**den (ihn)**	**die (sie)**	**das**	**die (sie)**
IO	**dem (ihm)**	**der (ihr)**	**dem**	**denen (ihnen)**

Examples:

A: Geben Sie mir den Schlüssel.
Give me the key.

B: Den finde ich im Augenblick nicht. (m. DO)
I can't find it just at the moment.

A: Der Chef verspricht mir immer wieder mehr Geld.
The boss is always promising me more money.

B: Dem kann man gar nichts mehr glauben. (m. IO)
You can't believe anything at all that he says.

A: Diese Milch ist sauer.
This milk is sour.

B: Die müssen wir wegwerfen. (f. DO)
We'll have to throw it away.

A: Frau Klimpel schwatzt sehr viel.
Frau Klimpel gossips a lot.

B: Ja, der erzähle ich nie (et)was. (f. IO)
Yes, I never tell her anything.

A: Er verkauft sein Geschäft.
He's selling his shop.

B: Wie bitte? Das glaube ich nicht. (n. DO)
What! I don't believe it.

A: Er hat zu viele Probleme mit seinem Geschäft.
He has too many problems with his business.

B: Dem ist er einfach nicht mehr gewachsen. (n. IO)
He simply can't cope (i.e. with the general situation)
any more.

A: Drüben sitzen die neuen Nachbarn.
The new neighbours are sitting over there.

B: Die kennen wir leider noch nicht. (plural DO)
Unfortunately we don't know them yet.

**A: Ich höre, die Kinder kriegen ein neues
Geschwisterchen.**
I hear the children are going to get a new little
brother or sister.

**B: Denen wollen wir aber eine Zeitlang noch
nichts davon sagen.** (plural IO)
We shan't tell them anything (about it) for a
while, though.

4 der and **die** are often used, particularly in spoken
German, before a forename or a family name, to refer
to individuals. With forenames this may imply intimacy,
and with family names it may have pejorative overtones:

Der Rudi muss abnehmen.
Rudi's got to lose weight.
Ich sehe die Anna heute Abend.
I'm seeing Anna this evening.
Dem Thomas schenke ich fünf Euro.
I'll give Thomas five euros.
Der Schmidt lässt seine Kunden immer warten.
Schmidt is always keeping his customers waiting.

This usage has no parallel in English. The English 'the'
before a family name, to mean the married couple or
family with that name, is entirely optional in German:

(Die) Schmidts sind nicht zu Hause.
The Schmidts are not at home.

5 A single **der**, **die**, or **das** can never suffice to cover a
series of nouns, particularly if they are of mixed gender

or number. But in both conversation and writing, it is common practice to omit **der**, **die**, **das** altogether with groups of two or more nouns, even if separated by **und**:

Das Frühstück ist fertig. Brot, Butter, Eier, Marmelade, Honig, Kaffee, Milch, Zucker, Salz und Pfeffer stehen auf dem Tisch.
Breakfast is ready. The bread, butter, eggs, jam, honey, coffee, milk, sugar, salt and pepper are on the table.

Exercise 22

Insert the correct variant of 'd. .' in the following sentences.

1 A Wie geht es den Geschwistern?
   B Von ... hören wir gar nichts.

2 A Wie lange müssen wir auf den Kaffee warten?
   B ... ist schon lange fertig!

3 Der Junge bekommt immer soviel Geld von mir. ... gebe ich jetzt nichts mehr.

4 A Bei diesem Wetter kann man gar nicht gut arbeiten.
   B ... sage ich auch.

5 A Unsere Tochter heiratet nächste Woche.
   B ... wünsche ich viel Spaß!

6 A Wie alt ist der Sohn von der Wirtin?
   B ... weiß ich nicht.

7 A Wie alt ist der Sohn von der Wirtin?
   B ... kenne ich nicht.

8 A Ich lese gern die BILD-Zeitung.
   B ... lese ich auch gern.

9 A Meine Eltern sind krank, aber sie wollen nicht zum Arzt.
   B ... kann man aber auch gar nicht helfen!

10 A Herr Schmidt verkauft mir saure Milch.
   B Bei ... kaufe ich nichts mehr!

9

USES OF THE PRESENT TENSE

1 The German present tense covers both the English ways of expressing 'present' ideas, as in:

I go to my mother's twice a week.
Don't delay me, I'm going home.

It is also used, as in the English sentences above, to express 'future' ideas, when the future seems like a clear extension of the present:

Nächsten Monat fahre ich in die Vereinigten Staaten.
I go to the States next month.
Ich fahre mit meinem Bruder in Urlaub.
I'm going on holiday with my brother.

2 When the future seems open, justifying a note of intention or conviction, the future tense with **werden** and the infinitive is used:

Ich werde nicht mehr so viel trinken.
I'm going to start drinking less.
Bei solcher Inflation wird alles bald viel mehr kosten.
With inflation like this, everything's going to cost a lot more soon.

Sometimes the future with **werden** is necessary for clarity. The following request:

Können Sie mir helfen, ich suche meine Koffer.
Can you help me? I'm looking for my suitcases.

could have the answer

Ich helfe Ihnen.
I'll help you.

9

Here the present tense has clear future meaning, the implication being **sofort** or **gleich**, 'at once', which might be added. But if the answer was, for example, 'I'll do my best', the present tense could be misleading ('I'm doing my best') and the future with **werden** is preferable:

Ich werde mein Bestes tun. I'll do my best.

3 Used together with a time reference, the German present tense indicates a state of affairs continuing from the past into the present. Contrast with English usage.

Ich kenne ihn seit sechs Jahren.
I have known him for six years.
Wie lange wohnen Sie schon hier?
How long have you been living here?
Wir wohnen hier seit 1992.
We've been living here since 1992.

43 PRESENT TENSE: IRREGULAR VERBS

There are several common verbs which are irregular in the present tense in the 2nd and 3rd persons singular. These must be learnt. The most useful ones are listed below, grouped according to the sound changes that take place. Only the 3rd person singular is given. The 2nd person is formed by inserting **-s-** before the final **-t** (unless the stem ends in **-s**, **-ss**, or **-ß**):

-en form		3rd person singular
fahren	to go (other than on foot), travel	**fährt**
fallen	to fall	**fällt**
halten	to hold	**hält**
schlafen	to sleep	**schläft**
schlagen	to beat, strike	**schlägt**
tragen	to carry, wear	**trägt**
verlassen	to leave	**verlässt**
wachsen	to grow	**wächst**

laufen	to run	**läuft**
lesen	to read	**liest**
sehen	to see	**sieht**
stehlen	to steal	**stiehlt**
essen	to eat	**isst**
geben	to give	**gibt**
helfen	to help	**hilft**
nehmen	to take	**nimmt**
sprechen	to speak	**spricht**
vergessen	to forget	**vergisst**
werfen	to throw	**wirft**

One common verb is irregular throughout the singular:

wissen	to know (facts)	**ich/er/sie/es weiß**
		du weißt

44 THE PRE-PRESENT

You will remember that auxiliary verbs (sections 34 and 35) are used as follows:

Start of sentence: End of sentence:
Finite auxiliary verb   →   Non-finite main verb
   (close to SU)   (**-en** form)

The pre-present follows a similar pattern. The finite verb is either **haben** or **sein**, which can be used as auxiliaries as well as independently. (To find out which to use, see section 45.) In statements this verb is usually the second element of the sentence, and in questions either the first or the second, depending on the type of question.

The non-finite main verb, or past participle, is made by taking the **-en** form, replacing the **-en** by **-t**, and putting **ge** before the stem. For example:

machen→ mach-en › ge-mach-t→ gemacht.

9

This type of verb is like 'climbed' in the English sentence 'we have climbed'.

If the stem of the verb itself ends in **t** or **d**, insert an **-e-** before the added **-t**, to make it easier to say. For example:

warten ('to wait')→ **wart-en**→ **ge-wart-et**→ **gewartet**

From now on we shall refer to the past participle as the **ge_(e)t** form.

Wir haben ein Bild gemalt.

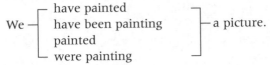

We ⎧ have painted ⎫
   ⎨ have been painting ⎬ a picture.
   ⎩ painted ⎭
     were painting

Wir sind in die Küche gerast.

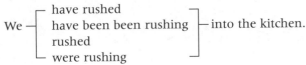

We ⎧ have rushed ⎫
   ⎨ have been been rushing ⎬ into the kitchen.
   ⎩ rushed ⎭
     were rushing

45 AUXILIARY VERB: 'SEIN' OR 'HABEN'?

9

The rule is quite simple. Use **sein** as the auxiliary if the process denoted by the **ge_(e)t** verb:

1 Denotes a process involving motion or a change of state (e.g. **kommen**, 'to come'; **springen**, 'to jump'; **sterben**, 'to die'; **werden**, 'to become') without, however, taking or implying a DO (thus excluding such verbs as **bringen**, 'to take, bring'; **reichen**, 'to hand'; **schicken**, 'to send'; **ziehen**, 'to pull').

2 Is either **sein**, 'to be', or **bleiben**, 'to stay, remain', which imply the opposite of motion or a change of state.

Otherwise use **haben** as the auxiliary.

Examples:
Ich bin hin und her gelaufen (motion).
I ran (or walked!) to and fro.
Ich bin zur Schule gegangen (motion)**, aber mein
Bruder ist zu Hause geblieben** (from **bleiben**).
I went to school but my brother stayed at home.
Meine Großmutter ist vier Wochen krank gewesen
(from **sein**).
My grandmother was ill for four weeks.
Dann ist sie gestorben (change of state).
Then she died.

The rule does mean that some verbs take either **sein**
or **haben**, according to the sense in which they are
being used:

Wir sind immer mit dem Zug gefahren.
(not implying a DO)
We always went by train.
Er hat einen eleganten Sportwagen gefahren.
(taking a DO)
He was driving an elegant sports car.

46 USES OF THE PRE-PRESENT

9

Knowing the pre-present is invaluable, because it enables
you to talk about almost any past event without ever
having to use the past tense (sections 59 and 66). For
the pre-present you only need the present tense of
haben or **sein** and one ge_(e)t form for each verb. The
pre-present covers all the four English constructions in:

We have bought a house.
We have been buying a house.
We bought a house.
We were buying a house.

The German for all the sentences above is simply:

Wir haben ein Haus gekauft.

Most verbs follow the pattern **ge_(e)t** to make the past participle. It is, for example, the pattern for most coinages from non-German sources (e.g. **gestartet, gestoppt, gelandet, gecheckt**). So **ge_(e)t** will always be used in this course as the symbol for the past participle verb form, despite the fact that some verbs don't follow this pattern. Here are some examples of the standard pattern:

-en form		stem	ge_(et) form
kaufen	to buy	**kauf**	**gekauft**
machen	to make, do	**mach**	**gemacht**
sagen	to say	**sag**	**gesagt**
zählen	to count	**zähl**	**gezählt**
baden	to bathe	**bad**	**gebadet**
blenden	to dazzle	**blend**	**geblendet**
bluten	to bleed	**blut**	**geblutet**
leisten	to achieve	**leist**	**geleistet**

1 Irregular forms of **ge_(e)t**

An irregular form in German often corresponds to an irregular form in an English verb from the same source (e.g. 'to swim, swum': **schwimmen, geschwommen**). Here are the main irregular past participles, grouped according to the changes that occur. Try to identify the changes for each group. Any particular oddities are underlined.

-en form		ge_(e)t form
brennen	to burn	**gebrannt**
bringen	to bring, take	**gebra<u>ch</u>t**
denken	to think	**geda<u>ch</u>t**
kennen	to know (people)	**gekannt**
wissen	to know (facts)	**gewusst**
essen	to eat	**gegessen**
fahren	to go (not on foot)	**gefahren**
fangen	to catch	**gefangen**

geben	to give	gegeben
halten	to hold	gehalten
kommen	to come	gekommen
laufen	to run	gelaufen
lesen	to read	gelesen
messen	to measure	gemessen
rufen	to call (out)	gerufen
schlafen	to sleep	geschlafen
schlagen	to hit, beat	geschlagen
sehen	to see	gesehen
stoßen	to bump	gestoßen
tragen	to carry, wear	getragen
treten	to step	getreten
wachsen	to grow	gewachsen
stehen	to stand	gest*anden*
gehen	to go	geg*angen*
brechen	to break	gebrochen
helfen	to help	geholfen
sprechen	to speak	gesprochen
sterben	to die	gestorben
treffen	to meet	getroffen
werden	to become	geworden
nehmen	to take	genommen
stehlen	to steal	gestohlen
leiden	to suffer	gelitten
pfeifen	to whistle	gepfiffen
schneiden	to cut	geschnitten
streiten	to quarrel	gestritten
bleiben	to stay, remain	geblieben
leihen	to lend	geliehen
scheinen	to seem, shine	geschienen
schreiben	to write	geschrieben
steigen	to climb	gestiegen
treiben	to drive, impel	getrieben

9

sitzen	to sit	**gese__ss__en**
schwimmen	to swim	**geschwommen**
finden	to find	**gefunden**
sinken	to sink	**gesunken**
springen	to jump	**gesprungen**
trinken	to drink	**getrunken**
bitten	to ask, request	**gebeten**
riechen	to smell	**gerochen**
schließen	to shut, close	**geschlossen**
liegen	to lie (recline)	**gelegen**
bieten	to offer	**geboten**
fliegen	to fly	**geflogen**
fliehen	to flee	**geflohen**
ziehen	to pull, draw	**gezogen**
lügen	to lie (fib)	**gelogen**
sein	to be	**ge__wes__en**

2 Effect of prefixes on the **ge_(e)t** form

Many German words are composites, consisting
of a central core with a distinctive meaning (the root), to
the front or rear of which are attached further syllables.
In the case of the **-en** form of a verb such as
bekommen ('to get'), the structure looks like this:

be	+	**komm**	+	**en**
prefix	+	root	+	suffix

The prefix, attached to the front, combines with the root to
produce the overall meaning of the verb; the root provides the
core of meaning of the verb; and the suffix, attached to the
end, carries the non-finite form ending. Suffixes are also used

to provide the present or past tense personal ending. Now see how the presence of a prefix affects the **ge_(e)t** form. The stressed syllables are marked with an accent, as observing the correct stress is the key to understanding prefixes and their effects.

TYPE I

-en form	ge_(e)t form	ge_(e)t form analysed		
		prefix	root	suffix
bekómmen	bekómmen	be	kómm	en
to get				
empfínden	empfúnden	emp	fúnd	en
to feel				
entspréchen	entspróchen	ent	spróch	en
to correspond				
erwárten	erwártet	er	wárt	et
to expect				
gehören	gehört	ge	hör	t
to belong				
misslíngen	misslúngen	miss	lúng	en
to fail				
verstéhen	verstánden	ver	stánd	en
to understand				
widerspréchen	widerspróchen	wider	spróch	en
to contradict				
zerstören	zerstört	zer	stör	t
to destroy				

9

TYPE II

-en form	ge_(e)t form	ge_(e)t form analysed		
		prefixes	root	suffix
ánkommen to arrive	**ángekommen**	án	ge	komm en
aúfstehen to get up	**aúfgestanden**	aúf	ge	stand en
aúsmachen to switch off	**aúsgemacht**	aús	ge	mach t
béitreten to join	**béigetreten**	béi	ge	tret en
eínladen to invite	**eíngeladen**	eín	ge	lad en
gégenzeichnen to countersign	**gégengezeichnet**	gégen	ge	zeichn et
míthelfen to assist	**mítgeholfen**	mít	ge	holf en
náchholen to catch up	**náchgeholt**	nách	ge	hol t
vórbeugen to avert	**vórgebeugt**	vór	ge	beug t
zúhören to listen	**zúgehört**	zú	ge	hör t

If you study the two tables carefully, you will see that:

the TYPE I verb prefixes, which are unstressed, do not permit the **ge_(e)t** form prefix **ge-** to be inserted between themselves and the root. They are inseparable from the root. Verbs with inseparable prefixes do not take the **ge-** at all;

the TYPE II verb prefixes, which are stressed, allow the prefix **ge-** to be inserted before the root, and so are called separable.

The **ge_(e)t** forms of both types are written as single words, e.g. **verstanden**, **ausgemacht**.

The suffix variations of both types of prefixed verbs (**-(e)t**, **-en**) follow this rule: if the unprefixed verb is irregular, e.g.

gestanden, so are any prefixed forms derived from it (e.g. **aufgestanden**, 'got up', **verstanden**, 'understood').

The two tables contain the main prefixes that are used exclusively as inseparable or separable prefixes, but they are not exhaustive. There are some prefixes (e.g. **über**, **um**, **unter**) which can appear in TYPE I or TYPE II verbs, producing verbs of completely different meaning, e.g. **umbáuen**, 'to build around, enclose'; **úmbauen**, 'to rebuild, convert'.

To help you use prefixed verbs correctly, all prefixed verbs are labelled I or II in the Mini-dictionary and word lists.

3 Verbs ending in **-ieren**

All verbs ending in (note the stress) **-íeren** (e.g. **telefoníeren, kontrollíeren, interessíeren, informíeren**) make the **ge_(e)t** form without the **ge-** but with the **-t** (e.g. **telefoníert**, etc).

9

Exercise 23

For each sentence, insert the correct form of 'sein' or 'haben' in the first gap, and the 'ge_(e)t' form of the given main verb in the second gap.

1 Er ... mir den Schlüssel ... (bringen)

2 Mein Freund ... heute in die Vereinigten Staaten ... (fliegen)

3 Unsere Eltern ... vor einigen Jahren ... (sterben)

4 Meine Mutter ... die Erdbeermarmelade in den Kühlschrank ... (stellen)

5 Das Kind ... vom Tisch ... (springen)

6 Ich ... heute den ganzen Tag zu Hause ... (bleiben)

7 Dieses Jahr ... die Miete für unsere Wohnung sehr ... (steigen)

8 Ich ... meiner Wirtin einen Brief ... (schicken)

9 Wir ... von meiner Schwester Geld ... (bekommen)

10 Du ... wirklich sehr groß ... (werden)

48 TIME EXPRESSIONS

9

1 Expressions for frequency

nie	never
je (jemals)	ever
selten	rarely
einmal	once
zweimal	twice (etc)
ab und zu	occasionally
manchmal	sometimes
regelmäßig	regularly
immer wieder	again and again
immer	always

2 General expressions for 'now'

jetzt	now (can refer to what is happening or what is imminent)
nun	now (seen as the final step in a series: also has non-temporal sense of 'well now')
im Augenblick **augenblicklich** **im Moment** **momentan**	at the moment
eben **gerade**	just now (a moment ago); (exactly) now, just (at the moment); now (presently), just (in a moment); as with English 'just', **eben** and **gerade** often also mean 'simply' or 'barely'
vorhin	a little time ago
neulich	recently (but only in the sense of a particular recent occasion in the speaker's mind)
letztens **in letzter Zeit**	recently
vor einiger Zeit	some time ago
sofort, gleich	straight away, immediately, at once
bald	soon
nachher	afterwards

3 General expressions related to 'then'

dann	then
damals	at that time
davor, vorher	before that
kurz davor	shortly before that

danach	after that, afterwards
kurz danach	shortly afterwards
früher	formerly

4 Time measured from 'now'

vor einem Monat	a month ago
vor einer Woche	a week ago
seit fünf Sekunden	for five seconds (i.e. starting five seconds ago, before now)
in drei Tagen	in three days (i.e. after three days)

5 Time measured from 'then'

einen Monat davor **einen Monat zuvor**	a month before, previously
seit vier Jahren	for four years (i.e. starting four years previously, before 'then')
nach zwei Wochen **zwei Wochen danach** **zwei Wochen später**	two weeks later

6 Expressions related to 'today'

heute	today
gestern	yesterday
vorgestern	the day before yesterday
heute vor einer Woche **heute vor acht Tagen**	a week ago today
gestern vor zwei Wochen **gestern vor vierzehn Tagen**	a fortnight ago yesterday
morgen	tomorrow
übermorgen	the day after tomorrow

heute in drei Wochen	three weeks today
morgen in acht Tagen	tomorrow week

YEARS, MONTHS, DAYS, DATES, AND TIME

1 Years (see also section 18): no preposition, or preceded, more formally, by **im Jahre**:

2010 werde ich zwanzig. I'll be twenty in 2010.
or
Er hat im Jahre 1995 geheiratet. He got married in 1995.

seit/vor/nach 2003 since/before/after 2003

2 Seasons: preposition **in** (all are m. nouns, so usually **im**)

	Frühling		spring
im	**Sommer**	in	summer
	Herbst		autumn
	Winter		winter

3 Months: preposition **in** (all are m. nouns, so usually **im**)

	Januar		**Juli**
	Februar		**August**
im	**März**	**im**	**September**
	April		**Oktober**
	Mai		**November**
	Juni		**Dezember**

4 Days: preposition **an** (all are m. nouns, so usually **am**)

	Sonntag		Sunday
	Montag		Monday
	Dienstag		Tuesday
am	**Mittwoch**	on	Wednesday
	Donnerstag		Thursday
	Freitag		Friday
	Sonnabend		Saturday
	or **Samstag**		

5 Dates

Without a preposition:

Heute ist der 1. März. (erste)
Today is the first of March.
Donnerstag ist der 3. Mai. (dritte)
Morgen ist der 7. November. (siebte)
Freitag ist der 19. Juli. (neunzehnte)
Übermorgen ist der 20. Oktober. (zwanzigste)

Dating a letter or document:

den 2. Januar 2000 (zweiten) (DO case)
den 30.8.2001 (dreißigsten Achten) (DO case)

With preposition **an**:

Am 15. Juni fahren wir in Urlaub. (fünfzehnten)
We're going on holiday on 15th June.

6 Time of day: preposition **um**

8.00	**acht Uhr**
8.05	**fünf nach acht**
8.08	**acht Minuten nach acht**
8.10	**zehn nach acht**
8.15	**Viertel nach acht** or **viertel neun**
8.20	**zwanzig nach acht**
8.25	**fünf vor halb neun**
8.30	**halb neun**
8.32	**zwei Minuten nach halb neun**
8.35	**fünf nach halb neun**
8.40	**zwanzig vor neun**
8.45	**Viertel vor neun** or **drei viertel neun**

Um Viertel nach eins kommt der Arzt.
The doctor's coming at a quarter past one.

The 24-hour clock, which is in very widespread use
for all sorts of formal purposes, is straightforward:

14.30   vierzehn Uhr dreißig
22.27   zweiundzwanzig Uhr siebenundzwanzig

Exercise 24

Establish in each case which of the sentences (a), (b),
or (c) is most compatible with the initial statement.

1 Im Augenblick habe ich keine Zeit.
   (a) Ich spiele in zwei Stunden Tennis.
   (b) Ich habe jetzt viel Arbeit.
   (c) Ich schlafe im Augenblick.

2 In zwei Wochen fahre ich in die Vereinigten
   Staaten.
   (a) Ich bin für zwei Wochen in den Vereinigten
       Staaten.
   (b) Der Urlaub in den Vereinigten Staaten ist zwei
       Wochen.
   (c) Ich fahre heute in vierzehn Tagen in die
       Vereinigten Staaten.

3 Übermorgen muss ich beim Metzger einkaufen.
   (a) In zwei Tagen kaufe ich ein Pfund Hackfleisch.
   (b) Übermorgen verkauft der Metzger sein
       Geschäft.
   (c) Übermorgen verkaufe ich Gemüse.

4 Seit gestern vor vierzehn Tagen ist seine Mutter
   krank.
   (a) Seine Mutter ist in vierzehn Tagen krank.
   (b) Seine Mutter ist schon zwei Wochen krank.
   (c) Vor vierzehn Tagen ist seine Mutter im Bett
       geblieben.

5 Frau Schmidt ist eben in die Stadt gegangen.
   (a) Frau Schmidt ist momentan in der Stadt.
   (b) Gerade ist Frau Schmidt in die Stadt gefahren.
   (c) Frau Schmidt will gleich in der Stadt spazieren
       gehen.

6 Früher hat Herr Kegel Bücher geschrieben.
   (a) Neulich hat Herr Kegel Bücher geschrieben.
   (b) Nachher schreibt Herr Kegel Bücher.
   (c) Herr Kegel hat damals gute Bücher geschrieben.

9

In English there is a range of reassurance tags, the choice of which is determined by the verb in each sentence:

He likes the painting, doesn't he?
So he likes the painting, does he?
He won't buy it, will he?
We shan't pay, shall we?
We're not going to pay, are we?

In German, on the other hand, one tag does for all sentences, though it varies from region to region and also according to the degree of formality.

In formal situations the tag would be **..., nicht wahr?** and this is often used in writing.

The most frequently used form is **..., nicht?** The initial comma is essential, otherwise the sentence becomes negative.

Most casual of all is **..., ne?**

Regional variants are **..., woll?** and **..., gell?**

When more reassurance is sought, **..., oder?** can be used, especially with negative sentences. However, this is far less common.

9

VOCABULARY

Study and learn the conversation below. You will need these new words:

die	**Ärztin (-nen)**	(female) doctor
	zum ersten Mal	for the first time
	jahrelang	for years
	plötzlich	suddenly
	unangenehm	unpleasant
der	**Schmerz (-en)**	pain
das	**Handgelenk (-e)**	wrist
	bemerken I	to notice
das	**Gelenk (-e)**	joint (here: wrist)
	steif	stiff
die	**Gelegenheit (-en)**	occasion
	passieren	to happen
der	**Schwager (-)**	brother-in-law
der	**Umzug (⁻e)**	removal
	meinen	to say (give an opinion)
der	**Beruf (-e)**	job
	benutzen I	to use
der	**Maurer (-)**	bricklayer
	etwa	(1) about (approximately); (2) perhaps (conjectural)
der	**Fliesenleger (-)**	tiler
	schon mal	ever
	von selbst	by itself
	röntgen	to X-ray
	wie gesagt	as (I) said
	erst mal	first of all
	untersuchen I	to examine
	allgemein	generally
das	**Herz (-en)**	heart
	abhören II	to check (heart, lungs)
der	**Blutdruck**	blood pressure
	messen	to measure
die	**Blutprobe (-n)**	blood test
	behandeln I	to treat
	überweisen I	to transfer, hand over
	schütteln	to shake

9

CONVERSATION

A doctor receives a new patient

PATIENT Guten Tag, Frau Doktor!

ÄRZTIN Guten Tag, Sie sind zum ersten Mal bei mir, nicht?

PATIENT Ja, ich bin jahrelang bei keinem Arzt gewesen.

ÄRZTIN Und was haben Sie denn jetzt so plötzlich?

PATIENT Vor einigen Tagen habe ich sehr unangenehme Schmerzen im rechten Handgelenk bemerkt, und das Gelenk ist auch ganz steif geworden.

ÄRZTIN Bei welcher Gelegenheit ist das passiert?

PATIENT Ich habe neulich meiner Schwester und meinem Schwager beim Umzug geholfen und sehr schwere Sachen getragen. Sofort danach habe ich es gemerkt. Die haben gemeint, ich soll zum Arzt gehen.

ÄRZTIN Haben Sie einen manuellen Beruf? ... mit anderen Worten, benutzen Sie Ihre Hände viel?

PATIENT Früher bin ich Maurer gewesen, aber seit etwa einem Jahr bin ich Fliesenleger.

ÄRZTIN Spielen Sie etwa Handball oder Tennis?

PATIENT Ja, ab and zu beides.

ÄRZTIN Haben Sie schon mal Probleme mit dem Handgelenk gehabt?

PATIENT Ja, vor etwa zwei Monaten, aber es ist von selbst besser geworden. Diesmal sind die Schmerzen viel stärker als vor zwei Monaten.

ÄRZTIN Hat man Ihnen das Handgelenk je geröntgt?

PATIENT Nein, wie gesagt, ich bin lange nicht mehr zum Arzt gegangen.

ÄRZTIN Ich werde Sie erst mal allgemein untersuchen ... Herz abhören ... Blutdruck messen ... Urin untersuchen ... eine

Blutprobe machen ....

PATIENT Warum denn das alles?

ÄRZTIN Sie waren doch so lange nicht beim Arzt...
und dann das Handgelenk röntgen...

PATIENT ... und dann werden Sie das Handgelenk
behandeln, nicht?

ÄRZTIN O nein! Dann überweise ich Sie an meinen
Kollegen Henschel. Der ist Orthopäde!

PATIENT [Schüttelt den Kopf!]

TRANSLATION

PATIENT Hello, doctor.

DOCTOR Hello. This is the first time you've come to see
me, isn't it?

PATIENT Yes, I haven't seen a doctor for years.

DOCTOR And what's the matter with you now all of a
sudden?

PATIENT A few days ago I noticed some very unpleasant
pains in my right wrist, and my wrist also got
quite stiff.

DOCTOR On what occasion did that happen?

PATIENT I was helping my sister and brother-in-law
with their house-moving recently and carrying
very heavy things. I noticed it immediately
afterwards. They said that I must go to the
doctor.

DOCTOR Do you have a manual job? ... in other words,
do you use your hands a lot?

PATIENT I used to be a bricklayer, but I've been a tiler for
about a year.

DOCTOR Do you play, say, handball or tennis?

PATIENT Yes, both now and again.

DOCTOR Have you ever had problems with your wrist
before?

PATIENT Yes, about two months ago, but it got better by
itself. This time the pains are much worse than
two months ago.

DOCTOR Has your wrist ever been X-rayed?

9

PATIENT   No. As I said, I haven't been to the doctor for a long time.

DOCTOR   First I'll give you a general examination ... check your heart ... measure your blood pressure ... check your urine ... do a blood test ....

PATIENT   Why all those things?

DOCTOR   Well, you said you hadn't seen a doctor for such a long time ... and then X-ray your wrist ...

PATIENT   ... and then you'll give me some treatment for the wrist, won't you?

DOCTOR   Oh no! Then I'll transfer you to my colleague Dr Henschel. He specialises in orthopaedics!

PATIENT   [Shakes his head!]

9

Week 10

- the 'possessor' case and a group of masculine nouns with unusual case endings
- more TYPE II verbs
- verb constructions with 'zu' ('to'), 'um … zu', 'ohne … zu', and 'statt … zu'
- how to express the 'obverse process' or passive
- auxiliary verbs in the pre-present, or perfect, tense
- the past tense of 'haben', 'sein', and the auxiliary verbs

50 THE POSSESSOR CASE

In English there are two ways of linking two nouns to show that one possesses the other:

A Friday's paper
John's wife's aunt
both companies' profits
women's rights

B the tip of the iceberg
the opinion of the judge
the end of the matter
brother of the deceased

In **A** the possessor is marked by apostrophe 's' (…'s). In **B** the nouns are linked by 'of'.

In German, possession is expressed by distinctive forms of d. ., of **ein**, of adjectives, and – for m. and n. singular nouns only – of the noun itself:

die Schwägerin meines Freundes
my friend's sister-in-law
die Ansichten beider Rechtsanwälte
the views of both lawyers
der Ruf des ehemaligen Politikers
the former politician's reputation
der Wagen einer alten Dame
an old lady's car

10

All the possessor (PO) forms are shown below:

	singular				plural
		m.	f.	n.	m. f. n.
	d. .	des	der	des	der
	(k)ein	(k)eines	(k)einer	(k)eines	keiner
d. .-type	dies. .	dieses	dieser	dieses	dieser
	jed. .	jedes	jeder	jedes	–
ein-type	unser	unseres	unserer	unseres	unserer
	Ihr	Ihres	Ihrer	Ihres	Ihrer

adjective after				
d. .	-en throughout			

adjective after				
ein	-en throughout			

adjective alone	-en	-er	-en	-er
noun ending	-(e)s	–	-(e)s	–

The (e) of the m. and n. singular noun endings is often inserted after monosyllabic noun stems.

10

51 PREPOSITIONS TAKING THE POSSESSOR CASE

As you saw in week 6, section 26, each preposition in German affects the case of the following noun or pronoun. A few common prepositions take the possessor (PO) case. To help you remember which they are, the English equivalents below all have 'of' after them:

außerhalb	outside of
innerhalb	inside of
jenseits	on the far side of (beyond)
statt	instead of
trotz	in spite of
während	in the course of (during)
wegen	because of, on account of

Though these prepositions are frequently used before nouns, there is no complete set of pronouns for use after PO prepositions. Instead there are a number of unusual forms. These are the most common:

stattdessen	instead (of it)
trotzdem	in spite of this, nevertheless
währenddessen	in the course of it/this
deswegen	because of this, consequently
meinetwegen	on my account, as far as I am concerned
unseretwegen	on our account
deinetwegen	on your account

wegen is also colloquially followed by the IO pronouns:

wegen mir	because of me
wegen uns	because of us
wegen dir	because of you
wegen dem	because of him

10

1 Most m. and n. nouns add **-(e)s** for the singular possessor case. However, some m. nouns, including common ones, do not add **-(e)s** for the possessor case, but add **-(e)n** for all cases, singular and plural, except the SU singular, which is the form given:

der Automat	machine (e.g. vending)	(and other 'imported' nouns ending in **-at**)
der Bauer	farmer	
der Franzose	Frenchman	(and other m nationality designations ending in **-e** like **der Pole**, but NOT **der Deutsche**, which follows different rules; see section 61)
der Held	hero	
der Herr	Mr, gentleman	(adds only **-n** in singular, **-en** in plural)
der Junge	boy	(the colloquial plural adds **-ns** throughout)
der Kollege	colleague	
der Kunde	customer	
der Mensch	person, human being, (plural) people	
der Nachbar	neighbour	
der Präsident	president	(and many other 'imported' nouns ending in **-ent**)
der Soldat	soldier	(see **Automat**)
der Student	student	(see **Präsident**)
der Tourist	tourist	(and other 'imported' nouns ending in **-ist**)

Many other nouns, particularly other imported nouns, follow the same pattern. All such nouns are followed in the Mini-dictionary not by the usual information on the plural, but by '(PO **-n**)' or '(PO **-en**)', for example:
der Tourist (PO **-en**) tourist.

2 A small group of m. nouns ending in **-e** add **-ns** for the singular PO case and **-n** in all other cases. Here are their singular SU cases:

der	**Buchstabe**	letter (of the alphabet)
der	**Gedanke**	thought
der	**Glaube**	belief
der	**Name**	name
der	**Wille**	will (determination)

These are marked in the Mini-dictionary with '(PO **-ns**)'.

53 USING TYPE II VERBS

We have already seen that TYPE II (separable) verbs need the **ge-** of the **ge-_(e)t** form to be inserted between the separable prefix and the root.

The same principle applies if the **-en** form is preceded by **zu** ('to'). This is also inserted between the prefix and the root. In both cases the resulting sequence is spoken and written as one word: **áusgegangen, áuszugehen.**

However, if a TYPE II verb is the finite verb of the sentence, the prefix is split off and appears right at the end of the sentence:

Ich lade meine Freunde für Sonnabend ein. (éinladen)
I'm inviting my friends for Saturday.
Er schlägt ein kaltes Mittagessen mit Brot, Käse und Wein vor. (vórschlagen)
He suggests a cold lunch with bread, cheese, and wine.
Ich helfe bei den Vorbereitungen für die Konferenz nicht mit. (míthelfen)
I'm not helping with the preparations for the conference.

Note that even **nicht**, which usually comes near the end of a sentence, must come before the separated prefix.

10

TYPE I (inseparable) verbs always remain intact:

Ich empfinde gar kein Mitleid mit dieser Frau. (empfínden)
I can feel no sympathy at all with this woman.

54 ZU + THE -EN FORM (INFINITIVE)

If a simple sentence contains both a finite verb and an -en form (infinitive), the -en form must stand right at the end of the sentence (see section 33):

Ich gehe zweimal in der Woche schwimmen.

The -en form is often accompanied by **zu**, just as 'to' often accompanies English infinitives. Whereas in English the verbs are usually near the beginning of a sentence, **zu** comes before the -en form at the end of the sentence. It is not possible to insert anything between **zu** and the -en form. Even stressed prefixes are pushed out of the way:

Er hofft, morgen zu kommen.
He hopes to come tomorrow.
Wir versuchen, ein neues Haus zu finden.
We are trying to find a new house.
Ich habe vor, meine Freunde für Sonnabend einzuladen.
I intend to invite my friends for Saturday.

Look at these more complex examples:

1 (a) **Er wird immer zögern,**   **mir seine Sorgen zu erzählen.**
He will always hesitate   to tell me his worries.

(b) **Ich habe neulich versucht,**   **den Chef für Montag einzuladen.**
I recently tried   to invite the boss for Monday.

2 (a) **Ich werde meine**   **uns ein Picknick**
       Mutter bitten,   **vorzubereiten.**
       I shall ask my mother   to prepare a picnic
                                 for us.

    (b) **Der Arzt hat mich**   **wegen des**
       überredet,   **Handgelenks zum**
                            Orthopäden zu gehen.
       The doctor   to go to the orthopaedic
          persuaded me   specialist with my wrist.

Sentences **1**(b) and **2**(a) show again how a separable
verb allows **zu** to slip between the prefix and root.

Each of the sentences above divides into two clear parts.
No bits of either part may stray into the other, so though
the **ge_(e)t** or **-en** form of the first part has to come last,
this means last in the relevant part.

In the **1** sentences, the SU of the first part becomes the
implied SU of the second part:

er – zögern – erzählen
ich – versuchen – einladen

This is not the case in the **2** sentences, however, where
the implied SU of the second part is the DO from the
first part:

ich – bitten – meine Mutter – vorbereiten
der Arzt – überreden – ich – gehen

10

Exercise 25

Complete the following by filling each double gap with the correct TYPE II verb from the column on the right. The short gap in each case is for the separable prefix, the long one for the rest of the verb.

Ich .... , eine Party zu geben.
Wir sind so viele, also ...... ich meine
Wohnung anders ... . Ich ...... nur
meine besten Freunde ... , aber wir
sind fünfzig. Diesmal ...... meine
Freunde mal nicht ... . Ich will alles
alleine machen. Um 8 Uhr ...... ich
sie ... . Dann können sie kommen.
Aber was sagen meine Freunde, sie ......
stattdessen ... , gar nicht zu essen,
sondern den ganzen Abend lang zu trinken.

anrufen
einladen
einrichten
mithelfen
vorhaben
vorschlagen

55 EXPRESSING PURPOSE

To express a link of purpose between the two parts of a sentence – '(in order) to, (so as) to' – the word **um** is placed at the beginning of the second part of the sentence. Below, the second parts of sentences from section 54 are modified in this way, with new first parts to make sense:

Er wird mich morgen besuchen,
He's visiting me tomorrow

um mir seine Sorgen zu erzählen.
(in order) to tell me his worries.

Ich bin zur Chefsekretärin gegangen,
I've been to the boss's secretary

um den Chef für Montag einzuladen.
(in order) to invite the boss for Monday.

Ich werde etwas Aufschnitt kaufen,
I'm going to buy some sliced meat

um uns ein Picknick vorzubereiten.
(so as) to prepare a picnic for us.

Ich muss besonders früh aufstehen,	**um wegen des Handgelenks zum Orthopäden zu gehen.**
I have to get up particularly early	(so as) to go to the orthopaedic specialist with my wrist.

It is common in English to drop 'in order' or 'so as' and say only 'to', but if the second part of the sentence is the purpose of the first, **um** is essential in German. Unlike sentences with **zu** but without **um**, the implied SU of the second (**um**) part must always be the SU of the first part. Also unlike sentences without **um**, the two parts can be switched around:

Um den Chef für Montag einzuladen,	**bin ich zur Chef-sekretärin gegangen.**
Um mir seine Sorgen zu erzählen,	**wird er mich morgen besuchen.**

When the order is reversed, the former second part, now coming first, affects the word order. As we saw in week 7, section 32, the verb must come second, whatever part of a statement comes first. The **um** part counts as such a part, so that the verb (**bin** and **wird** in the examples above) comes next, followed by the subject (**ich** and **er**).

56 MORE USEFUL EXPRESSIONS

10

Like **um**, both **ohne** and **statt** can be used to start the second part of a sentence. They mean 'without (...-ing)' and 'instead of (...-ing)' respectively. Like **um** sentences, **ohne** and **statt** sentences must have the same subject in both parts, and the sequence of the parts can be reversed.

Ich kann kein Picknick vorbereiten,	**ohne etwas Aufschnitt zu kaufen.**
I can't prepare a picnic	without buying some sliced meat.

Er wird mich morgen besuchen,
He's going to visit me tomorrow

statt mir seine Sorgen am Telefon zu erzählen.
instead of telling me his worries on the telephone.

Exercise 26

I Die Dame geht in die Stadt.
Sie kauft ein.

Die Dame geht in die Stadt, um einzukaufen.

The following pairs of sentences make up a story. Link the two sentences in each pair with 'um … zu', 'ohne … zu', or 'statt … zu', as appropriate, as above.

2 Fräulein Schmidt steht früh auf.
Sie geht mit ihrem Hund spazieren.

3 Mittags kommt sie nach Hause und arbeitet im Garten.
Sie isst nicht.

4 Am Nachmittag geht sie ins Kino.
Sie fragt ihre Mutter nicht.

5 Sie sieht gerne Filme.
Sie kommt auf andere Gedanken.

6 Am Abend kommt ihr Freund.
Er will sie ins Restaurant einladen.

7 Sie verlässt das Restaurant während des Essens.
Sie bezahlt nicht.

8 Er bleibt im Restaurant sitzen und isst beide Portionen.
Er läuft nicht zu seiner Freundin.

10

57 THE OBVERSE PROCESS (PASSIVE)

In German you can use the auxiliary finite verb **werden** together with the **ge_(e)t** form of a verb to express the obverse process (or passive):

Das Haus wird in diesen Tagen eingerichtet.
The house is being furnished at present.
Ich werde oft mitten in der Nacht angerufen.
I'm often rung up in the middle of the night.

In the obverse process, the usual logical progression from the 'doer' to person(s) or thing(s) affected (generally the DO) is turned upside down, so that the affected person or thing becomes the SU:

My father is showing the slides.
becomes
The slides are being shown (by my father).

The obverse process is useful either to draw particular attention to the 'doer', or when the 'doer' is not worthy of attention, or is unidentified. For example:

Die Dias werden von meinem Vater gezeigt.
The slides are being shown by my father (and not, say, by my brother).
Jetzt werden die Dias gezeigt.
The slides are now being shown (by persons insignificant or unknown).

The use of the obverse process in German differs from English in two respects:

1 In English a DO noun or pronoun can be turned into the SU of a sentence:

The slides are being shown.

So can an IO noun or pronoun:

The guest is being shown the slides.

In German the IO cannot become the SU. Although almost the same sequence of words is possible as in English, any IO noun or pronoun must stay in the IO case:

Dem Gast werden die Dias gezeigt.

The subject remains what would be the DO in the active sentence, i.e. **die Dias**, as can be seen from the plural verb **werden**.

2 In German the obverse process is possible with verbs that have no DO and need only a 'doer'. If the 'doer' can't be identified, the obverse process can be used without an SU (or with the impersonal **es** as the SU):

    Heute Abend wird gesungen.
or **Es wird heute Abend gesungen.**
    There's some singing this evening.

    Jetzt wird schnell gegessen!
or **Es wird jetzt schnell gegessen!**
    Now you're going to eat fast!

This means that sentences like:

The children are now being forgiven.
The students are being helped a lot.

containing verbs that take the IO case in German (see week 4, section 21) must be translated:

    Den Kindern wird jetzt verziehen.
or **Es wird den Kindern jetzt verziehen.**

    Den Studenten wird sehr geholfen.
or **Es wird den Studenten sehr geholfen.**

10

Because both the future tense and the obverse process are formed with **werden**, **werden** is not normally used twice in the future obverse process:

Wir werden nächste Woche in Französisch geprüft (werden).
We're going to be examined in French next week.

58 MORE ON THE PRE-PRESENT

To form the pre-present of the sentence:

Ich muss den Nachbarn helfen.
I have to help the neighbours.

the auxiliary verb **muss** has to become pre-present. However, instead of the **ge_(e)t** form of **müssen**, the **-en** form is used:

Ich habe den Nachbarn helfen müssen.
I had to help the neighbours.

The **-en** form of the auxiliary stands right at the end of the sentence, after the **-en** form of the main verb (**helfen**). The same applies to **dürfen**, **können**, **mögen**, **sollen**, **wollen**, and **lassen**.

So, 'I got my car washed' becomes:

Ich habe meinen Wagen waschen lassen.

All of these verbs have an alternative **ge_(e)t** form which is used when they are not auxiliaries. For example:

A: Kannst du geduldig warten?
  Are you able to wait patiently?
B: Nein, das habe ich nie gekonnt.
  No, I've never been able (to do) that.
Wir haben unser Gepäck am Bahnhof gelassen.
We left our luggage at the station.

10

All these 'independent' **ge_(e)t** forms begin with **ge-** and (oxcept **lasson**) ond with **-t**: **gedurft**, **gekonnt**, **gemocht**, **gemusst**, **gesollt**, **gewollt**, and **gelassen**.

When **werden** is used as an auxiliary to form the obverse process, the **ge_(e)t** form is simply **worden**, but when **werden** is used independently ('to become') the **ge_(e)t** form is **geworden**:

Die Dias sind von meinem Vater gezeigt worden.
The slides were shown by my father.
Die Kunden sind heutzutage sehr frech geworden.
Customers have become very cheeky these days.

59   INTRODUCING THE PAST TENSE

Apart from the advantages of using the pre-present as a means of referring to the past (section 46), it is also what Germans are most likely to use in everyday conversation. However, it involves using at least two verbs, sometimes three (as in section 58), and occasionally four.

The alternative is to use the past tense, which employs one verb fewer than the equivalent pre-present. The past tense is often used when the main verb is **sein** or **haben**, to avoid two forms of the same verb in one sentence (e.g. **er ist ... gewesen**; **ich habe ... gehabt**). The past tense of the auxiliary verbs is also often preferred to the pre-present, as it reduces the number of verbs in a sentence from a minimum of three to two. Compare the following:

pre-present	past tense
Ich bin vier Wochen krank gewesen.	**Ich war vier Wochen krank.**

I have been/was ill for four weeks.

Wir haben viel Pech gehabt.	**Wir hatten viel Pech.**

We have been/were very unlucky.

10

Ich habe den Nachbarn
helfen müssen.

Ich musste den
Nachbarn helfen.

Die Dias sind von
meinem Vater
gezeigt worden.

Die Dias wurden von
meinem Vater gezeigt.

Here are the past tenses of **haben**, **sein** and the auxiliary verbs:

	haben	sein
ich/er/sie(she)**/es**	hatte	war
wir/Sie/sie(they)	hatten	waren
du	hattest	warst

	dürfen	können
ich/er/sie(she)**/es**	durfte	konnte
wir/Sie/sie(they)	durften	konnten
du	durftest	konntest

	mögen	müssen
ich/er/sie(she)**/es**	mochte	musste
wir/Sie/sie(they)	mochten	mussten
du	mochtest	musstest

	sollen	wollen
ich/er/sie(she)**/es**	sollte	wollte
wir/Sie/sie(they)	sollten	wollten
du	solltest	wolltest

	lassen	werden
ich/er/sie(she)**/es**	ließ	wurde
wir/Sie/sie(they)	ließen	wurden
du	ließest	wurdest

The 1st and 3rd persons singular, which are always identical in the past tense, have four patterns in the above. Two of them are significant for learning German past tenses in general (see section 66), while a third is typical of another small group. The four patterns are:

10

1	**sein, lassen**	The stem changes (**war, ließ**) and is used without any ending.
2	**sollen, wollen**	The stem stays the same and is followed by **-t-** and the ending **-e**.
3	**haben, dürfen, können, mögen müssen**	The stem changes (**hat-, durf-, konn-, moch-, muss-**) and is followed by **-t-** and the ending **-e**.
4	**werden**	A new stem (**wurd-**) appears and is followed by the ending **-e**.

Pattern **1** is the one followed by the large number of verbs that change stem in the past tense (like English 'come/came'). We shall call these 'new stem verbs'.

Pattern **2** is the model for most verbs, which simply take the stem of the **-en** form and add **-t-**, followed by an ending. These are 'same stem verbs', like 'rush/rushed'.

Pattern **3** is a mixture of **1** and **2**, taking a new stem yet adding **-t-** always followed by an ending, somewhat akin to the English 'kneel/knelt', 'buy/bought'.

10

VOCABULARY

Learn the following conversation. You will need these new words:

die	Freundin (-nen)	girlfriend
die	Silvesterfahrt (-en)	New Year's Eve trip
der	Winterprospekt (-e)	winter brochure
	anbieten II	to offer
	preiswert	reasonably priced
das	Allgäu	mountainous area (in Southern Bavaria)
der	Preis (-e)	price
	reichhaltig	varied
der	Ausflug ('-e)	excursion
die	Abendveranstaltung (-en)	evening entertainment, event
das	Neujahrsfrühstück (-e)	New Year's Day breakfast
der	Sonderpreis (-e)	special price
die	Unterkunft ('-e)	accommodation
das	Doppelzimmer (-)	double room
das	Einzelzimmer (-)	single room
das	Silvesterfestessen (-)	New Year's Eve banquet
die	Skimöglichkeit (-en)	opportunity for skiing
	hin und zurück	there and back, i.e. return (of journey)
	sorgen für	to see to
die	Übernachtung (-en)	overnight stay
der	Hinweg (-e)	outward journey
das	Gleiche	the same
die	Rückfahrt (-en)	return journey
	unterwegs	on the way
	genügend	sufficiently
	anhalten II	to stop, pull up
	jeweils	each time
	einnehmen II	to eat, take, consume

die	Erfrischung (-en)	refreshment
der	Gasthof (-̈e)	inn
der	Löwe (PO -n)	lion
	unterbringen II	to accommodate
der	Grundpreis (-e)	basic price
	enthalten I	to contain, include
die	Dusche (-n)	shower
der	Zuschlag (-̈e)	additional charge
	nicht in Frage kommen	to be out of the question
die	Veranstaltung (-en)	item of entertainment, event
	einbegriffen	included
der	Geschmack (-̈e)	taste
	tagsüber	during the daytime
	tanzen	to dance
	gesellig	sociable
das	Beisammensein	being with other people
der	Gesellschaftsraum (-̈e)	lounge
	genießen I	to enjoy
die	Möglichkeit (-en)	opportunity
das	Skifahren	skiing
das	Festessen (-)	banquet
der	Tanz (-̈e)	dance
	veranstalten I	to arrange, put on
	nach Wunsch	as required, to order
das	Feuerwerk	fireworks
	loslassen II	to set off
das	Sektfrühstück	champagne breakfast
	klingen	to sound
	beschränken I	to limit
	anstrengend	energetic, strenuous
der	Teilnehmer (-)	participant
die	Leute	people
das	Gegenteil	opposite
die	Gruppe (-n)	group
die	goldene Hochzeit (-en)	golden wedding
	feiern	to celebrate
	besprechen I	to discuss, talk over

10

CONVERSATION

Enquiring at a coach tour company about a short New Year holiday

JUNGER MANN Meine Freundin und ich sind daran interessiert, eine Silvesterfahrt zu machen.

FRÄULEIN Gut, ich zeige Ihnen unseren Winterprospekt. Wir bieten dieses Jahr eine sehr preiswerte Fahrt mit Luxusbus nach Oberstdorf im Allgäu an, sieben Tage vom 28. Dezember bis zum 3. Januar inklusiv.

JUNGER MANN [Liest aus dem Winterprospekt]

---

7 Tage Silvesterfahrt mit Luxusbus ins Allgäu

5 Nächte in Oberstdorf

reichhaltiges Programm mit Ausflügen, Abendveranstaltungen und Neujahrssektfrühstück

Sonderpreis €790,–

Unterkunft in Doppelzimmern Einzelzimmer €30,– extra Silvesterfestessen €85,– extra Skimöglichkeiten

---

JUNGER MANN Was wird da alles für den Preis angeboten?

FRÄULEIN Ja, da ist erst mal die Fahrt hin und zurück im Luxusbus. Für alles wird gesorgt ... eine Übernachtung in einem netten Hotel auf dem Hinweg und das Gleiche auf der Rückfahrt ....

JUNGER MANN Wie wird unterwegs gegessen?

FRÄULEIN Es wird natürlich genügend oft angehalten, und das Mittagessen wird jeweils während einer längeren Pause in einem Gasthof eingenommen. Andere Erfrischungen werden im Bus serviert .... Ja, und in Oberstdorf selbst wird man im Gasthof Zum Löwen untergebracht. Der Grundpreis enthält die Unterbringung in Doppelzimmern mit Dusche und Toilette, aber es werden auch Einzelzimmer angeboten für einen Zuschlag von €30,–. Aber das kommt für Sie wohl nicht in Frage ...?

JUNGER MANN Was für Veranstaltungen sind im Preis einbegriffen?

FRÄULEIN Für jeden Geschmack wird gesorgt .... Tagsüber werden drei kleinere Ausflüge gemacht, und jeden Abend wird getanzt, oder man kann das gesellige Beisammensein in der Bar oder im Gesellschaftsraum genießen. Es gibt auch Möglichkeiten zum Skifahren, aber das muss extra bezahlt werden.

JUNGER MANN Und zu Silvester und am Neujahrstag selbst ...?

FRÄULEIN Silvester gibt es Tanz, und um elf Uhr wird eine besondere Show veranstaltet. Silvester wird auch um acht Uhr ein Festessen nach Wunsch serviert für einen Zuschlag von €85,–. Um Mitternacht wird dann das Feuerwerk losgelassen. Am 1. Januar wird ab neun Uhr ein Sektfrühstück eingenommen.

JUNGER MANN Das klingt alles sehr schön. Und sind noch Plätze frei?

FRÄULEIN Ja, wir haben noch sechs Plätze frei. Wir mussten die Zahl der Teilnehmer wegen der Größe unseres Busses auf dreißig beschränken.

JUNGER MANN Bei solch einem anstrengenden Programm sind die anderen Teilnehmer doch bestimmt alles junge Leute ....

10

FRÄULEIN	**O nein, ganz im Gegenteil! Sechzehn der Teilnehmer fahren als Gruppe, um Silvester eine goldene Hochzeit zu feiern.**
JUNGER MANN	**O! Das muss ich doch noch mal mit meiner Freundin besprechen ....**

TRANSLATION

YOUNG MAN	My girlfriend and I are interested in doing a New Year's Eve trip.
ASSISTANT	Right, I'll show you our winter brochure. This year we're offering a very reasonable trip by luxury coach to Oberstdorf in the Allgäu, seven days from 28th December to 3rd January inclusive.
YOUNG MAN	[Reads from the winter brochure]

---

7 day New Year's Eve trip
to the Allgäu by luxury coach

5 nights in Oberstdorf

Varied programme with excursions,
evening entertainments and
New Year's Day champagne breakfast

Special price €790,–

Accommodation in double rooms
Single room €30,– extra
New Year's Eve banquet €85,– extra
Opportunities for skiing

YOUNG MAN	What sort of things do you get for the price?
ASSISTANT	Well, first of all there's the outward and return journey in a luxury coach. Everything is taken care of ... an overnight stop in a nice hotel on the way out and the same on the return journey ....
YOUNG MAN	How are the meals provided on the journey?

10

ASSISTANT There are sufficient stops, of course, and lunch is always taken in an inn during a fairly long break. Other refreshments are served in the coach …. Well, and in Oberstdorf itself you're accommodated in the Lion Inn. The basic price includes accommodation in double rooms with shower and toilet, but single rooms are also available at an extra charge of €30,–. But you wouldn't be interested in that, I suppose …?

YOUNG MAN What sort of entertainments are included in the price?

ASSISTANT Every taste is catered for …. In the daytime there are three shortish excursions, and there's dancing every evening, or you can enjoy the company in the bar or the lounge. There are also opportunities to ski, but you have to pay extra for that.

YOUNG MAN And on New Year's Eve and New Year's Day themselves …?

ASSISTANT On New Year's Eve there's a dance, and at eleven o'clock a special show is put on. And on New Year's Eve there's also a banquet served to order at eight o'clock at an extra charge of €85,–. Then at midnight the fireworks are set off. On 1st January from nine o'clock onwards you can have a champagne breakfast.

YOUNG MAN That all sounds very nice. And are there still places available?

ASSISTANT Yes, we still have six places vacant. We have had to restrict the number of participants to thirty because of the size of our coach.

YOUNG MAN With such a strenuous programme I suppose the other participants are all young people ….

ASSISTANT Oh no, just the opposite! Sixteen of the participants are going as a group to celebrate a golden wedding on New Year's Eve.

YOUNG MAN Oh! I'll have to talk that over again with my girlfriend after all ….

10

Week 11

- words used in front of nouns to express quantity ('all the', 'a little', etc) or to identify them (e.g. 'the same')
- making adjectives into nouns
- linking sentences using joining words which affect the word order of the attached sentence
- reflexive pronouns ('myself', 'yourself', etc)
- the use of reflexive pronouns with verbs to form reflexive verbs

60 QUANTIFIERS AND IDENTIFIERS

As well as the **d. .-** and **ein**-type words of section 28, there is a set of common expressions used before nouns which quantify or identify them. These are grouped below according to whether they are used (a) before any type of noun; (b) before uncountable nouns (e.g. 'flour'); (c) before countable nouns in the singular (e.g. 'shop'); or (d) before countable nouns in the plural (e.g. 'shops').

As these expressions vary in their endings, in the information given for each you are referred where necessary to the sets of endings 1, 2, and 3 from week 7, section 29, and week 10, section 50 for the PO case.

As with the units of measurement in week 8, section 36, where there is 'of' in English there is usually nothing in German.

(a) Before any type of noun

the same (identical)	**d. . selb. .**	Written as one word, **der**, **die**, **das** with its usual endings, **selb. .** with set 1 endings.
the same (alike)	**d. . gleich**	Two separate words, **gleich** having set 1 endings.
all (of) the, the whole (of the)	**d. . ganz**	**ganz** means 'entire', so it also follows **ein**, **mein**, etc. It takes set 1 or 2 endings as required.

Ich bin in derselben* Gruppe wie du.
I'm in the same group as you.
Ich habe das gleiche* Kleid wie du gekauft.
I've bought the same dress as you.
Die ganze Arbeit hat er alleine geschafft.
He's managed all the work on his own.
Meine ganzen Bücher sind nass geworden.
All my books have got wet.
Ein ganzes Jahr hat er dafür gebraucht.
He took a whole year for it.

* In practice there is a lot of overlap between **d. . selb. .** and **d. . gleich**

(b) Before uncountable nouns

little	**wenig**	No ending required.
a little	**etwas**	No ending required.
some	**einig. .**	Takes set 3 endings.
a bit of	**ein bisschen**	Really a n. noun, so **ein** has its usual endings.
a drop of	**ein Tropfen**	A m. noun, so **ein** has its usual endings.
enough	**genug** **genügend**	No ending required.
much, a lot of	**viel**	No ending required.
all (of) the, the whole (of the)	**d. . ganz**	See (a) above.
all (the)	**all. .**	Takes set 1 endings, but PO **-en** before m. and n. nouns with PO ending **-(e)s**.
all that/this, all my, etc	**all d. . /dies. .** **all mein, usw.**	**all** has no ending.

für wenig Geld for little money
mit etwas Salz with a little salt
vor einiger Zeit some time ago
mit einem bisschen Papier with a bit of paper

11

mit einem Tropfen Öl with a drop of oil
Wir haben genug Wein. We have enough wine.
bei viel Arbeit with a lot of work
bei allem guten Willen with the best will in the world
trotz allen Komforts in spite of all the comfort
wegen all der Unruhe because of all that noise

(c) Before countable nouns in the singular

the same	**d. . selb. .**	See (a) above.
any, some or other	**irgendein**	Endings of **ein**.
another (one more)	**noch ein**	**ein** has usual endings.
another (a different one)	**ein. . ander**	**ander** takes set 2 endings.
the whole (of the)	**d. . ganz**	See (a) above.

Heute kommt irgendein Vertreter von der Versicherung.
Some representative or other from the insurance company is coming today.
Heute kommt noch ein Vertreter von der Versicherung.
Another (one more) representative from the insurance company is coming today.
Heute kommt ein anderer Vertreter von der Versicherung.
Another (different) representative from the insurance company is coming today.

(d) Before countable nouns in the plural

a pair of	**ein Paar**	a n. noun, so **ein** has its usual endings, and the following noun has the same case.
the two	**d. . beid. .**	**beid. .** takes set 1 endings.

both	**beid. .**	Takes set 3 endings.
a few	**ein paar**	No endings, though a following IO noun may need **-(e)n**.
some	**einig. .**	Takes set 3 endings.
	mehrer. .	Takes set 3 endings.
many	**viel. .**	Takes set 3 endings.
enough	**genug**	See (b) above.
	genügend	
all (of) the	**all. .**	Takes set 3 endings, but any following adjective adds **-en** in all cases.

von einem Paar alten Schuhen
from an old pair of shoes
wegen der beiden Damen
because of the two ladies
mit beiden Händen
with both hands
vor ein paar Wochen
a few weeks ago

für einige gute Freunde for some good friends
für mehrere gute Freunde for several good friends
für viele gute Freunde for many good friends
für alle guten Freunde for all the good friends

11

61 MAKING ADJECTIVES INTO NOUNS

Adjectives in German are often converted into nouns. In English this is limited to denoting collective categories of people ('the disabled', 'the sick') and some abstracts, ('the good, the bad, and the indifferent'), but in German the usage is almost unrestricted. In the last Conversation (see page 151) there was the phrase:

das Gleiche auf der Rückfahrt
the same on the return journey

Here the adjective **gleich**, given an initial capital letter, has become a n. noun, the automatic gender for all adjectival nouns that do not refer specifically to male or female beings.

Adjectival nouns take the adjective endings described in week 7, section 29. For instance, 'a German' is **ein Deutscher** if a man, but **eine Deutsche** if a woman, because the noun is derived from the adjective **deutsch**.

Adjectival nouns can be created as needed. Many of them are based on two non-finite forms of the verb: the **ge_(e)t** form, with which you are already familiar, and the **-end** form. Whereas the **ge_(e)t** form implies completion, the **-end** form implies incompleteness and simultaneity.

For example, **gefangen** means 'caught' or 'captured' and **überlebend** means 'surviving'. Used as adjectival nouns, they become **der Gefangene** (or **die Gefangene**), 'prisoner', and **der Überlebende** (or **die Überlebende**), 'survivor'. Any such nouns listed in the Mini-dictionary are marked 'adj', to show that they must be given adjective endings.

Another common use of adjectives as nouns is in combination with **etwas**, 'something', and **nichts**, 'nothing'. In these cases the adjective has the endings given in section 29 set 3.

11

Die Stunde soll mit etwas Einfachem anfangen.
The lesson must start with something simple.
Alles war ruhig, nichts Wesentliches ist geschehen.
Everything was quiet; nothing important happened.

On the other hand **alles**, 'everything', having the n. **-es**
already incorporated, is followed by an adjectival noun
using the section 29 set 1 endings:

Ich wünsche dir alles Gute zum Geburtstag.
I wish you all the best for your birthday.
In allem Praktischen war er der Klassenbeste.
In everything practical he was the best in the class.

62 ATTACHED SENTENCES

A sentence can contain a phrase which is attached to its
core and yet has a separate identity. The first such
phrases we looked at ended simply with **zu + -en** form.
Other phrases enclosed their contents between
link-words or joiners like **um**, **ohne**, and **statt** and
the **zu + -en** form.

As well as such 'attached phrases', however, there are
what we shall call 'attached sentences' – sentences
which contain a finite verb of their own, even though
they are attached to a central or core sentence.

1 The simplest way of linking an attached sentence to a
core sentence, so that the two are interdependent, is to
place the attached sentence next to the core sentence
with nothing except a comma in between – and with no
effect on the word order of either. For example:

**Der Arzt sagt, ich soll nur Fisch oder mageres
Fleisch essen.**
The doctor says I must only eat fish or lean meat.
Die haben gemeint, ich soll zum Arzt gehen.
They said I must go to the doctor.

Reverse the sequence of the sentences and the word order in the main sentence changes:

Ich soll nur Fisch oder mageres Fleisch essen, sagt der Arzt.

The entire attached sentence constitutes the DO of the main sentence.

2 The scope for linking sentences is immeasurably widened by the use of link-words or joiners to introduce the attached sentence. Here is a small set of joiners:

und	and
aber	but
oder	or
sondern	but (on the contrary)
sondern ... auch	but ... also

These can be used to join any comparable words or phrases to each other and can also link sentence to sentence. They function like their English equivalents and generally have no effect on the word order:

Es gibt auch Möglichkeiten zum Skifahren, aber das muss extra bezahlt werden.

If any of these joiners are used to link sentences where the word order has already been affected by some other factor (see section 63 below), the new word order will be retained for the sentence attached by **und**, **aber**, etc.

Take care when choosing between **aber** and **sondern**, both of which mean 'but':

If the sense is 'not only ... but also', the German must be **nicht nur ... sondern auch**.

11

If the sense is 'not ... but (on the contrary)', the German must be **nicht** (or another form of the negative, such as **kein**) ... **sondern**:

Er schickt keinen Brief, sondern er will mit mir persönlich sprechen.
He's not sending a letter but intends to speak to me personally.

3 The joiner **denn** is a rule unto itself. Like the joiners in **2** it doesn't affect word order, but it can't link anything except sentences. An attached sentence it introduces must stand after the core sentence.

Er kann mir nicht böse sein, denn er hat selbst Schuld daran.
He can't be cross with me, since it's his own fault.

The meaning of **denn** is explanatory, and it may be translated by 'as', 'since', or 'for'.

Nowadays there is a clear tendency in spoken German, as opposed to written German, for the joiner **weil** (see section 63) to be used like **denn** when it introduces an attached sentence after the core sentence, leaving the word order of the following sequence as it was:

Ich kann ihm nicht böse sein, weil ich habe selbst Schuld daran.
I can't be cross with him, because it's my own fault.

11

1 d. . joiners

	singular			plural	translation
	m.	f.	n.	m. f. n.	
SU	**der**	**die**	**das**	**die**	who, which, that
DO	**den**	**die**	**das**	**die**	who(m), which, that
IO	**dem**	**der**	**dem**	**denen**	to/for whom, to/for which
PO	**dessen**	**deren**	**dessen**	**deren**	of whom, of which, whose

These joiners are identical with the **d. .** words described in section 41, plus **dessen** and **deren** for the possessor case. They relate the attached sentence to a noun in the core or preceding sentence.

The joiner is singular (m., f., or n.) or plural to match the relevant noun in the core sentence, but the choice of case is determined by the role of the joiner in the attached sentence. There it may stand by itself as SU, DO, IO, or PO, or be in tandem with a preposition. The following examples show the principles involved:

SU **Ich bringe meinen Sohn, der nach Berlin fährt, zum Bahnhof.**
I'm taking my son, who's going to Berlin, to the station.
Das Fleisch, das auf dem Tisch liegt, kannst du für den Hund nehmen.
You can take the meat that's on the table for the dog.

DO **Mein Chef, für den ich seit zehn Jahren arbeite, ist sehr unsympathisch.**
My boss, for whom I've been working for ten years, is very unpleasant.
Wir haben den Urlaub, den wir auf Zypern verbracht haben, ganz toll gefunden.
We found the holiday (that) we spent in Cyprus quite fantastic.

11

IO **Meine Schwiegertochter, der ich gestern Blumen geschenkt habe, hat sie zum Blumengeschäft zurückgebracht.**
My daughter-in-law, to whom I gave some flowers yesterday, took them back to the florist's.
Der Verwandte, bei dem ich wohne, ist wie ein Vater zu mir.
The relative who(m) I live with is like a father to me.

PO **Hans, dessen Frau aus Ägypten kommt, lernt Chinesisch!**
Hans, whose wife comes from Egypt, is learning Chinese!
Die Frau, deren Auto falsch geparkt ist, versucht mit dem Polizisten zu flirten.
The woman whose car is illegally parked is trying to flirt with the policeman.

As in all the above examples, the finite verb of the attached sentence, i.e. the sentence introduced by the joiner, must stand at the end of the attached sentence. This rule applies to all the types of attached sentences described in this section.

Finally, when the attached sentence is related to a noun in the main sentence by a preposition, and that noun is not a living being, the **d. .** joiner has the alternative **wo(r)-**. (This is like the **da(r)-** described in week 8, section 40.)

Die Fehler, über die ich gerade lache, sind eigentlich überhaupt nicht witzig.
or
Die Fehler, worüber ich gerade lache, sind eigentlich überhaupt nicht witzig.
The mistakes I'm just laughing about aren't really funny at all.

2 dass, ob, and w. . joiners

The **w. .** joiners are **wann, warum, was, welch . .,
wer, wen** ('whom'), **wessen** ('whose'), **wem** ('to
whom'), **wie,** and **wo.** These joiners enable the entire
contents of the attached sentence to be the SU or DO
of the main sentence:

SU **Dass wir heute Abend kein Essen im Haus
    haben, ist nicht meine Schuld.**
    or
    **Es ist nicht meine Schuld, dass wir heute
    abend kein Essen im Haus haben.**
    It's not my fault that we've no food in the
    house this evening.

DO **Kannst du mir sagen, ob er morgen kommt?**
    Can you tell me whether he's coming tomorrow?

SU **Wann er morgen aufsteht, ist vollkommen egal.**
    or
    **Es ist vollkommen egal, wann er morgen
    aufsteht.**
    It's completely immaterial when he gets up
    tomorrow.

DO **Weißt du zufällig, wessen Regenschirm hier
    liegt?**
    Do you happen to know whose umbrella this is here?

This category of attached sentences includes cases
where the attached sentence may not appear to be
the object of the core sentence, although it really is,
because an optional word has been omitted:

Ich bin froh (darüber), dass er endlich zu Hause ist.
I'm glad (about the fact) that he's home at last.

Here, in English 'about the fact' sounds artificial, but
including the optional **darüber** would sound natural in
German. This way of producing a 'complete' core

sentence uses **da(r)-** to stand for the object of a preposition (**über**). The full object is then stated in the attached sentence introduced by **dass.**

When the preposition is essential to the sense of an idiom the construction with **da(r)-** in the core sentence is mandatory, as in the following:

Wir sind dafür, dass das Licht ausgemacht wird.
We are for the light being switched off.
Mein Vater ist dagegen, dass ich den Führerschein mache.
My father is against me (my) taking my driving test.

Here the sense depends entirely on **für** and **gegen**, but there are also many combinations of verb + preposition and adjective + preposition where, though the sense is clear from the verb or adjective, usage requires the preposition to be stated (and therefore **da(r)-** in the core sentence). Examples include **bestehen auf**, 'to insist on'; **einverstanden mit**, 'agreeable to':

Ich bestehe darauf, dass er sofort bezahlt.
I insist on him (his) paying immediately.
Er ist damit einverstanden, dass sie den Führerschein macht.
He's agreeable to her taking her driving test.

Nor is the **da(r)-** + preposition construction limited to cases where the attached sentence is introduced by the joiner **dass.** The expression **abhängen von**, 'to depend on', is often followed by attached sentences introduced by **ob, wo, wie**, etc:

Meine Entscheidung hängt davon ab, ob der Versuch gelingt.
My decision depends on whether the attempt succeeds.

Do not confuse **dass** with **das**; **dass** is always a joiner.

Exercise 27

Revise the following mini-story by using 'dass' to introduce each attached sentence. The first one is done for you.

1 Fritz schlägt vor, Ernst soll ihm helfen.→ Fritz schlägt vor, dass Ernst ihm helfen soll.

2 Ernst bittet darum, Fritz soll solche Vorschläge nicht machen.

3 Fritz besteht darauf, Ernst soll endlich mal etwas tun.

4 Ernst findet die Arbeit so anstrengend, er verletzt sein Handgelenk plötzlich.

5 Jetzt hat Fritz solches Mitleid, er schickt Ernst zum Arzt.

6 Der Arzt sieht sofort, Ernst ist einfach faul!

3 Prepositional joiners

These fulfil the same function at the beginning of an attached sentence as a preposition does before a noun. One or two are identical or nearly identical to the equivalent prepositions:

Bis fünf Uhr ...	(**bis** preposition)
Till five o'clock ...	
Bis er kommt, ...	(**bis** joiner)
Till he comes ...	
Während des Konzerts ...	(**während** preposition)
During the concert ...	
Während das Orchester spielt, ...	(**während** joiner)
While the orchestra is playing ...	
Nach dem Essen ...	(**nach** preposition)
After the meal ...	
Nachdem wir gegessen haben, ...	(**nachdem** joiner)
After we have dined ...	
Vor Weihnachten ...	(**vor** preposition)
Before Christmas ...	
Bevor wir anfangen, ...	(**bevor** joiner)
Before we begin ...	

11

Others are more remote from the preposition with equivalent meaning:

Wegen des schlechten Wetters ...   (**wegen** preposition)
Because of the bad weather ...
Weil das Wetter schlecht ist, ...   (**weil** joiner)
Because the weather is bad ...
Trotz meiner Erkältung ...   (**trotz** preposition)
In spite of my cold ...
Obwohl ich erkältet bin, ...   (**obwohl** joiner)
Although I have a cold ...

Most prepositional joiners relate either to (a) time or (b) causality. Here are the most important ones:

(a) Time

als	when (single period or point of time in the past)
bevor	before
bis	till, until
nachdem	after
seitdem	since
sobald	as soon as
während	while
wenn	whenever (repeated periods or points of time in the past or present)

(b) Causal connection

da	as, since
damit	so that, in order that (purpose)
obwohl	although
ohne dass	without
so dass	so that (effect), with the result that
statt dass	instead of
während	whereas
weil	because
wenn	if
wo	seeing that

11

It is important not to use **so dass** for every 'so that', but only where a consequence is being referred to:

Ich habe meinen Hausschlüssel verloren, so dass ich nicht ins Haus komme.
I've lost my front door key, so (that) I can't get into the house.

Where purpose or intention is meant, use **damit**:

Er hat das Schloss ausgetauscht, damit ich mit meinem Hausschlüssel nicht ins Haus komme.
He's changed the lock so that I can't get into the house with my front door key. (i.e. in order to prevent me)

ohne dass and **statt dass** are used when the subject of the attached sentence is different from the subject of the core sentence (cf. section 56):

Ich kann kaum anfangen zu lesen, ohne dass mich eins der Kinder stört.
I can barely start reading without one of the children disturbing me.
Meine Eltern haben mir den Englischkurs bezahlt, statt dass ich mein eigenes Geld dafür nehmen musste.
My parents paid for the English course for me instead of my having to use my own money for it.

11

Exercise 28

Rewrite the following so that each contains an attached sentence introduced by 'bevor', 'bis', 'nachdem', 'obwohl', 'während', 'weil', as appropriate. The first one is done for you.

1 Vor dem Essen muss man die Hände waschen.→
  Bevor man isst, muss man die Hände waschen.

2 Nach dem Essen soll man eigentlich nicht schlafen.

3 Während des Essens darf man nicht zu viel reden.

4 Trotz des vielen Redens hat er eigentlich nicht viel gesagt.

5 Wegen des schönen Wetters müssen wir endlich im Garten arbeiten.

6 Bis zum Anfang des Programms kannst du noch schön in der Küche helfen!

7 Wegen deines hohen Blutdrucks musst du weniger arbeiten.

8 Trotz seines hohen Blutdrucks läuft er jeden Tag.

64 REFLEXIVE PRONOUNS

If the SU of a sentence needs to become the DO or IO of the same sentence too, i.e. to be turned back on itself (hence the term reflexive), English uses '(to/for) myself, yourself, themselves', etc.

For the 1st person singular and plural and for the 2nd person singular, German uses the DO and IO pronouns you learnt in sections 15, 20 and 31:

		DO	IO
Ist	singular	**mich**	**mir**
Ist	plural	**uns**	**uns**
2nd	singular	**dich**	**dir**

Wir kaufen uns für nächsten Sommer einen Wohnwagen. (IO)
We're buying (for) ourselves a caravan for next summer.

Du siehst furchtbar müde aus, du musst dich mehr schonen. (DO)
You look terribly tired. You've got to spare yourself more.

For the 3rd person singular and plural and for the 2nd person plural, the special form **sich** is used, whether for the DO or IO:

Meine Eltern haben mir den Brief nicht gegeben, sondern ihn für sich behalten. (DO)
My parents didn't give me the letter but kept it for themselves.

Mein Bruder hat sich einen neuen Sportwagen angeschafft. (IO)
My brother has got himself (lit. acquired for himself) a new sports car.

Wenn Sie sich nicht etwas mehr schonen, machen Sie sich kaputt. (DO)
If you don't spare yourself a bit more you'll wear yourself out.

NOTE:
(a) The plural reflexive pronouns, as well as meaning 'ourselves, yourselves, themselves', can also mean 'each other, one another':

Weil wir im selben Alter sind, haben wir uns sofort geduzt.
Because we're the same age we addressed each other with 'du' immediately.

(b) The reflexive pronouns are used in all cases where the required pronoun relates to the subject of the sentence, even when English would not use a '-self' pronoun. Remember to use **sich** and not the DO/IO pronouns for the 2nd person plural and 3rd person singular and plural:

Er hat nicht genug Geld bei sich.
He hasn't got enough money on him.

11

Jetzt haben Sie Ihren besten Freund gegen sich.
Now you've got your best friend against you.

(c) The German equivalent of the English 'myself' etc used to emphasise a point is **selbst**:

Probier diesen Kuchen, ich habe ihn selbst gemacht.
Try this cake – I made it myself.

65 REFLEXIVE VERBS

There are parallels between the use of reflexive pronouns with verbs in English and in German:

Er hat sich verletzt und muss zum Arzt (gehen).
He's hurt himself and has to go to the doctor.

However, in German the combination verb + reflexive pronoun (reflexive verb) often occurs where you would not expect one in English.

1 Where English has 'get + verb ending in -ed'. Some common examples:

to get annoyed	**sich ärgern**
to get dressed (to dress)	**sich anziehen II**
to get drunk	**sich betrinken I**
to get excited	**sich aufregen II**
to get lost	**sich verirren I**
	sich verlaufen I
to get ready	**sich vorbereiten II**
to get shaved (to shave)	**sich rasieren**
to get undressed	**sich ausziehen II**
to get used/accustomed (to)	**sich gewöhnen (an) I**
to get washed (to have a wash)	**sich waschen**

In attached sentences, where the finite verb comes last, the reflexive pronoun is quite likely to come immediately after the joiner, before the SU to which it relates.

11

Während mein Bruder sich wäscht, ziehe ich mich an.

or

Während sich mein Bruder wäscht, ziehe ich mich an.

While my brother's having a wash, I'll get dressed.

However, if the subject of the attached sentence is itself a pronoun, it must precede the reflexive pronoun:

Während er sich wäscht, ziehe ich mich an.

While he's having a wash, I'll get dressed.

2 Where English has 'be + verb ending in -ed' (or an adjective with similar meaning), where the process indicated is often a state of mind. The most common examples are:

to be ashamed	**sich schämen**
to be embarrassed	**sich genieren**
to be frightened (of)	**sich fürchten (vor)**
to be interested (in)	**sich interessieren (für)**
to be pleased (at)	**sich freuen (über)**
to be surprised	**sich wundern**

Er bittet seine Mutter nicht um Geld, weil er sich geniert.

He's not asking his mother for money because he's embarrassed.

Er findet die Ferien langweilig, denn er interessiert sich für nichts.

He finds the holidays boring, since he's not interested in anything.

Ich gratuliere, ich freue mich sehr über Ihren Erfolg.

I congratulate (you). I'm very pleased at your success.

Ich wundere mich, dass du bei so schönem Wetter im Haus bleibst.

I'm surprised that you're staying inside the house in such lovely weather.

11

3 As equivalent to a range of English expressions, some referring to mental states or processes:

to apologise	**sich entschuldigen I**
to approach	**sich nähern**
to be, be situated	**sich befinden I**
to catch a cold	**sich erkälten I**
to complain	**sich beklagen I**
to feel (e.g. sad)	**sich fühlen**
to hurry	**sich beeilen I**
to imagine (delusion)	**sich (IO) einbilden II**
(mental image)	**sich (IO) vorstellen II**
to long (for)	**sich sehnen (nach)**
to look forward (to)	**sich freuen (auf)**
to remember	**sich erinnern (an) I**
to say thank you, express one's thanks	**sich bedanken I**

Der Junge ist noch so klein, ich habe ihn mir größer vorgestellt.
The boy is still so small. I imagined him taller.
Ich habe Hunger, ich freue mich sehr auf das Essen.
I'm hungry. I'm looking forward to the meal (literally, to the food).

4 Some ideas are conveyed in German by impersonal reflexive phrases with the subject **es**, for example:

to be, to be about, to be a matter of	**sich handeln um**

11

Ich muss Sie leider stören, es handelt sich um Ihren Sohn ...
I'm sorry to have to trouble you; it's about your son ...
Bei der Silvesterfahrt handelt es sich um eine Sieben-Tage-Tour.
The New Year's Eve trip is (a matter of) a seven-day tour.
Im Allgäu lebt es sich sehr angenehm.
Life is very pleasant in the Allgäu.

Study and learn the dialogue that follows. You will need these new words:

der	Fehler (-)	fault
	sich beschweren I	to complain
	erscheinen I	to appear
der	Kassenbon (-s)	till receipt
der	Kauf (¨e)	buying, purchase
die	Reklamation (-en)	complaint (here implying replacement or refund)
der	Aufkleber (-)	sticker
der	Anfang (¨e)	beginning
	pfeifen	to whistle
der	Pfeifton	whistling
	auftauchen II	to turn up, appear
der	Ton (¨e)	sound
	sich (DO) anhören II	to sound
das	Gerät (-e)	(piece of) equipment
	überhaupt	(here) actually
die	Ordnung	order
	einwandfrei	perfect
	genau	precisely, for certain
	versuchen I	to try
	allerdings	though, mind you
	ersetzen I	to refund
das	Exemplar (-e)	copy
	vorrätig	in stock
	bestellen I	to order
	sich (IO) anhören II	to listen to
	reichen	to hand
	sich vertun I	to make a mistake, slip up

11

A customer returns a faulty CD to the shop

VERKÄUFER Ja, bitte schön?

KUNDIN Guten Tag! Ich habe mir vorgestern bei Ihnen eine CD mit Popmusik gekauft, die leider einige Defekte hat. Da die CD ziemlich teuer war, wollte ich mich jetzt beschweren.

VERKÄUFER Um was für eine CD handelt es sich denn?

KUNDIN Es ist das neueste Konzert von den Pur-Tops, das gerade erst erschienen ist.

VERKÄUFER Darf ich mal den Kassenbon sehen, den Sie beim Kauf bekommen haben, denn ohne Bon gibt es keine Reklamation.

KUNDIN Das Dumme ist, daß ich den Bon einfach nicht finden kann, aber Sie sehen, der Aufkleber mit dem Preis befindet sich noch auf der Hülle.

VERKÄUFER Ja, aber trotzdem .... Also, um welche Defekte handelt es sich denn?

KUNDIN Also, am Anfang gibt es einen hohen Pfeifton, der immer wieder auftaucht. Und dann hat die CD Stellen, wo man überhaupt nichts hört. Und wenn mal die Musik da ist, liegt das Ganze viel zu hoch im Ton.

VERKÄUFER Das hört sich nicht gut an, aber ist Ihr Gerät denn überhaupt in Ordnung?

KUNDIN O ja, das Gerät ist einwandfrei. Das weiß ich ganz genau, weil mein Bruder, der Musik studiert, seine CDs gespielt hat, nachdem ich es mit dieser versucht habe.

VERKÄUFER Na gut. Ich kann allerdings kein Geld ersetzen, sondern Ihnen nur ein neues Exemplar derselben CD geben, wenn wir sie noch vorrätig haben. Sonst muss ich sie bestellen .... Aber erst muss ich mir selbst die CD anhören.

11

KUNDIN **Bitte schön. [Sie reicht ihm die CD-Hülle und er macht sie auf.]**

VERKÄUFER **Aber das ist doch kein Pur-Tops-Konzert, sondern das Klarinettenquintett von Mozart!**

KUNDIN **O, da muss ich mich aber entschuldigen, ich habe mich vertan! Ich habe die Falsche mitgebracht!**

TRANSLATION

ASSISTANT Yes please?

CUSTOMER Hello! The day before yesterday I bought a CD of pop music here, which unfortunately has some faults. As the CD was rather expensive I wanted to complain now.

ASSISTANT What sort of CD is it?

CUSTOMER It's the latest concert by the Pur-Tops, which has only just come out.

ASSISTANT Can I see the till receipt that you got at the time of purchase, since we can't do anything about complaints without a receipt.

CUSTOMER The stupid thing is that I just can't find the receipt, but you can see that the sticker with the price on it is still on the case.

ASSISTANT Yes, but still …. Well, what were the faults?

CUSTOMER Well, at the beginning there's a high-pitched whistling sound that keeps coming back. And then there are places on the CD where you can't hear anything at all. And when the music actually is there, everything is pitched much too high.

ASSISTANT That doesn't sound good, but is your equipment actually in order?

CUSTOMER Oh yes, the equipment is perfect. I know that for certain, because my brother, who's a music student, played his CDs after I had been trying with this one.

ASSISTANT Oh, all right. Mind you, I can't refund cash

11

but only give you a new copy of the same CD, if we still have it in stock. Otherwise I'll have to order it .... But first I've got to listen to the CD.

CUSTOMER   Here you are. [She hands him the CD case and he opens it]

ASSISTANT   But this isn't a Pur-Tops concert, it's Mozart's Clarinet Quintet!

CUSTOMER   Oh, I really must apologise. I've made a mistake! I've brought the wrong one!

11

Week 12

- *more on the formation and uses of the past tense*
- *the 'pre-past' tense (in English 'had walked', etc)*
- *the 'oblique past' tense of auxiliary verbs (in English, 'would', 'might', etc)*
- *conditional statements, using the present ('if he stays, we will ...'), the oblique past ('if he stayed we would ...'), and the oblique pre-past ('if he had stayed, we would have ...')*
- *the obverse (passive) use of 'zu' + the infinitive*
- *affective words essential to idiomatic German*

66 MORE ON THE PAST TENSE

This tense, already introduced in week 10, section 59, is an alternative to the pre-present (perfect) for expressing past time. Which tense you use depends on: (a) the need to keep a sentence short by using one word fewer (the past tense instead of the pre-present); (b) the usefulness or not of having the main verb where otherwise there would only be an auxiliary verb; (c) creating variety in longer structures with main and attached sentences; (d) the rhythm of a sentence; and (e) regional speech habits.

Unlike in English, the choice is not determined by whether the particular time concerned is seen as isolated from the present (English past tense) or as involving the present (English pre-present tense). German often mixes the pre-present and past tenses, even within the scope of a core sentence with an attached sentence:

past tense	pre-present
Als ich ankam,	**hat sie mich zu einer Tasse Kaffee eingeladen.**
When I arrived	she invited me to (have) a cup of coffee.

12

As indicated in section 59, two sets of endings are used, (a) one for past tenses having the same stem as the **en** form, (b) the other with past tenses having new stems:

	same-stem verbs	new-stem verbs
singular		
1st person	**-(e)te**§	no ending
3rd person	**-(e)te**§	no ending
2nd person	**-(e)test**§	**-(e)st***
plural		
lst/2nd/3rd	**-(e)ten**§	**-en**

§ **e** is inserted when the stem ends in **-d** or **-t**
* **e** is inserted when the stem ends in **-s**, **-ss**, or **-ß**

Was du lasest, kam von der Kirche.
What you were reading came from the church.
Die Kinder machten ziemlich viel Krach, während er redete.
The children were making quite a lot of noise while he was speaking.

While making the past tense of same-stem verbs is simple, the past tense stems of new-stem verbs have to be learned (see section 67).

As well as (a) and (b) above, there are (c) a few new-stem verbs that take the same-stem verb endings:

-en form		past tense stem
brennen	to burn	**brann-**
bringen	to bring, take	**brach-**
denken	to think	**dach-**
kennen	to know (people)	**kann-**
wissen	to know (facts)	**wuss-**

Dass du ihn kanntest, wusste ich nicht.
I didn't know that you used to know him.

67 PAST TENSE VERBS THAT CHANGE STEM

Like the **ge_(e)t** form of irregular verbs (see section 47), these have to be learnt by heart. Note that some of the new stems are the same as the stem of the **ge_(e)t** form (past participle), while others change yet again.

Here are most of the commonly used verbs listed in week 9, section 47, grouped according to whether or not the stem is the same as the **ge_(e)t** form.

1 New stems the same as the **ge_(e)t** form

-en form		past tense stem
stehen	to stand	**stand**
leiden	to suffer	**litt**
pfeifen	to whistle	**pfiff**
schneiden	to cut	**schnitt**
streiten	to quarrel	**stritt**
bleiben	to stay, remain	**blieb**
leihen	to lend	**lieh**
scheinen	to seem, shine	**schien**
schreiben	to write	**schrieb**
steigen	to climb	**stieg**
treiben	to drive, impel	**trieb**
riechen	to smell	**roch**
schließen	to shut, close	**schloss**
bieten	to offer	**bot**
fliegen	to fly	**flog**
fliehen	to flee	**floh**
ziehen	to pull, draw	**zog**
lügen	to lie (fib)	**log**

2 New stems different from the **ge_(e)t** form, which is given for comparison. Note that if the main vowel in the stem of the **-en** form is **-e-** or **-i-** (but not together), the

12

past tense stem is almost certain to contain the vowel **-a-**. Though this is not true of **wissen** (**wuss-**) or **gehen** (**ging**), it works for all the other verbs in group (c) of section 66, for **stehen** in **1** of this section, and for the verbs in the following list:

-en form		past tense stem	ge (e)t form
essen	to eat	**aß**	**gegessen**
fahren	to go (not on foot)	**fuhr**	**gefahren**
fangen	to catch	**fing**	**gefangen**
geben	to give	**gab**	**gegeben**
halten	to hold	**hielt**	**gehalten**
kommen	to come	**kam**	**gekommen**
laufen	to run, walk	**lief**	**gelaufen**
lesen	to read	**las**	**gelesen**
messen	to measure	**maß**	**gemessen**
rufen	to call (out)	**rief**	**gerufen**
schlafen	to sleep	**schlief**	**geschlafen**
schlagen	to hit, beat	**schlug**	**geschlagen**
sehen	to see	**sah**	**gesehen**
stoßen	to bump, push	**stieß**	**gestoßen**
tragen	to carry, wear	**trug**	**getragen**
treten	to step, kick	**trat**	**getreten**
wachsen	to grow	**wuchs**	**gewachsen**
gehen	to go	**ging**	**gegangen**
brechen	to break	**brach**	**gebrochen**
helfen	to help	**half**	**geholfen**
sprechen	to speak	**sprach**	**gesprochen**
sterben	to die	**starb**	**gestorben**
treffen	to meet	**traf**	**getroffen**
nehmen	to take	**nahm**	**genommen**
stehlen	to steal	**stahl**	**gestohlen**
sitzen	to sit	**saß**	**gesessen**
schwimmen	to swim	**schwamm**	**geschwommen**

12

finden	to find	fand	gefunden
singen	to sing	sang	gesungen
sinken	to sink	sank	gesunken
springen	to jump	sprang	gesprungen
trinken	to drink	trank	getrunken
bitten	to ask, request	bat	gebeten
liegen	to lie (recline)	lag	gelegen

Exercise 29

Rewrite the following pairs of sentences, turning the first one in each pair into an attached sentence introduced by 'während' ('while') and using the second as the core sentence. Use the past tense in the attached sentence and the pre-present in the core sentence. The first pair is done for you.

1 Ich laufe durch die Stadt.
Meine Schwester schläft.

Während ich durch die Stadt lief, hat meine Schwester geschlafen.

2 Fritz arbeitet im Garten.
Sein Bruder hört sich Pop-Musik an.

3 Hanna schreibt einen Brief.
Ihre Freundin geht schwimmen.

4 Otto trinkt Milch.
Sein Bruder Bruno trinkt Schnaps.

5 Frau Krause spricht mit ihrem Nachbarn.
Ein Einbrecher stiehlt ihr Geld vom Küchentisch.

6 Die Eltern streiten sich oben im Haus.
Die Kinder halten unten im Haus eine Party.

7 Anton spricht mit den Eltern.
Susanne stößt den Hund ins Wasser.

12

68 THE PRE-PAST ('I HAD BEEN,' ETC)

This is formed with the past tense of **sein** or **haben** plus the **ge_(e)t** form. (For whether to use **sein** or **haben**, see week 9, section 45.) The pre-past (or pluperfect) is used as in English (e.g. 'had walked/had been walking') to make the sequence of events clear:

Als ich ankam, hatten sie (schon) gegessen.
When I arrived they had (already) eaten.
When I arrived they had (already) been eating.

as opposed to

Sobald ich ankam, aßen sie.
When (i.e. After) I arrived they ate.

and

Als ich ankam, aßen sie (schon/gerade).
When I arrived they were (already/just) eating.

It is also used to refer to situations or events preceding a point or period of time that is already in the past:

Bis vorgestern hatten wir keine Briefe von ihm bekommen.
Up to the day before yesterday we hadn't received any letters from him.

69 THE OBLIQUE PAST TENSE

Most English auxiliary verbs are available in oblique/non-oblique pairs (e.g. 'will/would', 'may/might', 'can/could'). The oblique member of the pair tends to suggest deference, hesitation, tentativeness, or politeness.

Oblique verbs are abundant in German, and are not restricted to auxiliary verbs. We begin here, however, by finding out how to form the oblique past tense of eight

12

auxiliaries, because these eight oblique past tenses are in constant idiomatic use. This use shows these verbs not just as auxiliaries, but as main verbs in their own right.

Note that despite its name, the meaning of the oblique past tense is NOT past, but vaguely present/future.

The 1st/3rd person singular is given below; for the 2nd person singular add **-st**, for the plural add **-n**.

past tense	oblique past tense	nearest English equivalents
hatte	**hätte**	would have, might have
war	**wäre**	would be, were (as in 'if I were you …')
wurde	**würde**	would
durfte	**dürfte**	might; (negative) shouldn't
konnte	**könnte**	could, might, would be able to
mochte	**möchte**	would like (to)
musste	**müsste**	ought to, should, would have to
sollte	**sollte**	ought to

Hättest du etwas dagegen?
Would you have any objection?
An deiner Stelle wäre ich böse.
In your place I would be cross.
Würden Sie bitte warten?
Would you please wait?
Er dürfte eigentlich nicht Auto fahren.
He shouldn't really be driving.
Er könnte sich verletzen.
He might hurt himself.
Ich möchte bitte eine Tasse Kaffee.
I'd like a cup of coffee, please.
Dieser Brief müsste übermorgen schon ankommen.
This letter should arrive the day after tomorrow.
Du solltest nicht so schnell fahren.
You oughtn't to drive so fast.

12

Apart from its idiomatic use with the auxiliary verbs, the main use of the oblique past tense is in some types of conditional statements (see section 71), and for this you need to know how to make the oblique past of all verbs, not just auxiliaries.

Same-stem verbs (see section 66) do have an oblique past, but because it is the same as the past tense it is usually avoided and replaced by **würde (-st, -n)**, 'would', plus the **-en** form of the verb required:

Wenn er ein neues Haus   baute, ...
or, preferred
Wenn er ein neues Haus   bauen würde
If he built a new house, ...

New-stem verbs, some of which are very common, are a different matter. The 1st and 3rd person singular oblique past is always distinguishable, and if the main vowel in the new stem is **a** or **o** or **u**, all forms differ from those of the past tense, because these vowels become **ä**, **ö**, and **ü** respectively. The new-stem verbs with same-stem endings behave similarly if the vowel can change.

-en form		**bleiben**	**kommen**	**ziehen**	**wissen**
past tense					
new stem		**blieb**	**kam**	**zog**	**wusste**
oblique past tense					
singular					
1st/3rd	(¨)e	**bliebe**	**käme**	**zöge**	**wüsste**
2nd	(¨)est	**bliebest**	**kämest**	**zögest**	**wüsstest**
plural					
1st/2nd/3rd	(¨)en	**blieben**	**kämen**	**zögen**	**wüssten**

71 THE CONDITIONAL: 'IF' STATEMENTS

A conditional statement consists of an attached sentence, usually beginning with **wenn** ('if'), or less commonly **falls** ('in case'), and a core sentence to express what happens if the condition is met. The order of the core and attached sentences can be reversed:

Wenn sie zu Hause bleibt, bringen wir ihr etwas Schönes mit.
If she stays at home we'll bring her something nice.
Wir bringen ihr etwas Schönes mit, wenn sie zu Hause bleibt.
We'll bring her something nice if she stays at home.

If the attached sentence (condition) comes first:

(a) An alternative to using a joiner and placing the verb last (see section 63) is to start the attached sentence with the verb, followed immediately by the SU:

Bleibt sie zu Hause, bringen wir ihr etwas Schönes mit.

It is important not to mistake this structure for a question (see week 5, section 22).

(b) The core sentence can start with **so** or **dann**:

Wenn sie zu Hause bleibt, so bringen wir ihr etwas Schönes mit.
Bleibt sie zu Hause, so bringen wir ihr etwas Schönes mit.
Wenn sie zu Hause bleibt, dann bringen wir ihr etwas Schönes mit.
Bleibt sie zu Hause, dann bringen wir ihr etwas Schönes mit.

12

There are three kinds of conditional statements in German, corresponding roughly to three similar kinds in English.

1 Odds are even on the condition being met, so neutral

Here the attached condition sentence has a finite verb in the present tense, and the core sentence has a finite verb in the present tense or the future.

Wenn die Bäume schnell wachsen, bekommen wir in zwei Jahren die ersten Früchte.
If the trees grow fast we'll get the first fruit in two years.
Wenn man ihm die Wahl eines Instruments überlässt, wird er bestimmt Klavier lernen.
If the choice of an instrument is left to him he'll definitely learn the piano.

2 Odds are against the condition being met, so remote

Here the finite verbs of both the attached conditional sentence and the core sentence can be:

either the oblique past tense of the main verb (section 70);

or the oblique past tense of **werden** (**würde, -st, -n**) plus the **-en** form of the main verb.

Either option is fine. As German is freer than English here, you just need to concentrate on incorporating one form or other of the oblique past tense into both sentences.

Wenn wir so einen Mann in den Club aufnehmen würden, würden wir in Schwierigkeiten kommen.
or
Wenn wir so einen Mann in den Club aufnähmen, kämen wir in Schwierigkeiten.
If we accepted a man like that into the club we'd get into difficulties.

12

There is no need for consistency between the attached and core sentences, and inconsistency is often preferred. **würde (-st, -n)** is, however, very common in everyday speech and useful for two reasons:

firstly, many verbs have no distinguishable oblique past tense (see section 70);

secondly, if you are not sure of the (oblique) past tense of a new stem verb, you can get round it by using **würde (-st, -n)**.

3 The condition cannot be met, because it relates to an 'opportunity' now past, so hypothetical

Here both the conditional sentence and the core sentence contain the oblique pre-past (see section 68). This means using **hätte (-st, -n)** or **wäre (-st, -n)** as appropriate (see week 9, section 45) with the **ge_(e)t** form of the main verb. Both **hätte** and **wäre** suggest 'would', which is present only in the core sentence in English, so care is needed.

Wenn wir das gewusst hätten, wären wir nicht gekommen.
If we had known that, we wouldn't have come.

12

Exercise 30

(a) Write out the conditional sentences from the left-hand column, adding to each the correct core sentence from the right-hand column.

(b) Write out the completed sentences a second time, deleting 'wenn' and starting with the finite verb. The first sentence is done for you in each case.

1 Wenn Emil in den Film geht, ... dann wird es zu kalt für uns alle.

   (a) Wenn Emil in den Film geht, dann sehe ich ihn mir auch an.

   (b) Geht Emil in den Film, dann sehe ich ihn mir auch an.

2 Wenn du die Fahrkarte besorgen würdest, ... dann wäre sie schwierig.

3 Wenn Peter nicht das Fenster schließt, ... dann wird es Krach geben.

4 Wenn dieser Mann nicht den Club verlässt, ... dann sehe ich ihn mir auch an.

5 Wenn die kleine Tochter nicht fernsehen dürfte, ... dann wirst du am Sonntag morgen schlafen können

6 Wenn der Vater in die Gaststube geht, ... dann hätten wir die Möglichkeit, am Wochenende in die Berge zu fahren.

7 Wenn du jetzt das Essen für Sonntag kochst, ... dann trinkt er immer zu viel.

12

72 MORE ABOUT THE OBVERSE PROCESS

You already know **zu + -en** form constructions in which the logical SU of the **-en** form verb in the attached phrase appears in the core sentence (see section 54):

Wir haben vor, morgen in die Berge zu fahren.
We intend to drive into the mountains tomorrow.
(we ... drive)
Ich möchte dich bitten, mir die Fahrkarte zu besorgen.
I'd like to ask you to obtain the ticket for me.
(you ... obtain)
Wir helfen ihnen, den Weg zu finden.
We'll help them to find the way.
(they ... find)

However, when the **zu + -en** construction is used in tandem with **sein**, the force of the resulting expression is that of the obverse process, with a further overlay of obligation, or permission, or possibility:

Die Ergebnisse sind sofort nach der Wahl bekannt zu machen.
The results are to be made known immediately after the election.
(the results must be made known)
Dieser Wein ist in jedem Supermarkt zu bekommen.
This wine is to be obtained at any supermarket.
(this wine can be obtained)
Dem Patienten ist nicht mehr zu helfen.
literally: The patient is not to be helped any further.
(meaning: the patient cannot be helped)
Sogar über den Direktor ist Kritik zu hören.
Criticism is even to be heard of the director.
(criticism can be heard)

12

This structure needs special care, because the corresponding English one – 'to' + basic form of verb does not express the obverse process, but only the future, or obligation, or both:

The meeting is to reconvene at 7.30.
(the meeting is going to/must reconvene)

73 AFFECTIVE WORDS

In German there are several short words, usually unstressed, which have no direct translation in English, and which are not strictly necessary to the 'factual' meaning of a sentence. It is essential to learn them in order both to speak idiomatic German and to understand the full meaning of what is being expressed.

How these affective words in German work is best illustrated by English expressions such as '(un)fortunately', 'sadly', and 'clearly', which are included in sentences not as part of their 'factual' meaning, but in order to show how speakers feel about that 'factual' meaning (and, often, how they hope to make the listener feel about it).

Our friends clearly can't finance the undertaking.

means that the fact stated is 'clear' to the speaker, and 'clearly' here is different from the same word in:

She stated her intentions clearly.

where it is part of the factual meaning.

The same is true of the two different uses of 'hopefully' in the following:

Hopefully he'll pass his driving test this time.
He embarked hopefully on his third attempt at a balloon crossing of the English Channel.

12

These expressions include words such as 'probably', 'possibly', by which speakers give their assessment of how likely their propositions are to be realised. Such expressions, then, are speakers' own comments on the content of what they are saying and German has similar expressions, such as **wahrscheinlich** ('probably'), **offensichtlich** ('clearly'), and **hoffentlich** ('hopefully').

However, German also has some common short words with more generalised affective meanings. They have few counterparts in English, except 'even.'

Here are the most common affective words in approximate descending order of frequency of use. It is impossible to illustrate their use out of context, so we can only give a rough description of the attitude each one expresses. Most of them are used, and underlined, in the Conversation on page 196.

doch	contradiction; objection; protest; persuasion
ja	acknowledgement by the speaker that the 'fact' being stated is well-known, accepted, obvious
wohl	belief that the 'fact' being stated, though not definite, is highly probable; assumption
mal	minimalisation of the 'fact' stated (cf. 'just')
denn	impatience/urgency for an answer/explanation
etwa	vagueness; uncertainty; disbelief; incredulity
auch	mark or expectation of surprise at the inclusion of something in some notional category or other (cf. 'even')
schon	mark or expectation of surprise at the relative prematurity of something on some notional scale or other (cf. 'even')

12

noch	mark or expectation of surprise at the relative 'overdueness' of something on some notional scale or other (cf. 'even')
eben (N. German) **halt** (S. German)	acceptance, acquiescence, resignation in face of the inevitability of the 'fact' being stated

The definitions above are not literal and are only given as a guide. Note, too, that all these words have other meanings, for example **(je)doch**, 'however'; **ja**, 'yes'; **wohl**, 'well'; **(ein)mal**, 'once'; **denn**, 'for'; **etwa**, 'about'; **auch**, 'also'; **schon**, 'already'; **noch**, 'still'; **eben**, 'just (now)'.

12

VOCABULARY

Study and learn the conversation that follows. You will need these new words:

der	Film (-e)	film
der	Fotoapparat (-e)	camera
	nämlich	you see
	voll	full
die	Sommerferien (plural)	summer holidays
das	Bild (-er)	photo, picture
	vorig	last
das	Taschengeld	pocket money
	sparen	to save
der	Schulausflug (-̈e)	school outing
	na gut	(oh,) all right
	verschieden	various
das	Dia (-s)	slide
	richtig	proper
der	Augenblick (-e)	moment
	im Augenblick	at present
	überreden I	to persuade
	hinterher	afterwards
der	Abzug (-̈e)	print
der	Klassenkamerad (PO -en)	classmate
die	Aufnahme (-n)	exposure, photo
	vierundzwanziger	with twenty-four
	reintun II	to put in
	so was	that sort of thing
	überhaupt	at all, in general
der	Zähler (-)	counter
	sich bewegen I	to move
	weiterdrehen II	to wind on
der	Auslöser (-)	shutter release
	drücken	to press
	egal ob	regardless of whether
	abgesehen davon	quite apart from that
	mach dir nichts daraus	don't worry about it
	kriegen	to get

12

A teenager with a camera problem

MÄDCHEN Vati, sag <u>mal</u>, könntest du mir <u>wohl</u> bitte einen Film für meinen Fotoapparat geben? Meiner ist nämlich voll. Ich habe ihn <u>schon</u> seit den Sommerferien darin und habe die letzten Bilder vorige Woche auf der Hochzeit von Marianne gemacht.

VATER Ich verstehe, du möchtest <u>wohl</u> dein Taschengeld sparen! Wenn ich dir einen Film gebe, brauchst du natürlich keinen zu kaufen.

MÄDCHEN Nein, so ist das nicht, aber wir haben heute einen Schulausflug, und ich möchte gern fotografieren können.

VATER Na gut. Ich habe verschiedene Filme. Was für einen wolltest du haben – für Dias oder richtige Bilder?

MÄDCHEN Im Augenblick habe ich einen Diafilm drin. Du weißt, du hattest mich überredet, Dias zu machen. Aber ich habe richtige Bilder lieber, und die sind <u>auch</u> für einen Schulausflug besser. Ich könnte dann hinterher <u>auch</u> Abzüge für meine Klassenkameraden machen lassen.

VATER Gut. Wieviele Aufnahmen möchtest du <u>denn</u> haben? Möchtest du einen vierundzwanziger Film haben oder einen sechsunddreißiger?

MÄDCHEN Gib mir <u>doch</u> einen vierundzwanziger, dann ist der Film schneller zu Ende, denn für einen Schulausflug brauche ich <u>doch</u> bloß zehn oder so.

VATER [Er reicht ihr einen Film.] So, da hast du deinen Film ....

MÄDCHEN ... und Vati, könntest du <u>mal</u> bitte den alten Film herausnehmen und den neuen reintun? Du weißt ja, ich kann so was gar

12

nicht gut ....

VATER Na gut .... [Er öffnet den Fotoapparat.]
Aber hier ist <u>doch</u> überhaupt kein alter
Film drin! Hast du <u>etwa</u> die ganze Zeit
ohne Film fotografiert?!

MÄDCHEN Was??!! O meine schönen Aufnahmen von
der Hochzeit und überhaupt aus den
ganzen Wochen seit den Sommerferien!
Und ich dachte die ganze Zeit, es wäre ein
Film drin! Der Zähler bewegte sich <u>doch</u>
immer weiter.

VATER Bei deinem Apparat geht der Zähler <u>eben</u>
weiter, wenn man weiterdreht und den
Auslöser drückt, egal ob ein Film drin ist
oder nicht. Abgesehen davon wüsste ich
nicht, wie ein Film überhaupt in deinem
Apparat hätte sein können. Ich habe
nämlich den alten Film am Ende der Ferien
selbst herausgenommen. Aber mach dir
nichts daraus! Du kriegst Abzüge von
meinen Hochzeitsbildern!

TRANSLATION

GIRL Daddy, (tell me,) could you give me a film for
my camera, please? (You see,) mine's full. I've
had it in since summer holidays, and I took the
last photos last week at Marianne's wedding.

FATHER I see, you want to save your pocket money! If
I give you a film you won't need to buy one,
of course.

GIRL No, it's not (like) that, but we've got a school
outing today, and I'd like to be able to take
some photographs.

FATHER Alright. I've got various films. What sort did
you want (to have): for slides or proper photos?

GIRL At present I've got a slide film in. (You)
remember, you'd persuaded me to take slides.
But I prefer proper photos, and they're better

12

for a school outing. Then I'd be able to get prints made for my classmates afterward.

FATHER Fine. How many exposures would you like (to have)? Do you want film with twenty-four or one with thirty-six?

GIRL Let me have one with twenty-four. (Then) the film will be finished more quickly, (since) I only need about ten for a school outing.

FATHER [He hands her a film.] Well, there's your film ...

GIRL ... and daddy, could you please just take the old film out and put the new one in? You know I'm no good at that kind of thing ....

FATHER Oh, alright .... [He opens the camera.] But there isn't any old film (at all) in here! Surely you haven't been taking photographs all this time without film in it?!

GIRL What??!! Oh, my lovely photos of the wedding, and from all these weeks since the summer holidays! And all the time I thought there was a film in it! But the counter kept moving on.

FATHER In your camera the counter does move on when you wind on and press the shutter release, regardless of whether there's a film in or not. Quite apart from that, I couldn't have imagined how a film could have been in your camera. (You see,) I took the old film out myself at the end of the holidays. But don't worry about it! You'll get prints of my photographs of the wedding!

12

Week 13

- *ways of translating the English '-ing' form ('doing', 'laughing', etc)*
- *link words such as 'therefore', 'however', etc*
- *the familiar plural form*
- *word order in sentences with two '-en' verb forms*
- *idiomatic use of impersonal expressions*
- *the oblique present tense*
- *tenses and word order in reported speech and enclosed attached sentences*

74 TRANSLATING THE ENGLISH '-ING' FORM ('BY DOING', 'IN SPITE OF DOING')

There are few direct German equivalents for the various uses of the English verb form ending in '-ing'. The only major exception is the **-end** form (see section 61) used as an adjective in front of the noun:

der lachende Polizist
the laughing policeman

You will find out more about this usage in section 82.

Most other English '-ing' forms have to be rephrased before they correspond to what is possible in German, and there is usually a simple alternative:

After talking to him I changed my mind.
After I talked to him I changed my mind.
Nachdem ich mit ihm gesprochen hatte, habe ich meine Meinung geändert.

Before leaving I gave them my phone number.
Before I left I gave them my phone number.
Bevor ich wegging, habe ich ihnen meine Telefonnummer gegeben.

However, 'by … -ing' and 'in spite of … -ing' do not have obvious alternatives corresponding to the German, which requires constructions like those in section 63 **3**(b).

13

1 'by ... -ing'

Use **indem** to introduce an attached sentence:

Ich konnte viel Geld sparen, indem ich Überstunden gemacht habe.
I was able to save a lot of money by doing overtime ('in that I did overtime').

2 'in spite of ... -ing'

Use **trotzdem** to introduce an attached sentence:

Ich konnte nicht viel Geld sparen, trotzdem ich Überstunden gemacht habe.
I wasn't able to save much money in spite of doing overtime ('in spite of that I did overtime').

These constructions make it easy for the core and attached sentences to have different subjects:

Wir konnten viel Geld sparen, indem du Überstunden gemacht hast.
We were able to save a lot of money by your doing overtime.

13

75 | LINE-OF-THOUGHT POINTERS

The last Conversation contained two examples of
nämlich, 'you see':

Meiner ist nämlich voll.
Ich habe nämlich den alten Film . . . selbst
herausgenommen.

nämlich is a line-of-thought pointer. It indicates that
the sentence containing it is an explanation of a
previous sentence.

Whereas the joiners you learnt in section 63 enable
attached sentences to be connected to other sentences,
line-of-thought pointers enable sentences of all kinds to
be bound into bigger chunks of German by pointing to
the way a train of thought is developing.

Below are the most common line-of-thought pointers,
grouped by function and with the nearest English
equivalents. They are given without examples, because
they can only be properly illustrated in longer texts. You
will find many examples in the Conversation at the end
of this week.

Most of these expressions can stand at the start or in
the middle of a sentence, but any restrictions on their
position are noted.

1 Consequential

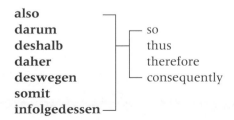

also
darum ⎤
deshalb ⎥ so
daher ⎥ thus
deswegen ⎥ therefore
somit ⎥ consequently
infolgedessen ⎦

13

NOTE: German **also** never means 'also', and German **so** on its own usually means 'in this way' (though before an adjective it means 'so').

2 Explanatory

denn (start only)	for
nämlich (middle only)	you see

3 Additive

außerdem	besides, furthermore,
überdies	moreover
zudem	
ebenfalls	likewise
gleichfalls	

4 Dismissive

ohnehin (middle only)	anyway, in any case
sowieso (middle only)	

5 Remonstrative

immerhin	after all
schließlich	
wenigstens	at least
jedenfalls	at any rate

6 Reservational

jedoch	however
doch (start only)	

13

7 Contrastive

andererseits	on the other hand,
dagegen	in contrast, by
hingegen	comparison

8 Concessive

allerdings	admittedly, to be sure,
freilich	though (final only),
	mind you

zwar ... aber	true ... but

NOTE: **zwar** in this sense is always followed by **aber**, **jedoch**, or some similar reservational pointer in a subsequent sentence.

9 Provocative

trotzdem	nevertheless,
dennoch	nonetheless

10 Alternative

sonst	otherwise
ansonsten	

es sei denn	unless, except that

NOTE: **es sei denn** is very close in sense to the joiner **wenn** ('if') followed by a negative (**nicht** or **kein**).

13

Exercise 31

Add an appropriate line-of-thought pointer from the list below to the second sentence of each pair. In some sentences more than one choice is possible, and then the Key gives the most apt word, with the others in brackets. Try putting the line-of-thought pointers at the start and in the middle, making any other necessary or desirable changes. The first example is done for you.

allerdings
andererseits
außerdem
deshalb
immerhin
jedoch
trotzdem

1 Emil weiß, dass Karl kommt.
Er plant eine Busfahrt mit ihm.

Deshalb plant er eine Busfahrt mit ihm.
Er plant deshalb eine Busfahrt mit ihm.

2 Karl möchte zur Nordsee.
Emil bucht eine Fahrt nach Berlin.

3 Berlin ist eine schöne Stadt.
Es gibt sehr viele Touristen.

4 Die Nordsee ist ruhig.
In Berlin gibt es viel zu sehen.

5 Das Brandenburger Tor ist sehr attraktiv.
Es ist historisch und politisch wichtig.

6 Warum ist es historisch und politisch wichtig?
Vor einiger Zeit war es das Tor zwischen Westen und Osten.

7 Karl wollte an die Nordsee.
Er hat Berlin sehr interessant gefunden.

13

CONVERSATION BETWEEN INTIMATES:
THE PLURAL

In section 31 the way to address intimates was only
given in the singular, i.e. for addressing just one person.
If you are talking to more than one person you know
intimately, or a group containing several such people,
you need to use these forms:

pronouns		possessive (ein-type, cf. **unser**)
SU	**ihr**	**euer**
DO	**euch**	
IO	**euch**	

verbs

-en form	present tense	past tense	oblique past tense	instructions/ requests
haben	**habt**	**hattet**	**hättet**	**habt**
sein	**seid**	**wart**	**wäret**	**seid**
dürfen	**dürft**	**durftet**	**dürftet**	–
sollen	**sollt**	**solltet**	**solltet**	–
lassen	**lasst**	**ließt**	**ließet**	**lasst**
sehen	**seht**	**saht**	**sähet**	**seht**
machen	**macht**	**machtet**	**machtet**	**macht**
reden	**redet**	**redetet**	**redetet**	**redet**

13

77 ATTACHED SENTENCES WITH TWO '-EN' FORMS

Attached sentences where the finite verb comes last (see section 63) will contain two **-en** forms if the pre-present or pre-past of certain auxiliary verbs is used (see section 58). Look at two examples from section 58:

Ich habe den Nachbarn helfen müssen.
Ich habe meinen Wagen waschen lassen.

If we turn them into attached sentences, where the finite verb (here **habe**) would normally stand last, the finite verb now stands immediately before the two **-en** forms:

Ich kam zu spät, weil ich den Nachbarn habe helfen müssen.
I came late because I had to help the neighbours.
Obwohl ich meinen Wagen habe waschen lassen, sah er hinterher immer noch schmutzig aus.
Although I got my car washed, it still looked dirty afterwards.

78 IMPERSONAL EXPRESSIONS

An impersonal expression consists of a verb used with the subject **es** (not standing for an identifiable n. noun). German and English impersonal expressions are often the same, but German also has a range of impersonal idioms outside the scope of English usage. You already know **es gibt** (see week 6, section 27) and **es handelt sich (um)** (see section 65). Here are some more examples:

Bei Nacht ging es über die Grenze.
I [or whoever the context indicates] crossed the frontier by night.
Während der Revolution kam es zu gefährlichen Unruhen.
During the revolution some dangerous disturbances occurred.

13

Bei unseren Exportplänen geht es nur um den Kurs.
As regards our export plans, it's solely a matter of the rate of exchange.

In the sentences above, **es** is obligatory, but it is optional in other idioms and is commonly left out in everyday speech.

Es ist mir zu warm, mach bitte das Fenster auf!
or
Mir ist zu warm, mach bitte das Fenster auf!
I'm too hot. Please open the window!

Es graut mir vor dem Schulanfang nach den Ferien.
or
Mir graut vor dem Schulanfang nach den Ferien.
I hate (the thought of) the start of school after the holidays.

79 THE OBLIQUE PRESENT TENSE

This tense is vital for reported speech (see section 80). In practice all you need to learn is the 3rd person singular. Simply take the stem of the **-en** form and add **-e**. (The sole exception is **sein**, which has the oblique 3rd person singular **sei**.) Verbs irregular in the 3rd person singular of the present tense are not so in the oblique present. The only plural form much used is **seien** (from **sein**).

-en form	3rd person singular present	3rd person singular oblique present
haben	**hat**	**habe**
sein	**ist**	**sei**
dürfen	**darf**	**dürfe**
sollen	**soll**	**solle**
lassen	**lässt**	**lasse**
sehen	**sieht**	**sehe**
machen	**macht**	**mache**
reden	**redet**	**rede**
tun	**tut**	**tue**

13

Directly quoted speech in German is no different from that in English. The speaker's words are placed within quotation marks.

In reported speech the original words spoken undergo changes in both English and German. For instance, if the speaker says 'I …', this becomes 'he' or 'she' in reported speech, while 'here' may remain 'here' or become 'there'.

German always uses the oblique tenses throughout for reporting speech. Here are some guidelines:

1 Every present tense verb in the speaker's actual words (including the present tenses of **haben** and **sein** used as part of the pre-present, and of **werden** as part of the future or obverse process) is replaced by EITHER the oblique present tense OR the oblique past tense.

The main aim is that the replacement verb should demonstrably be the oblique tense. This means that many oblique present tense forms are no use, because they are the same as the present tense. In these cases the oblique past tense (even if the same as the non-oblique past tense) is better.

However, the oblique present tense has one form that is much used in reported speech, the 3rd person singular (see section 79). This is always different from the 3rd person present tense because it ends in **-e** instead of **-t**. This form is constantly used in newspapers and on radio and TV, but less in everyday speech. For example:

Actual words	**Der Minister: „Ich nehme die ganze Verantwortung auf mich, denn der Fehler wird schwere Folgen haben."**
Reported speech	**Der Minister sagte, er nehme die ganze Verantwortung auf sich,**

13

denn der Fehler werde schwere Folgen haben.
The Minister said he was taking the whole responsibility upon himself, for the error would have grave consequences.

Actual words	**Monika: „Ich nehme keinen Regenschirm mit, sonst lasse ich ihn bestimmt irgendwo liegen."**
Reported speech	**Monika sagte, sie nehme/nähme keinen Regenschirm mit, sonst lasse/ließe sie ihn bestimmt irgendwo liegen.** Monika said she wasn't taking an umbrella. Otherwise she would be certain to leave it somewhere.
Actual words	**Die Freunde: „Wir sind heute zu euch gekommen, weil wir euch seit langem nicht gesehen haben."**
Reported speech	**Unsere Freunde sagten, sie seien/wären heute zu uns gekommen, weil sie uns seit langem nicht gesehen hätten.** Our friends said they had come to (see) us today because they hadn't seen us for a long time.

NOTE:

(a) The oblique past tense is preferred in conversation.

(b) Just as **würde (-st, -n, -t)** plus the **-en** form of the main verb is useful in conditional statements (see section 71), it is also a useful substitute in reported speech, especially when no clear oblique form is available:

Actual words	**Die Nachbarn: „Wir erwarten unsere Tochter mit Mann und Kindern aus Würzburg für die Weihnachtsferien."**

13

| Reported speech | **Unsere Nachbarn sagten, sie würden ihre Tochter mit Mann und Kindern aus Würzburg für die Weihnachtsferien erwarten.** |
| | Our neighbours said they were expecting their daughter with her husband and children from Würzburg for the Christmas holidays. |

2 Every past tense verb in the speaker's actual words is replaced by the **ge_(e)t** form of that verb together with either the oblique present tense or the oblique past tense of **haben** or **sein**. The rule for the choice of auxiliary is the same as for the pre-present (section 45):

Actual words	**Peter: „Ich fand nur drei Kunden vor, als ich das Geschäft aufmachte."**
Reported speech	**Peter sagt, er** $\left\{ \begin{array}{l} \textbf{habe} \\ \textbf{hätte} \end{array} \right\}$ **nur drei Kunden vorgefunden, als er das Geschäft aufgemacht** $\left\{ \begin{array}{l} \textbf{habe} \\ \textbf{hätte.} \end{array} \right.$
	Peter said he found only three customers (waiting) when he opened the shop.

Actual words	**Die Zwillinge: „Wir gingen zusammen bis zum Markt, wo wir uns dann trennten."**
Reported speech	**Die Zwillinge sagten, sie** $\left\{ \begin{array}{l} \textbf{seien} \\ \textbf{wären} \end{array} \right\}$ **zusammen bis zum Markt gegangen, wo sie sich dann getrennt hätten."**
	The twins said they went together as far as the market, where they then separated.

If the speaker's actual words already contain the past tense of **haben** or **sein** as part of the pre-past (see section 68), these are simply replaced by their oblique past tenses:

| Actual words | **Die Gäste: „Wir waren zum Strand gegangen und als wir uns zum Sonnen** |

hingelegt hatten, fing es plötzlich an
zu regnen."

Reported speech Die Gäste sagten, sie wären zum Strand gegangen, und als sie sich zum Sonnen hingelegt hätten, $\left\{\begin{array}{l}\text{hätte}\\\text{habe}\end{array}\right\}$ es plötzlich angefangen zu regnen.
The guests said they had gone to the beach and when they had lain down to sunbathe it suddenly started raining.

3 When a speaker's actual words contain an instruction or request form of the verb, there is no hard and fast rule about how to report this indirectly. The natural way is to use either the oblique past tense **möchte** or some form of the verb **sollen**, oblique or non-oblique, as seems to fit the case:

Actual words **Arzt: „Essen Sie nur Fisch oder mageres Fleisch!"**

Reported speech **Der Arzt sagt, ich soll nur Fisch oder mageres Fleisch essen.**
The doctor says I must only eat fish or lean meat.

Actual words **Schwester und Schwager: „Geh zum Arzt!"**

Reported speech **Die haben gemeint, ich soll zum Arzt gehen.**
They said I must go to the doctor.

Actual words **Arzthelferin: „Herr Doktor, schauen Sie bitte doch noch einmal bei Herrn Sinke vorbei."**

Reported speech **Meine Helferin hat gesagt, ich sollte bei Ihnen noch einmal vorbeischauen.**
My assistant told me to visit you again.

Actual words **Hempels: „Bitte besuchen Sie uns doch, sobald wir das Haus eingerichtet haben!"**

13

Reported speech	**Hempels haben gesagt, wir möchten sie besuchen, sobald sie das Haus eingerichtet hätten.**
	The Hempels said we must visit them as soon as they had furnished the house.

81 WORD ORDER IN REPORTED SPEECH

Most of the examples in section 80 required no change in the word order in reported speech. This is because no joiners were used to introduce the attached reported speech sentences. This is only possible with statements and instructions. Even these are often introduced by **dass**, and all reported questions must start with one of the joiners from section 63 (**2**). In these cases the verb of the attached reported speech sentence must stand at the end:

Actual words	**Mann: „Ich halte gar nichts von den Freunden unserer Kinder."**
Reported speech	**Mein Mann sagt, dass er gar nichts von den Freunden unserer Kinder halte/hielte.**
	My husband says that he doesn't think much of our children's friends.

Actual words	**Er: „Wie lange wirst du noch einkaufen?"**
Reported speech	**Er fragte sie, wie lange sie noch einkaufen** $\begin{cases} \textbf{werde} \\ \textbf{würde.} \end{cases}$
	He asked her how long she would go on shopping.

Actual words	**Ich: „Geben Sie meinem Sohn noch eine Chance?"**
Reported speech	**Ich fragte ihn, ob er meinem Sohn noch eine Chance** $\begin{cases} \textbf{gebe} \\ \textbf{gäbe.} \end{cases}$
	I asked him whether he would give my son another chance.

13

Exercise 32

For each example of reported speech, say which of the statements (a), (b), or (c) comes closest to the situation described.

1 Der Minister sagt, er habe den Brief vor drei Wochen zwar gesehen, aber er sei nicht überzeugt gewesen.
(a) Es gibt einen Brief.
(b) Es gibt keinen Brief.
(c) Ein Brief ist angekommen.

2 Monika sagt, sie habe ihren Regenschirm zuerst an der Schule liegen gelassen, ihn dann aber später abgeholt.
(a) Sie hat ihren Regenschirm verloren.
(b) Sie bringt ihren Regenschirm zur Schule.
(c) Sie hat ihren Regenschirm noch.

3 Die Freunde sagen, sie hätten uns lange nicht gesehen und würden uns gern besuchen.
(a) Die Freunde besuchen uns.
(b) Die Freunde möchten uns besuchen.
(c) Die Freunde möchten uns nicht sehen.

4 Die Nachbarn sagen, ihre Tochter spiele im Orchester die Klarinette und ginge bald auf eine Reise nach England.
(a) Die Tochter geht auf Ferien nach England.
(b) Die Tochter spielt Klarinette in England.
(c) Die Nachbarn fahren nach England.

5 Peter sagt, er habe nur zwei Kunden am Morgen gehabt; am Nachmittag seien noch vier schwierige Kunden gekommen und er sei deshalb am Abend sehr müde gewesen.
(a) Peter hat sechs nette Kunden gehabt.
(b) Peter ist froh, dass es Abend ist.
(c) Peter bedient seine Kunden freundlich.

6 Die Zwillinge sagen, sie seien auf den Markt gegangen und hätten sich Pullover gekauft; einer von ihnen habe noch ein T-Shirt gekauft.
(a) Die Zwillinge haben zwei Pullover und zwei T-Shirts gekauft.
(b) Die Zwillinge haben sich auf dem Markt getrennt.
(c) Einer der Zwillinge hat einen Pullover und ein T-Shirt.

13

7 Die Gäste sagen, sie hätten sich erst am Strand
sonnen wollen; sie hätten dann einen Ausflug
machen wollen, aber die Sonne sei für alles zu
heiß gewesen.

(a) Die Gäste haben einen Ausflug gemacht.

(b) Die Gäste haben sich gesonnt.

(c) Die Gäste konnten das alles nicht machen.

82 ENCLOSED ATTACHED SENTENCES

Section 63 (**1**) on **d. .** -type joiners showed how they
link the attached sentence which they introduce to a
noun in a preceding sentence. Some attached sentences
can be placed before the noun to which they relate rather
than after it.

Attached sentences placed before the noun must have
that noun as their subject. The principles will be clear
if we take an example from section 63 where the
d. . -type joiner is in the SU case:

**Das Fleisch, das auf dem Tisch liegt, kannst du für
den Hund nehmen.**
You can take the meat that's on the table for the dog.

The attached sentence could appear as follows:

**Das [auf dem Tisch liegende] Fleisch kannst du für
den Hund nehmen.**

Three things have happened to the attached sentence:

(a) the joiner **das** has gone,

(b) the finite verb **liegt** has changed into the non-finite
form **liegend** (see sections 61 and 74), and

(c) **liegend** has acquired the ending needed by
adjectives after **d. .** words (see week 7, section 29), since

13

although **liegend** is not an adjective it has to be treated like one on the analogy **das frische Fleisch** → **das ... liegende Fleisch.**

Otherwise the word order is the same as in the original attached sentence, with **liegend** occupying the position of the verb **liegt.** The enclosed attached sentence would be the same if the 'time' of the whole changed:

Das Fleisch, das auf dem Tisch lag, konntest du für den Hund nehmen.
Das [auf dem Tisch liegende] Fleisch konntest du für den Hund nehmen.
You were able to take the meat that was on the table for the dog.

There are restrictions on which type of word may appear last in these attached sentences (which we shall call 'enclosed' because they fit between any **d. .-** or **ein-**type of word and the noun they relate to). Each type of final word corresponds to a different type of original sentence with its own characteristics. Here are the five types with examples (always showing first the original attached sentence from which the enclosed attached sentence is derived):

1 Adjective

Der Verlust der Reisepässe war eine Angelegenheit, die dem Reiseleiter äußerst unangenehm war.
The loss of the passports was a matter that was extremely embarrassing to the courier.
Der Verlust der Reisepässe war eine [dem Reiseleiter äußerst unangenehme] Angelegenheit.

Here the verb **war** from the original attached sentence has disappeared in the enclosed attached sentence.

2 -end form of almost any verb except **sein** and the auxiliary verbs (in their auxiliary function)

Teilnehmer, die bis morgen auf ihre Ergebnisse hier warten, werden eingeladen, im Hotel zu übernachten.
Participants who are waiting here until tomorrow for their results are invited to spend the night in the hotel.
[Bis morgen auf ihre Ergebnisse hier wartende] Teilnehmer werden eingeladen, im Hotel zu übernachten.

This enclosed attached sentence does not *appear* enclosed at the front end. Only the **d. .** joiner and the tense and person of **warten** disappear here.

3 ge_(e)t form of any verb that can have a DO

Das östliche Mittelmeer, das oft von meinen Bekannten als Lieblingsreiseziel ausgesucht wird, werde auch ich mir dieses Jahr vornehmen.
This year I'm also going to visit the eastern Mediterranean, which is often chosen by my friends as a favourite destination.
Das [oft von meinen Bekannten als Lieblingsreiseziel ausgesuchte] östliche Mittelmeer werde auch ich mir dieses Jahr vornehmen.

Zündkerzen, die zu selten ausgewechselt wurden, können einen dann im Stich lassen.
Spark plugs that have been changed too infrequently can (then) leave you in the lurch.
[Zu selten ausgewechselte] Zündkerzen können einen dann im Stich lassen.

Here, the attached sentence becoming enclosed loses both the **d. .** joiner and the finite auxiliary verb **werden**.

4 ge_(e)t form of verb making the pre-present with **sein**

Die Stadt wird von einer Krankheit bedroht, die in der Gegend noch nie vorgekommen ist.

13

The town is threatened by a disease that has never before appeared in the area.
Die Stadt wird von einer [in der Gegend noch nie vorgekommenen] Krankheit bedroht.

This type of enclosed sentence loses the **d. .** joiner and the finite auxiliary verb **sein** from the original attached sentence. The process represented by the **ge_(e)t** form has the connotation of completion (sections 44, 61).

5 zu + -end form of any verb that can take a DO

To understand this properly you should first look again at section 72, from which the following examples derive:

Die Ergebnisse, die sofort nach der Wahl bekannt zu machen sind, werden im Rathaus ausgehängt.
The results, which are to be made known immediately after the election, will be posted in the town hall.
Die [sofort nach der Wahl bekannt zu machenden] Ergebnisse werden im Rathaus ausgehängt.

Die Kritik, die über den Direktor zu hören war, war unberechtigt.
The criticism that was to be heard about the director was unfounded.
Die [über den Direktor zu hörende] Kritik war unberechtigt.

Here, the **d. .** joiner and **sein** disappear when the attached sentence is enclosed.

With all the examples above, it is essential first to isolate the enclosed attached sentence, then to establish which type of standard attached sentence it is similar to. Finally you need to understand it along the same lines as our translations of the original attached sentences. Enclosed attached sentences are found in profusion in German, especially in all types of writing, so there is a great incentive to face the challenge they pose.

VOCABULARY

Study the conversation on the next page, trying to relate each step in the discussion to what you have learnt. You will need these words:

	vorhaben II	to have planned
	genau	precisely
	hier ist nichts los	nothing's going on here
	um ... herum	about
	erzählen	to tell
	zustehen II	to be due
	vorschießen II	to advance (money)
	meines Erachtens	in my opinion
	wahnsinnig	crazy
	umgehen (mit) II	to deal (with)
das	**Verhältnis (-se)**	(plural) means
	ausgeben II	to spend
	grillen	to grill
	geeignet	suitable
	je	each
	besorgen I	to obtain
	so (et)was	things like that
die	**Tiefkühltruhe (-n)**	(chest) freezer
	toll	great
	sich verschulden I	to get into debt, go into the red
	überübermorgen	the day after the day after tomorrow
	übernachten I	to stay the night
	aufkommen II	to (be liable to) pay
	was = etwas	something
	übrigens	by the way
der	**Eintritt**	admission
	dabei wegkommen (mit) II	to get away (with)
	nicht in Frage kommen	to be out of the question
der	**Vorschuss (¨e)**	advance

13

	gewiss	certainly
	anspruchslos	undemanding
die	**Unterhaltung (-en)**	entertainment
	in die Tasche greifen	to dip into one's pocket
	losfahren II	to set out, come out
	abholen II	to collect, pick up
die	**Erziehung**	education, upbringing
die	**Sparsamkeit**	thrift

CONVERSATION

A family controversy over the children's spending

VATER **Was habt ihr denn heute abend vor?**

SOHN **Das wissen wir noch nicht ganz genau. Hier in Vossdorf ist heute nichts los, aber in Wunsdorf soll es eine große Disko geben. Die wäre allerdings ziemlich teuer, so um die zehn Euro herum pro Person, hat uns die Brigitte erzählt ...**

MUTTER **... und deswegen wollt ihr also nicht hin ....**

TOCHTER **... O doch, wenn ihr uns das uns für die nächsten vier Wochen zustehende Taschengeld vorschießen würdet.**

VATER **Ihr habt eine meines Erachtens wahnsinnige Art, mit Geld umzugehen. Ihr lebt total über euere Verhältnisse. So viel braucht ihr doch wohl nicht für einen einzigen Abend auszugeben!**

MUTTER **Ja, Vater hat ganz Recht!**

SOHN **Es geht leider nicht nur um heute Abend! Morgen gibt's nämlich ein Barbecue bei Eckels, und der Franz hat gesagt, wir möchten doch etwas zum Grillen geeignetes Fleisch und je zwei Liter Bier besorgen.**

13

MUTTER	So was braucht ihr doch nicht zu kaufen! Ich werde für euch ein paar Sachen aus der Tiefkühltruhe holen, und Bier könnt ihr auch von hier mitnehmen.
TOCHTER	O, das wäre toll! Ich glaube, wir müssen uns trotzdem verschulden, denn überübermorgen gibt die Brigitte eine tolle Party bei sich, und da wir auch dort übernachten dürfen, müssen wir ihrer Mutter natürlich ein Geschenk mitbringen.
MUTTER	Wenn es sich um ein Geschenk für die Mutter handelt, braucht ihr doch nicht dafür aufzukommen! Ich besorge morgen was Schönes in der Stadt.
VATER	Was möchtest du denn sonst noch finanzieren, Ilse?
SOHN	Übrigens brauchen wir für heute Abend nicht nur den Eintritt sondern auch das Geld für ein Taxi hinterher von Wunsdorf bis nach Hause. Das sind immerhin fünfzehn Kilometer, und mit weniger als fünfundzwanzig Euro kommen wir nicht dabei weg.
VATER	Das kommt zusammen auf etwa fünfundvierzig Euro. Das kommt überhaupt nicht in Frage, mit oder ohne Vorschuss!
MUTTER	Was Vater sagt, ist ganz gewiss richtig, ihr müsstet viel anspruchsloser sein. Andererseits, für eine harmlose Unterhaltung mit Freunden einmal in der Woche braucht ihr nicht in euere eigene Tasche zu greifen. Den Eintritt können wir bezahlen. Außerdem sagt Vater immer, er führe nachts ganz gern los, um euch von irgendwo abzuholen. Also könnt ihr auch das Taxigeld sparen!
VATER	Und das soll nun Erziehung zu Sparsamkeit sein!

13

TRANSLATION

FATHER So what have you got on this evening?

SON We don't quite know yet. There's nothing going on here in Vossdorf, but there's supposed to be a big disco in Wunsdorf. It's pretty expensive though, about ten euros per person, so Brigitte told us …

MOTHER … and so therefore you're not intending to go ….

DAUGHTER Oh we are, if you'd advance us the pocket money that's due to us for the next four weeks.

FATHER You've got a way of dealing with money that's crazy in my opinion. You're living completely beyond your means. You're not telling me that you need to spend that much on a single evening!

MOTHER Yes, father's absolutely right!

SON Unfortunately it's not just a matter of this evening. You see, tomorrow there's a barbecue at the Eckels, and Franz said could we get some meat that's suitable for grilling and two litres of beer each.

MOTHER But you don't need to buy things like that! I'll take a few things out of the freezer for you, and you can take some beer from here, too.

DAUGHTER Oh, that would be great! I think we'll have to go into the red even so. You see, the day after the day after tomorrow Brigitte's putting on a fantastic party at her house, and as we're allowed to stay the night there we've obviously got to take her mother a present.

MOTHER If it's a present for the mother, you don't have to spend your money on it! I'll get something nice in the town tomorrow.

FATHER And what else were you thinking of underwriting, Ilse?

SON By the way, for this evening we don't only need the admission but also the money for a taxi home from Wunsdorf afterwards. After all, that's fifteen kilometres, and we shan't get away with

13

less than twenty-five euros.

FATHER That comes to about forty-five euros. That's quite out of the question, with or without an advance!

MOTHER What father says is certainly right. You ought to be a lot less demanding. On the other hand, you don't need to dip into your own pockets for a bit of harmless entertainment with friends once a week. We can pay the admission charge. Moreover, father's always saying how he's happy to come out at night to pick you up from somewhere or other. So you'll even be able to save the taxi fare!

FATHER And that's what you call bringing them up to be thrifty!

13

Reading practice

Hier geht es um die Wurst

Was ist älter: das Frankfurter Würstchen oder das Wiener Würstchen?

Richtige Antwort: das Frankfurter Würstchen.

Metzger Johann Georg Lahner kommt aus Frankfurt und ist Erfinder vom Frankfurter Würstchen. 1904 geht er nach Wien. Sein 'Frankfurter' Würstchen ist sehr bald in Wien bekannt als Wiener Würstl.

(Reading level: weeks 5 to 6)

VOCABULARY

die	Antwort (-en)	answer
der	Erfinder	inventor
	Wien/Wiener	Vienna/Viennese
das	Würstchen (-)	diminutives of 'die Wurst':
das	Würstl (-) (Austrian)	sausage

London auf die Schnelle

Piccadilly Circus, Hyde Park, Big Ben, Madame Tussaud und die Tate Gallery. Das sind die bekanntesten Stellen in London für den Ausländer. Der neue London-Katalog von ATLASTRIPS bietet in Kooperation mit British Air Holidays Kurztrips in die britische Metropole. Individuell und flexibel kann der Gast seinen Urlaub planen.

Theater und Musicals am Abend, Sightseeing-Touren, Lunch oder Shopping auf der Portobello Road. London bietet Unterhaltung pur. Ein gemütliches Hotel ist da sehr wichtig. Es gibt über 30 Hotels: vom simplen bis zur Luxusklasse. Eine Übernachtung mit englischem Frühstück im 2-Sterne-Hotel London Crown kostet etwa 53 Euro; das 3-Sterne-Hotel Regal nimmt für Übernachtung und Frühstück etwa 90 Euro. Das 4-Sterne-Hotel Gresham House direkt am Hyde Park ist luxuriös und kostet etwa 250 Euro.

Man kann von London auch relativ schnell in die Universitätsstädte Oxford und Cambridge kommen. Sie sind wunderschön und so typisch englisch. London, Oxford und Cambridge sind eine Reise wert.

(Reading level: weeks 5 to 6)

VOCABULARY

	bieten	to offer
	gemütlich	cosy, comfortable
die	Reise (-n)	trip, journey
	auf die Schnelle	at speed
	über	more than
	wert	worth

Wein ist im Kommen

Die Deutschen trinken wieder öfter ein Glas Wein statt ein Glas Bier oder ein Glas Sekt. Der Weinkonsum steigt wieder nach der Stagnation in den letzten Jahren. Solche Präferenzen gehen oft Hand in Hand mit Gesundheitstrends. Milch und Fruchtsäfte profitieren in diesem Jahr auch.

Der nasse Sommer ist schlecht für die Brauereien und für die alkoholfreien Getränkehersteller. Man hat einfach nicht solchen Durst. Jeder Deutsche trinkt etwa 3,2 Liter weniger Bier und etwa 1,6 Liter weniger Mineralwasser als im letzten Jahr.

Aller Alkoholkonsum außer Wein ist jetzt niedriger, er steht bei 163,6 Liter pro Person, das sind etwa 2,8 Liter weniger als im letzten Jahr. Dasselbe ist der Fall bei alkoholfreien Getränken, die Deutschen trinken 1,9 Liter weniger und sind jetzt bei 225,5 Liter pro Kopf.

Absolutes Lieblingsgetränk der Bundesbürger aber ist Bohnenkaffee mit 164,5 (Vorjahr 164,6) Litern pro Kopf. Der Teekonsum steigt um 0,5 auf 25,5 Liter.

(Reading level: weeks 6 to 7)

VOCABULARY

	außer	except
die	Brauerei (-en)	brewery
	dasselbe	the same
der	Durst	thirst
die	Gesundheit	health
	letzt	last
der	Saft (¨e)	juice
	steigen (um … auf)	to increase (by … to)
das	Vorjahr	previous year

Versteigerung bei der Lufthansa

Der Auktionator von der Lufthansa: „Fünfzig Euro zum Ersten, fünfzig Euro zum Zweiten und niemand mehr?" Der Versteigerer schwingt den Hammer. „… fünfzig Euro zum Dritten." Es ist kurz nach zwölf Uhr mittags. Die Auktion in Mannheim beginnt gerade. Etwa 150 Koffer und Taschen, mehrere Kinderwagen, Dutzende von Sonnenschirmen und Tennisschlägern liegen vor ihm. Das dauert fünf bis sechs Stunden ohne Pause, und er arbeitet so schnell wie möglich.

Einmal im Monat, immer am Samstag ab zwölf Uhr, versteigert der Auktionator für die Deutsche Lufthansa AG herrenloses Fundgut. Die Lufthansa wartet drei Monate auf die Besitzer dieser Sachen. In der Zeit sucht die Lufthansa die Besitzer, aber eben meistens vergeblich. Scheinbar gehören diese Sachen niemandem.

Die Koffer z.B. kauft man immer geschlossen, also mit allem Inhalt. Das ist am interessantesten. Keiner kennt den Inhalt. Ist der Koffer „schwer" oder „sehr schwer" oder „nicht so schwer"? Der Preis für einen geschlossenen Koffer ist etwa 50 Euro. Die Preise sind selten höher als 80 Euro. Es sind ja genug Koffer da.

Vierzig Millionen Gepäckstücke transportiert die Lufthansa im Jahr. Nur jedes Zehntausendste ist herrenlos trotz intensiver Suche nach dem Besitzer. Von einer Million Koffern und Taschen gehen also etwa einhundert verloren.

Die Adressen von den Besitzern in den Koffern sind willkommener als nasse Handtücher oder stinkende Nahrungsmittel…. Und der Zoll sucht im Fundgut Waffen und Rauschgift. Wirklich wertvolle Sachen und Geld sind fast nie in den Koffern. Trotzdem kann der neue Käufer für seine 50 Euro eben Glück oder Pech haben.

(Reading level: weeks 6 to 7)

VOCABULARY

	AG (Aktiengesellschaft)	plc
	arbeiten	to work
der	Auktionator (-en)	auctioneer
	beginnen	to begin
	(zum) Beispiel, z.B.	for example, e.g.
das	Fundgut	lost property
das	Gepäckstück (-e)	piece of luggage
der	Hammer (-)	hammer
das	Handtuch (¨er)	towel
	herrenlos	ownerless
der	Kinderwagen (-)	pram
	meistens	generally
	mittags	noon
	möglich	possible
das	Nahrungsmittel (-)	food
das	Rauschgift (-e)	drug
	scheinbar	apparently
	schwingen	to swing
der	Sonnenschirm (-e)	parasol
	stinken	to stink
die	Suche	search
die	Tasche (-n)	bag
der	Tennisschläger (-)	tennis racquet
	vergeblich	in vain
	verloren gehen	to get lost
der	Versteigerer (-)	auctioneer
	versteigern I	to auction
die	Versteigerung	auction
die	Waffe (-n)	weapon
	wertvoll	valuable
	willkommen	welcome
	wirklich	really
der	Zoll (¨e)	customs

Leistungstest für deutsche Schulen

Die Kultusminister wollen ihre Schulen regelmäßig testen lassen. Im internationalen Vergleich sind deutsche Schulen jetzt schlechter als die im Ausland. Am schlechtesten sind die Leistungen in Mathematik, dann folgen die Naturwissenschaften und dann Lesen. Später folgen Fremdsprachen, Geschichte, Geographie und Schreiben. Bei einer internationalen Vergleichsstudie in der achten Klasse in Mathematik erreichen deutsche Schüler nur den 16. Platz unter 26 Ländern – deutlich hinter Russland und Tschechien.

Außerdem sind sie im Schnitt älter als Schüler in anderen Ländern. Ein deutscher Schüler beginnt sein Schulleben erst mit sechs Jahren. Normalerweise soll er mit 18 Jahren fertig sein, aber ein deutscher Schüler kann „sitzen bleiben" und muss dann das Schuljahr wiederholen. Das ist viel üblicher als in anderen Ländern. Dadurch wird ein deutscher Schüler vielleicht erst mit 20 Jahren fertig.

In Nordrhein-Westfalen beginnt die Schulministerin mit einem eigenen Programm. Noten und Zeugnisse sollen vergleichbar sein. Fachlehrer sollen die Arbeiten in Parallelklassen korrigieren. Keine Schule soll „leichter" als eine andere sein.

(Reading level: weeks 7 to 8)

VOCABULARY

die	Arbeit (-en)	piece of work, (examination) paper
das	Ausland	abroad
	deutlich	clearly, significantly
	erreichen	to attain, reach
der	Fachlehrer (-)	specialist teacher
die	Fremdsprache (-n)	foreign language
die	Geschichte	history
die	Klasse (-n)	class
	korrigieren	to correct, mark
der	Kultusminister (-)	education minister
die	Leistung (-en)	performance
das	Lesen	reading
die	Naturwissenschaft (-en)	natural sciences, biology
	normalerweise	normally
die	Note (-n)	mark
	Russland	Russia
	im Schnitt	on average
das	Schreiben	writing
das	Schuljahr (-e)	school year
	sitzen bleiben II	to repeat a year
	Tschechien	the Czech Republic
	üblich	usual
der	Vergleich (-e)	comparison
	vergleichbar	comparable
	wiederholen I	to repeat
das	Zeugnis (-se)	report, certificate

Jeder vierte Deutsche ist Allergiker

Jeder vierte Deutsche über 14 Jahren leidet bereits unter Allergien. Dies findet man in einer Krankenkassenstudie. Am meisten ist es der Heuschnupfen. Etwa sechs Millionen Bundesbürger leiden daran. Etwa 2,3 Millionen leiden an einer Sonnenallergie; 2,2 Millionen reagieren allergisch auf Tierhaare. 1,9 Millionen haben eine Allergie gegen bestimmtes Essen, 2,1 Millionen gegen Staub im Haus.

 Die Hälfte der Allergiker hat jetzt einen anderen Lebensstil. Neun Prozent fahren nur noch zu bestimmten Zeiten in den Urlaub, sieben Prozent essen nur noch ganz normal, fünf Prozent haben keine Haustiere mehr. Allergien sind außerdem teuer: Ein Drittel der Allergiker bezahlt 50 Euro im Monat mehr für die Bekämpfung der Symptome.

(Reading level: weeks 7 to 8)

VOCABULARY

die	Allergie (-n)	allergy
die	Bekämpfung	alleviation
	bereits	already
das	Haustier (-e)	pet
der	Heuschnupfen	hay fever
die	Krankenkasse (-n)	health insurance (organisation)
der	Lebensstil	lifestyle
	leiden unter	to suffer from
	reagieren	to react
der	Staub	dust
das	Tierhaar (-e)	animal hair
der	Urlaub (-e)	holiday

Die Sucht nach dem Handy

Macht das Handy den Körper kaputt? „Elektroskeptiker"
vermuten Gefahren für die Gesundheit durch den Mobilfunk. Gibt
es wirklich ein Risiko? Ein Forscherteam aus Kamp-Lintfort will
darüber informieren. Die ersten Resultate sollen im nächsten Jahr
bekannt werden.

Das Handy erwärmt Körperzellen beim Gebrauch. Zu viel Wärme
bringt Gefahren. Der Biologe Wojtysik erklärt: „Da gehen die Zellen
kaputt, das Eiweiß verklumpt. Wie ein gebratenes Schnitzel, das ist
vergleichbar." Doch keine Angst, das Handy röstet seinen Besitzer
nicht.

Seit einem Dreivierteljahr wollen nun die Forscher genauer sein.
Freiwillige Studenten oder Wissenschaftler lassen mit sich
experimentieren. Es gibt Zellversuche, aber keine Tierversuche.

Australische Forscher haben Experimente mit Tieren gemacht. In
einer Studie im Auftrag der australischen Telekom haben Mäuse
„Strahlen" von Mobilfunkgeräten bekommen, und die
Wissenschaftler haben vermehrten Krebs festgestellt.

(Reading level: weeks 8 to 9)

VOCABULARY

	im Auftrag	on behalf (of)
	Australien	Australia
der	Biologe (-n)	biologist
	braten	to fry
das	Eiweiß	protein
	erwärmen I	to heat
	experimentieren	to experiment
das	Handy (-s)	mobile phone
	feststellen II	to discover
der	Forscher (-)	researcher
	freiwillig	voluntary
der	Gebrauch	use
die	Gefahr (-en)	danger
der	Körper (-)	body
der	Krebs (-e)	cancer
die	Maus (¨e)	mouse

das	**Mobilfunkgerät (-e)**	mobile phone
das	**Resultat (-e)**	result
	rösten	to roast
das	**Schnitzel (-)**	cutlet, schnitzel
der	**Skeptiker (-)**	sceptic
der	**Strahl (-en)**	ray, emission
die	**Sucht (¨e)**	addiction
das	**Tier (-e)**	animal
	verklumpen I	to get lumpy
	vermehrt	increased
	vermuten I	to suspect
der	**Versuch (-e)**	experiment
die	**Wärme**	heat
der	**Wissenschaftler (-)**	scientist
die	**Zelle (-n)**	cell

Erdbeeren: Hoher Gesundheitswert

Der hohe Gesundheitswert von Erdbeeren basiert nicht nur auf dem großen Vitamingehalt, vor allem an Vitamin C, sondern auch auf dem Reichtum an den verschiedenen lebenswichtigen Mineralstoffen wie z.B. Kalium, Calcium, Magnesium, Phosphat und Silizium. Erdbeeren sind auch sehr gut für die Verdauung (harntreibend und entschlackend) und für die Darmtätigkeit aufgrund des Pektingehaltes.

(Reading level: weeks 8 to 9)

VOCABULARY

	aufgrund	by virtue (of)
	basieren auf	to be based on
die	Darmtätikgeit	bowel activity
	entschlackend	purgative
die	Erdbeere (-n)	strawberry
der	Gehalt	content
die	Gesundheit	health
	harntreibend	diuretic
das	Kalium	potassium
	lebenswichtig	important (to life)
der	Mineralstoff (-e)	mineral
das	Phosphat	phosphate
der	Reichtum	wealth
das	Silizium	silicon
die	Verdauung	digestion

Größeres Drogen-Risiko: 1712 Opfer in einem Jahr

Die Drogensituation in Deutschland hat sich sehr verschlechtert: Zum ersten Mal ist die Zahl der Rauschgifttoten im letzen Jahr wieder angestiegen – auf 1712 Todesopfer. Gleichzeitig hat der Konsum synthetischer Modedrogen wie Ecstasy durch immer jüngere Konsumenten in alarmierender Weise zugenommen.

Damit wurden 147 Menschen mehr als im Vorjahr Opfer ihrer Sucht – ein Anstieg um fast zehn Prozent. Zwanzig junge Menschen sind durch Ecstasy gestorben. Von den fast 17 200 registrierten Erstkonsumenten nahmen 44 Prozent synthetische Drogen. Die höchste Konsumrate war LSD (plus 54,3 Prozent), danach Amphetamin-Derivate mit 52,2 Prozent. Ecstasy gehört dazu.

Die Ecstasy-Menge, die die Polizei gefunden hat, ist explosionsartig um 80 Prozent gewachsen. Bei allen anderen Rauschgiften sind die Fundmengen gesunken – bei Heroin von 933 auf 898 Kilo.

Die politischen Parteien auf der Linken kritisieren. Die jungen Drogensüchtigen haben mehr Angst vor polizeilicher Verfolgung als den Wunsch nach Hilfe. Dies treibt sie in die Kriminalität. Die Parteien auf der Rechten lehnen jede Entkriminalisierung des Drogenkonsums ab. Stattdessen fordern sie mehr Präventions- und Therapieangebote.

(Reading level: weeks 9 to 10)

VOCABULARY

	ablehnen II	to reject
	ansteigen II	to increase
der	Anstieg (-e)	increase
die	Droge (-n)	drug
die	Entkriminalisierung	decriminalisation
	explosionsartig	explosively
	fast	almost
die	Fundmenge (-n)	quantity found
	gleichzeitig	simultaneously
die	Hilfe	help
der	Konsument (PO -en)	consumer
die	Kriminalität	crime
	kritisieren	to criticise
die	Linke (see section 61)	the Left
das	Opfer (-)	victim
die	Partei (-en)	(political) party
	polizeilich	by the police
das	Präventionsangebot (-e)	preventive measure
das	Rauschgift (-e)	drug
die	Rechte (see section 61)	the Right
das	Risiko (-s/Risiken)	risk
das	Therapieangebot (-e)	therapeutic measure
das	Todesopfer (-)	fatality, death
der	Tote (see section 61)	dead person
die	Verfolgung	pursuit
	verschlechtern I sich	to deteriorate
die	Weise (-n)	way, manner
der	Wunsch (¨e)	wish
	zunehmen II	to increase

Reizende Leute

Weder Hopfers noch Bremsers haben erwartet, dass sie nach nur drei Tagen ihres Ferienaufenthaltes so gute Freunde finden. Als sich Hopfers in ihrem Zimmer über die erste Begegnung mit Bremsers unterhalten haben, hat er gesagt: „Da haben wir wirklich die richtigen Leute kennen gelernt. Der Mann ist wirklich interessant im Gespräch und die Frau finde ich einfach reizend. Und die Großzügigkeit, mit der sie uns an der Bar bewirtet haben!" Und die so hochgelobten Bremsers haben zur gleichen Zeit etwas Ähnliches über die Hopfers gesagt.

Nicht dass sich Hopfers und Bremsers nur während der ersten Ferienwoche sehr oft getroffen haben. Auch in der zweiten Woche haben sie jeden Abend zusammengesessen, geredet, gelacht und getrunken. Herr Hopfer hat gemeint: „Am nettesten sind Bremsers, wenn sie beschwipst sind, dann macht sie die überraschendsten Kommentare und er wirkt so komisch mit schwerer Zunge. Aber durch diese Trinkabende wird unser Geld bald nicht mehr reichen und ich glaube, dass die Bremsers auch langsam zu wenig Geld für diese teuren Abende haben." Ähnliche Gedanken bei Bremsers, die dann angefangen haben, sich Abende mit Hopfers ohne Wein recht langweilig vorzustellen.

In der dritten Woche haben sich beide Paare gegenseitig einfach langweilig, dumm und geizig gefunden. Am Ende der Woche haben sie sehr herzlich Abschied genommen und sich versprochen, in Verbindung zu bleiben ….

(Reading level: weeks 10 to 11)

VOCABULARY

	Abschied nehmen	to say farewell/goodbye
der	**Aufenthalt (-e)**	stay
die	**Begegnung (-en)**	meeting, encounter
	beschwipst	tipsy
	bewirten I	to invite, entertain
	gegenseitig	one another
	geizig	mean, miserly
die	**Großzügigkeit**	generosity
	hochgelobt	highly praised
	kennen lernen	to get to know
	komisch	funny
	reichen	to last
	reizend	delightful, charming
	überraschend	surprising
	unterhalten I sich	to converse
die	**Verbindung (-en)**	contact
	weder ... noch	neither ... nor
	wirken	to have an effect
die	**Zunge (-n)**	tongue

Was Männer abtörnt: Aussehen ist wichtiger als Charakter

Nun wissen wir, was Männer an Frauen absolut nicht mögen: Frauen, die alles besser wissen (und damit vielleicht die eigene Meinung vehement vertreten können?) sind für Männer doch tatsächlich „Abtörner Nummer eins". Dicht darauf folgen Körpergeruch (68 Prozent) und schlechte Zähne (62 Prozent). Auch vulgäre Sprachgewohnheiten gefallen den Männern nicht. So lautet jedenfalls das Resultat einer Umfrage, die das Münchner Magazin „freundin" veröffentlicht hat.

Die angeblich weibliche Vorliebe, langfristige Zukunftspläne zu machen, hält fast jeder zweite Mann für „absolut unsexy". Nach der Umfrage ist der Kaufrausch vieler Frauen immerhin noch für 42 Prozent der Männer ein Ärgernis.

Nicht weiter überraschend: Die Herren legen viel Wert auf das Aussehen. Optische Gesichtspunkte wie eine gute Figur (61 Prozent) oder Miniröcke (59 Prozent) – natürlich mit langen Beinen (58 Prozent) – stehen ganz oben auf ihrer Wunschliste.

(Reading level: weeks 10 to 11)

VOCABULARY

	abtörnen	to turn off
	angeblich	allegedly
das	Ärgernis (-se)	(source of) irritation
das	Aussehen (-)	appearance
das	Bein (-e)	leg
	dicht	close
	folgen	to follow
der	Gesichtspunkt (-e)	point of view
die	Gewohnheit (-en)	habit
der	Kaufrausch	spending mania
der	Körpergeruch	body odour
	langfristig	long-term
	lauten	to say
die	Liste (-n)	list
	(eine) Meinung vertreten I	to express (an) opinion
	Münchner	(of/from) Munich
der	Rock (¨e)	skirt
die	Umfrage	opinion poll
	veröffentlichen I	to publish
die	Vorliebe	preference
	weiblich	female, feminine
	Wert legen auf	to set store by
der	Zahn (¨e)	tooth
die	Zukunft	future

Autoklau nahm deutlich ab

Die Zahl der Kfz-Diebstähle hat wegen elektronischen Wegfahrsperren im letzten Jahr weiter deutlich abgenommen. Offiziellen Informationen zufolge lag der Rückgang bei 14,6 Prozent. Danach wurden im letzten Jahr 110 764 Fahrzeuge gestohlen, im Jahr davor waren es 129 652. Während im letzten Jahr davon 40 090 auf Dauer verschwunden blieben, waren es im vorletzten 46 301. Dies ist eine Abnahme von 9,1 Prozent.

Bei Langfingern waren die Marken VW (12 237), Mercedes (6 227), BMW (4 220) und Audi (3 955) am gefragtesten. In der Luxusklasse gingen die Diebstähle in den vergangenen Jahren bereits drastisch zurück. Im letzten Jahr lag die Zahl der entwendeten und weiter gesuchten Porsche bei 302. Jedes dritte gestohlene Fahrzeug wurde im Ausland entwendet.

Die Entwicklung zeigt, dass sich der serienmäßige Einbau der Wegfahrsicherung, der seit über einem Jahr für alle Neufahrzeuge vorgeschrieben ist, sehr gelohnt hat. Seitdem ist der Polizei kein Fall bekannt, in dem ein Dieb diese Sicherung überwunden hat und mit dem Auto wegfahren konnte.

Nachforschungen ergaben, dass in solchen Fällen entweder ein Diebstahl vorgetäuscht, das Fahrzeug abgeschleppt oder der Schlüssel entwendet worden war.

(Reading level: weeks 11 to 12)

VOCABULARY

	abnehmen II	to decrease
	abschleppen II	to tow away
der	Autoklau	car theft
der	Dieb (-e)	thief
der	Diebstahl (¨e)	theft
der	Einbau	installation, fitting
	entwenden I	to steal
die	Entwicklung (-en)	development, situation
das	Fahrzeug (-e)	vehicle
der	Fall (¨e)	case
	gefragt	in demand
das	Kfz (Kraftfahrzeug)	vehicle
der	Langfinger (-)	thief
	lohnen sich	to be worth while
die	Marke (-n)	type, make
der	Rückgang (¨e)	decrease
	serienmäßig	standard
	überwinden I	to defeat
	vergangen	past
	verschwunden bleiben	to disappear permanently
	vorletzt	last but one
	vorschreiben II	to prescribe
	vortäuschen II	to fake
	wegfahren II	to drive away
die	Wegfahrsicherung	immobiliser
die	Wegfahrsperre	immobiliser
	zufolge	according (to)

Unruhestand: Jeder elfte Rentner geht noch zur Arbcit

Jeder elfte Rentner geht noch zur Arbeit. Dies ist das Zwischenergebnis einer Langzeitstudie von drei Professoren. Sie hatten 2 000 Männer und Frauen aus Wuppertal, Solingen und Remscheid im Alter von 60 bis 80 Jahren befragt.

Grund für die Studie sei die ständig wachsende Zahl älterer Menschen in der Gesellschaft, erklärte Professor Wächter, der die Untersuchung leitet. Man habe das Freizeitverhalten der Rentner näher beobachten wollen. Doch was Wächter und seine Kollegen fanden, hatte mit „Ruhestand" oft nichts zu tun. Dabei sei das Geldverdienen für arbeitende Rentner nicht das Hauptmotiv. Älteren Leuten gehe es oft um „soziale Anerkennung".

„Auf der anderen Seite rechnen viele Betriebe fest mit der günstigen Rentnerarbeit", sagte die wissenschaftliche Mitarbeiterin Eva Walter. Bei 400-Euro-Jobs bekämen die Sozialversicherungskassen keinen Cent. Stundenlöhne seien sehr niedrig: Urlaubs-, Weihnachts- oder Krankengeld würden nor- malerweise nicht bezahlt. Dabei sei die Rentnerarbeit oft erstklas- sig. Walter: „Die Leute haben Berufserfahrung, sind pünktlich und zuverlässig. Das wünscht sich jeder Personalchef."

„Die von uns befragten Rentner kamen oft durch Zeitungsannoncen an ihren Job." Vielfach sei die Nachfrage der Betriebe so groß gewesen, dass die Rentner zwischen mehreren Angeboten auswählen konnten.

(Reading level: weeks 12 to 13)

die	Anerkennung	recognition
das	Angebot (-e)	offer
	auswählen II	to choose
	befragen I	to question
	beobachten I	to observe
die	Berufserfahrung (-en)	(job) experience
der	Betrieb (-e)	firm
	erklären I	to explain
	erstklassig	first class
das	Freizeitverhalten	leisure behaviour
die	Gesellschaft (-en)	society
	günstig	good value
das	Hauptmotiv (-e)	main motive
das	Krankengeld (-er)	sick pay
die	Langzeitstudie (-n)	long-term study
	leiten	to lead
die	Mitarbeiterin (-nen)	(female) colleague
die	Nachfrage (-n)	demand
	pünktlich	punctual
der	Rentner (-)	pensioner
der	Ruhestand	retirement
die	Sozialversicherungs-kasse (-n)	social insurance fund
	ständig	constantly
der	Stundenlohn (¨e)	hourly pay
der	Unruhestand	(pun) non-retirement state, state of restlessness
die	Untersuchung (-en)	investigation
	wissenschaftlich	academic
die	Zeitungsannonce (-n)	newspaper advert
	zuverlässig	reliable
das	Zwischenergebnis (-se)	provisional result

Türkei diskriminiert Deutsche

Nach der Kritik des türkischen Ministerpräsidenten an der „Diskriminierung" von Türken in Deutschland hat der Bundestagsabgeordnete Hirsch am Montag die „Diskriminierung" von Deutschen in der Türkei beklagt.

Die Lage von deutschen Frauen, die mit Türken verheiratet seien, stehe trotz jahrelanger Kritik immer noch in „krassem Gegensatz" zu den Lebensumständen von Türken in der Bundesrepublik, erklärte Hirsch, der mehrere Benachteiligungen auflistete. So müssten deutsche Frauen alle zwei Jahre ihre Aufenthalts- und Arbeitserlaubnis gegen hohe Kosten erneuern lassen. Beim Tod des Ehemannes oder einer Scheidung gebe es keine gesicherte Aufenthaltsrechte. Auch ein Wahlrecht werde nicht gewährt.

„Diese Diskriminierung kann nicht länger toleriert werden und wird die Beziehungen zwischen beiden Staaten belasten."

(Reading level: weeks 12 to 13)

die	**Arbeitserlaubnis (-se)**	work permit
die	**Aufenthaltsgenehmigung (-en)**	residence permit
	belasten I	to burden
die	**Benachteiligung (-en)**	disadvantaging
die	**Beziehungen (pl)**	relations
der	**Bundestagsabgeordnete (adj)**	(German) MP
	diskriminieren	to discriminate against
der	**Ehemann (¨er)**	husband
	erneuern I	to renew
	gewähren I	to grant
die	**Lage (-n)**	situation
die	**Lebensumstände (pl)**	living conditions
der	**Ministerpräsident (PO -en)**	prime minister
die	**Scheidung (-en)**	divorce
der	**Tod**	death
	tolerieren	to tolerate
die	**Türkei**	Turkey
	türkisch	Turkish
das	**Wahlrecht**	right to vote, franchise

Key to exercises

Week 3

Exercise 4: 1 Der Vater liebt die Wirtin. 2 Es ist harmlos!
3 Er kauft die Zeitung. 4 Sie macht die Betten. 5 Die Tochter
holt das Auto. 6 Sie ruft die Katze und den Hund. 7 Die
Katze und der Hund kommen. 8 Die Wirtin bringt Wasser.
9 Vater, Wirtin, Tochter, Hund und Katze trinken das Wasser.

Week 4

Exercise 5: 1 Sie kaufen ein Haus und machen Wohnungen.
2 Eine Wohnung hat keine Küche. 3 Das ist ein Problem
und sie bauen eine Küche. 4 Eine Wohnung hat kein
Wasser. 5 Das ist auch ein Problem, aber der Vater installiert
ein Wassersystem. 6 Eine Wohnung hat keine Elektrizität.
7 Das ist kein Problem. Der Sohn ist Elektriker. 8 Eine
Wohnung hat eine Küche, Wasser, Elektrizität und (einige)
Schränke, aber keine Fenster. 9 Das ist kein Problem, es ist
eine Katastrophe.

Exercise 6: 2 Zwei Brote kosten €5 (fünf Euro).
3 Zwei Würste kosten €3 (drei Euro). 4 Zwei Uhren kosten
€170,00 (hundertsiebzig Euro). 5 Zwei Zeitungen kosten
€3,50 (drei Euro fünfzig). 6 Zwei Betten kosten €688 (sechs-
hundertachtundachtzig Euro). 7 Zwei Schränke kosten
€1 010 ((ein)tausendzehn Euro). 8 Zwei Messer kosten
€7,50 (sieben Euro fünfzig). 9 Zwei Rosen kosten €4,30 (vier
Euro dreißig). 10 Zwei Autos kosten €36 000,00
(sechsunddreißigtausend Euro).

Exercise 7: Ich bringe meinem Vater ein Buch. Ich gebe es
ihm im Flur. Ich schenke meinem Bruder einen Hund und
wünsche ihm einen guten Tag.

Week 5

Exercise 8: 1 Was 2 Wann 3 Wen 4 Wo 5 Wer 6 Wie 7 Warum

Exercise 9:

Verkäufer Bitte schön …?
  Fremde Guten Tag. Haben Sie einen Führer?
Verkäufer Was für einen Führer?
  Fremde Einen Stadtführer.
Verkäufer Ich weiß es nicht. Fragen Sie bitte den Chef.
  Fremde Guten Tag. Ich suche einen Stadtführer. Haben
          Sie so etwas?
    Chef Ja sicher. Die Stadtführer sind drüben. Gucken
          Sie dort …
  Fremde Es ist verrückt. Ich finde Stadtführer von
          Frankfurt, Gießen, Marburg und Kassel, aber ich
          finde keinen Stadtführer von Bunsenheim.
    Chef Natürlich nicht. Warum brauchen wir
          Stadtführer von Bunsenheim? Wir wohnen hier
          und kennen die Stadt!

Exercise 10: 2 größer 3 jünger 4 klüger 5 wärmer
6 länger 7 netter

Week 6

Exercise 11: Der Verbrecher steht mit einem Pinsel und
einer Palette in der Hand vor einem Bild. Auf dem Bild sind
mehrere Sachen. Auf einer Tischdecke liegt ein Brot, neben
dem Brot ist ein Glas und hinter dem Brot ist eine Flasche
mit einem Korken. Auf der Flasche ist ein Etikett. Was ist
aber für den Verbrecher am wichtigsten? Die Feile in
dem/im Brot, natürlich!

Exercise 12: Der Einbrecher geht bis an die Haustür. Er
klopft an die Tür. Niemand kommt zur Tür. Er geht um das
Haus und guckt durch die Fenster. Er findet ein Auto ohne
Nummernschild zwischen dem Haus und der Garage. Er
geht zurück an die Haustür. Er steckt eine Feile zwischen die
Tür und den Rahmen. Er öffnet die Tür mit der Feile und
geht in den Flur. Ihm gegenüber auf der Treppe sitzt ein
Skelett mit einer Axt in der Hand.

Exercise 13:

Hotelgast Was gibt es im Fernsehen heute Abend?
  Kellner Ich weiß es nicht.
Hotelgast Gucken sie bitte in die Fernsehzeitung.
  Kellner Es gibt keine Fernsehzeitung diese Woche.
Hotelgast Gibt es eine Tageszeitung?
  Kellner Ja, hier ist eine Tageszeitung … aber sie ist
         leider von gestern.

Week 7

Exercise 14: 2 Nein, sie ist mit ihrer Schwester bei Müllers eingeladen. 3 Nein, der Vater kommt ohne unser Geschenk für die Mutter. 4 Nein, ich esse den Kuchen mit einer Tasse Kaffee. 5 Nein, er geht mit seinem Stadtführer durch Frankfurt. 6 Nein, ich mache das Abendbrot ohne meine Tochter. 7 Nein, sie geht ohne ihren Bruder zur Tante. 8 Nein, wir kaufen die Wurst ohne eine Cola.

Exercise 15: 1 Keiner, (Jeder) 2 Welche 3 Keinen, Diesen 4 Keinen, Diesen 5 (Jeder), Dieser 6 Solches, Welches 7 Welches 8 Jeder, Dieser 9 Welche, Jede

Exercise 16:

  She Will you please go and do the shopping?
   He Certainly! Have you got a shopping list for me?
  She No, I'll tell you everything … First please bring a
      small white loaf and ten fresh rolls from the baker.
   He They're cheaper at Marktkauf, and we're going there
      this afternoon.
  She All right. Then buy half a pound of mince and 250
      grams of boiled ham at the butcher's.
   He They always serve me badly at the butcher's. I
      would rather buy meat in the old town, and we also
      have to go there this afternoon.
  She All right. Then I need lettuce, one and a half pounds
      of small, firm tomatoes, a nice cucumber, ten
      pounds of potatoes and a pound of French beans
      from the greengrocer's.
   He The things for the salad and the other vegetables

aren't urgent, and after all there's (a) market
tomorrow.

She All right, but I definitely need eggs from Edeka.

He No, you don't need (them). We still have a lot.
We'll (then) get eggs from the market, too.

She All right, then you don't need to go shopping.

Exercise 17: 2 Hol bitte ein kleines Weißbrot vom Bäcker.
Das Weißbrot kaufe ich lieber bei Marktkauf. 3 Hol bitte 250
Gramm gekochten Schinken vom Metzger. Den gekochten
Schinken kaufe ich lieber in der Altstadt. 4 Hol bitte einen
Kopfsalat vom Gemüsegeschäft. Den Kopfsalat kaufe ich
lieber auf dem Markt. 5 Hol bitte zwanzig Eier von Edeka.
Die Eier kaufe ich lieber auf dem Markt. 6 Hol bitte eine
schöne Gurke vom Gemüsegeschäft. Die Gurke kaufe ich
lieber auf dem Markt. 7 Hol bitte zehn frische Brötchen vom
Bäcker. Die Brötchen kaufe ich lieber bei Marktkauf. 8 Hol
bitte ein halbes Pfund Hackfleisch vom Metzger. Das
Hackfleisch kaufe ich lieber in der Altstadt. 9 Hol bitte zehn
Pfund Kartoffeln vom Gemüsegeschäft. Die Kartoffeln kaufe
ich lieber auf dem Markt. 10 Hol bitte ein Pfund grüne
Bohnen vom Gemüsegeschäft. Die grünen Bohnen kaufe ich
lieber auf dem Markt.

Week 8

Exercise 18: 1 kann 2 müssen 3 darf 4 muss 5 darf 6 darf
7 kann

Exercise 19: 1 damit 2 darauf 3 danach 4 dazu 5 dafür
6 daneben 7 dagegen 8 dazwischen 9 dahinter 10 davor

Exercise 20: 1 tue/stelle 2 sind/liegen 3 tue/lege 4 tun/
stellen 5 tue/stelle 6 sind/stehen 7 tue/lege 8 tue/stecke
9 tue/lege 10 ist/liegt 11 sind/liegen 12 tue/lege 13 tue/stelle

Exercise 21: Now look! I'll keep the refrigerator clear as far
as possible. Then you'll be able to find everything quite easily.
I'm putting the chicken for Sunday, the frozen raspberry flan
and the two oven-ready meals into the freezer compartment.

You can eat the oven-ready meals tomorrow and the day after. The plum tart and the dish with cream are at the top. I'm also putting the two bottles of wine there … Oh, there's just a little space there still, I can put the carton of yoghurt in between. I'm putting the four bottles of beer in the bottom of the door, and two cartons of milk are next to them. I'm putting the packet of boiled ham, the salami and the liver sausage in the middle. They're for evenings, of course … Eggs? … I'm putting the eggs singly in the top of the door, of course, twelve of them. I'm putting two pieces of butter in the top compartment in the door. I'll leave the third one out to get soft. The flat container with three sorts of cheese is in the middle, and a tube of mayonnaise and the sliced cheese are behind it. The cucumber, the lettuce, the grapes and the tomatoes are at the bottom, and I'm putting the bag of oranges, one cauliflower and the sprouts in the vegetable compartment right at the bottom. I'll put a little jar of honey and a jar of strawberry jam a little higher in the door … My goodness, how full the refrigerator is again!

Week 9

Exercise 22: 1 denen 2 der 3 dem 4 das 5 der 6 das 7 den 8 die 9 denen 10 dem

Exercise 23: 1 hat/gebracht 2 ist/geflogen 3 sind/gestorben 4 hat/gestellt 5 ist/gesprungen 6 bin/geblieben 7 ist/gestiegen 8 habe/geschickt 9 haben/bekommen 10 bist/geworden

Exercise 24: 1 (b) 2 (c) 3 (a) 4 (b) 5 (a) 6 (c)

Week 10

Exercise 25: Ich habe vor, eine Party zu geben. Wir sind so viele, also richte ich meine Wohnung anders ein. Ich lade nur meine besten Freunde ein, aber wir sind fünfzig. Diesmal helfen meine Freunde mal nicht mit. Ich will alles alleine machen. Um 8 Uhr rufe ich sie an. Dann können sie kommen. Aber was sagen meine Freunde, sie schlagen stattdessen vor, gar nicht zu essen, sondern den ganzen Abend lang zu trinken.

Exercise 26: 2 Fräulein Schmidt steht früh auf, um mit ihrem Hund spazieren zu gehen. 3 Mittags kommt sie nach Hause und arbeitet im Garten, statt zu essen. 4 Am Nachmittag geht sie ins Kino, ohne ihre Mutter zu fragen. 5 Sie sieht gerne Filme, um auf andere Gedanken zu kommen. 6 Am Abend kommt ihr Freund, um sie ins Restaurant einzuladen. 7 Sie verlässt das Restaurant während des Essens, ohne zu bezahlen. 8 Er bleibt im Restaurant sitzen und isst beide Portionen, statt zu seiner Freundin zu laufen.

Week 11

Exercise 27: 2 ..., dass Fritz solche Vorschläge nicht machen soll. 3 ..., dass Ernst endlich mal etwas tun soll. 4 ..., dass er sein Handgelenk plötzlich verletzt. 5 ..., dass er Ernst zum Arzt schickt. 6 ..., dass Ernst einfach faul ist!

Exercise 28: 2 Nachdem man gegessen hat, soll man eigentlich nicht schlafen. 3 Während man isst, darf man nicht zu viel reden. 4 Obwohl er viel geredet hat, hat er eigentlich nicht viel gesagt. 5 Weil das Wetter schön ist, müssen wir endlich im Garten arbeiten. 6 Bis das Programm anfängt, kannst du noch schön in der Küche helfen! 7 Weil du hohen Blutdruck hast, musst du weniger arbeiten. 8 Obwohl er hohen Blutdruck hat, läuft er jeden Tag.

Week 12

Exercise 29: 2 Während Fritz im Garten arbeitete, hat sich sein Bruder Pop-Musik angehört. 3 Während Hanna einen Brief schrieb, ist ihre Freundin schwimmen gegangen. 4 Während Otto Milch trank, hat sein Bruder Bruno Schnaps getrunken. 5 Während Frau Krause mit ihrem Nachbarn sprach, hat ein Einbrecher ihr Geld vom Küchentisch gestohlen. 6 Während sich die Eltern oben im

Haus stritten, haben die Kinder unten im Haus eine Party gehalten. 7 Während Anton mit den Eltern sprach, hat Susanne den Hund ins Wasser gestoßen.

Exercise 30: 2 (a) Wenn du die Fahrkarte besorgen würdest, dann hätten wir die Möglichkeit, am Wochenende in die Berge zu fahren. (b) Würdest du die Fahrkarte besorgen, dann hätten wir die Möglichkeit, am Wochenende in die Berge zu fahren. 3 (a) Wenn Peter nicht das Fenster schließt, dann wird es zu kalt für uns alle. (b) Schließt Peter nicht das Fenster, dann wird es zu kalt für uns alle. 4 (a) Wenn dieser Mann nicht den Club verlässt, dann wird es Krach geben. (b) Verlässt dieser Mann nicht den Club, dann wird es Krach geben. 5 (a) Wenn die kleine Tochter nicht fernsehen dürfte, dann wäre sie schwierig. (b) Dürfte die kleine Tochter nicht fernsehen, dann wäre sie schwierig. 6 (a) Wenn der Vater in die Gaststube geht, dann trinkt er immer zu viel. (b) Geht der Vater in die Gaststube, dann trinkt er immer zu viel. 7 (a) Wenn du jetzt das Essen für Sonntag kochst, dann wirst du am Sonntag morgen schlafen können. (b) Kochst du jetzt das Essen für Sonntag, dann wirst du am Sonntag morgen schlafen können.

Week 13

Exercise 31: 2 Jedoch bucht Emil eine Fahrt nach Berlin. Emil bucht jedoch eine Fahrt nach Berlin. (trotzdem, allerdings) 3 Allerdings gibt es sehr viele Touristen. Es gibt allerdings sehr viele Touristen. (deshalb, jedoch, außerdem) 4 Andererseits gibt es in Berlin viel zu sehen. In Berlin gibt es andererseits viel zu sehen. (jedoch) 5 Außerdem ist es historisch und politisch wichtig. Es ist außerdem historisch und politisch wichtig. (andererseits) 6 Immerhin war es vor einiger Zeit das Tor zwischen Westen und Osten. Es war immerhin vor einiger Zeit das Tor zwischen Westen und Osten. 7 Trotzdem hat er Berlin sehr interessant gefunden. Er hat trotzdem Berlin sehr interessant gefunden. (jedoch, allerdings, andererseits)

Exercise 32: 1 (a) 2 (c) 3 (b) 4 (b) 5 (b) 6 (c) 7 (c)

Mini-dictionary

Numbers are not included in the Mini-dictionary. The cardinal numbers are to be found in section 18 and the ordinal numbers in week 7, section 30. I indicates TYPE I (inseparable prefix) verbs; II indicates TYPE II (separable prefix) verbs.

GERMAN–ENGLISH

ab und zu occasionally, now and again

der **Abend (-e)** evening

das **Abendbrot (-e)** supper

abends in the evenings

die **Abendveranstaltung (-en)** evening entertainment/event

aber but

der **Abfall (-̈e)** rubbish, waste, garbage

abgesehen (davon) apart (from that)

abhängen II (von) to depend (on)

abholen II to collect, pick up

abhören II to listen to, check (e.g. heart)

abnehmen II to lose weight

der **Abzug (-̈e)** print, copy

ach! oh!

achten (auf) to pay attention (to), keep an eye (on)

(das) Ägypten Egypt

die **Ahnung (-en)** idea, clue, notion

all all

alle zwei Tage every other day

allein(e) alone

allerdings admittedly, mind you, … though

alles everything

das **Allgäu** (mountainous area in Southern Bavaria)

allgemein general, in general

als than, as, when

also so, therefore, well

alt old

das **Alter (-)** age

die **Altstadt** old (part of) town

am = an dem

an at, on, to, by, on to, up to

anbieten II to offer

ander. . other, different

andererseits on the other hand

ändern to change, alter

anderthalb one and a half

der **Anfang (-̈e)** beginning, start

anfangen II to begin, start

der **Anfänger (-)** beginner

die **Angelegenheit (-en)** matter, affair, business

angenehm pleasant

die **Angst (-̈e)** fear, anxiety, worry

anhalten II to stop, pull up

anhören II sich to listen to, sound

ankommen II to arrive

anrufen II to ring up, call, telephone

anschaffen II to get, acquire, obtain, buy

die **Ansicht (-en)** view, opinion

ansonsten otherwise, apart from that

anstatt instead (of)

anstrengend strenuous, energetic

antworten to answer

anziehen II to put on (clothes)

anziehen II sich to get dressed

die **Apfelsine (-n)** orange

der **April** April
arbeitslos unemployed
ärgern sich to get annoyed
arm poor
der **Arzt** (¨e) doctor (male)
die **Arzthelferin** (-nen) doctor's
receptionist
die **Ärztin** (-nen) doctor (female)
auch also, too, even
auf on, on top of, on to
der **Aufkleber** (-) sticker
aufkommen II to (be liable
to) pay
aufmachen II to open
die **Aufnahme** (-n) exposure,
photo, shot
aufnehmen II to accept,
admit
aufpassen II to pay attention,
take note, watch
aufregen II sich to get
excited/worked up
der **Aufschnitt** sliced (cold) meat
aufstehen II to get up
auftauchen II to turn up,
appear
der **Augenblick** (-e) moment,
instant
im Augenblick/
augenblicklich at the moment
der **August** August
aus out of, from
der **Ausflug** (¨e) excursion,
outing
ausgeben II to spend
ausgehen II to go out
aushängen II to post, put up,
display
der **Ausländer** (-) foreigner
der **Auslöser** (-) shutter release
ausmachen II to put out,
switch off
aussehen II to look, appear
außerdem besides, moreover,
furthermore

außerhalb outside (of)
äußerst extremely
die **Aussicht** (-en) view, prospect
aussuchen II to choose, select
austauschen II to exchange
auswechseln II to replace
ausziehen II sich to get
undressed
das **Auto** (-s) car
der **Automat** (PO -en) machine
(e.g. vending)
die **Axt** (¨e) axe

der **Bäcker** (-) baker
baden to bathe, swim
der **Bahnhof** (¨e) station
bald soon
die **Banane** (-n) banana
die **Bar** (-s) bar
bauen to build
der **Bauer** (PO -n) farmer
der **Baum** (¨e) tree
der **Becher** (-) cup, mug, carton
bedanken I sich to say 'thank
you', express one's thanks
bedeuten I to mean
bedienen I to serve
bedrohen I to threaten
beeilen I sich to hurry (up)
befinden I sich to be, be
situated
begegnen I to meet
behalten I to keep
der **Behälter** (-) container
behandeln I to treat
bei with, at, in
beid. . both, two
das **Beisammensein** being with
people, get-together
beitreten II to join
bekannt known, well-known,
acquainted
der **Bekannte (adj)** acquaintance,
friend
beklagen I sich to complain

bekommen I to get, obtain
bemerken I to notice
benutzen I to use
der **Berg (-e)** mountain, hill
der **Beruf (-e)** job, trade,
  profession, occupation
beschränken I to limit, restrict
beschweren I sich to complain
der **Besitzer (-)** proprietor, owner
besonder. . special
besonders especially
besorgen I to get, obtain
besprechen I to discuss, talk
  over
besser better
bestehen I (auf) to insist (on)
bestellen I to order
die **Bestellung (-en)** order
am **besten** best of all
bestimmt definite
besuchen I to visit, attend
betrinken I sich to get drunk
das **Bett (-en)** bed
der **Beutel (-)** bag
bevor before
bewegen I sich to move
bezahlen I to pay for
das **Bier** beer
das **Bierchen (-)** (nice) little beer
bieten to offer
das **Bild (-er)** picture, photograph
billig cheap, inexpensive
der **Bindfaden** string
bis until, up to
ein bißchen a bit
bist (you) are
bitte please
bitten (um) to ask (for),
  request
bitte schön? yes please?
bitte schön! here you are!
blass pale
der **Bleistift (-e)** pencil
blenden to dazzle
die **Blume (-n)** flower

das **Blumengeschäft (-e)** florist's
der **Blumenkohl** cauliflower
der **Blutdruck** blood pressure
bluten to bleed
die **Blutprobe (-n)** blood test
der **Boden (-̈)** floor, ground
die **Bohne (-n)** bean
grüne Bohnen French beans
böse angry, naughty, wicked
brauchen to need
brechen to break
breit wide
brennen to burn
der **Brief (-e)** letter
bringen to bring, take
das **Brot (-e)** bread, loaf
das **Brötchen (-)** roll
der **Bruder (-̈)** brother
das **Buch (-̈er)** book
der **Buchstabe (PO -ns)** letter
  (of the alphabet)
der **Bus (-se)** bus, coach
die **Butter** butter
die **Buttersoße** butter sauce

der **Cent (-s)** cent
die **Chance (-n)** chance
checken to check
der **Chef (-s)** boss
die **Chefsekretärin (-nen)** boss's
  secretary, personal assistant
chinesisch Chinese
die **CD** compact disc
die **CD-Hülle** CD case
der **Club (-s)** club
die **Coca-Cola (-)** Coca-Cola

d. . the
d. . selb. . the same
da there, then, as
das **Dach (-̈er)** roof
dafür for it, instead
dagegen against it, on the
  other hand
daher from there, therefore

dahin (to) there
dahinter behind it
damals then, at that time
die **Dame (-n)** lady
damit with it, in order that, so that
danach after that, afterwards
daneben next to it
danke (schon)! thank you!
dann then
darüber over it, above it, about it
darum round it, therefore, so
das that
dauern to last
davor before it
dazu to it, with it
dazwischen between them
die **Decke (-n)** ceiling
der **Defekt (-e)** fault
denken to think
denn for, as, since, then
dennoch nevertheless, yet
deren whose, of whom
deshalb therefore
dessen whose, of whom
deswegen on account of it, therefore
der **Deutsche (adj)** German
der **Dezember** December
das **Dia (-s)** slide
dich you
der **Dienstag** Tuesday
dies. . this
dir to/for you
der **Direktor (-en)** director
doch but, however, after all
der **Donnerstag** Thursday
das **Doppelzimmer (-)** double room
dort there
dorthin (to) there
die **Dose (-n)** can, tin, jar
draußen outside
das **Drittel (-)** third

drüben over there
der **Druck (¨e)** pressure
drücken to press
du you
dumm silly, stupid
dunkel dark
durch through, by
dürfen may, to be allowed/able
die **Dusche (-n)** shower
duzen to say 'du'

eben just, just now, simply
ebenfalls likewise
ebenso just as
die **Ecke (-n)** corner
Edeka (chain of small supermarkets)
egal all the same, immaterial, regardless
ehemalig former
das **Ei (-er)** egg
eigen own
eigentlich really, actually
eilen to be urgent
ein a, one
einbegriffen included
einbilden II sich to imagine
der **Einbrecher (-)** burglar
einfach simple
eingeladen invited
einig. . some, a few
einkaufen II to do the shopping
die **Einkaufsliste (-n)** shopping list
einladen II to invite
einmal once
einnehmen II to eat, take, consume
einrichten II to furnish, arrange
der **Eintritt (-e)** admission
einverstanden agreed
einwandfrei perfect, faultless, flawless

einzeln separate, one by one, single

das **Einzelzimmer (-)** single room

das **Eisfach ("er)** freezer compartment

elegant elegant

der **Elektriker (-)** electrician

die **Elektrizität** electricity

empfehlen I to recommend

empfinden I to feel

endlich finally, at last

der **Englischkurs (-e)** English course

enthalten I to contain, include

die **Entscheidung (-en)** decision

entschuldigen I sich to apologise

Entschuldigung! excuse me!

die **Entschuldigung (-en)** excuse, apology

entsprechen I to correspond

er he

meines Erachtens in my opinion

die **Erdbeermarmelade** strawberry jam

der **Erfolg (-e)** success

die **Erfrischung (-en)** refreshment

das **Ergebnis (-se)** result

erinnern I sich (an) to remember

erkälten I sich to catch a cold

erkältet sein to have a cold

die **Erkältung (-en)** cold

erscheinen I to appear

ersetzen I to replace

erst first, only

erwarten I to expect, await

erzählen I to tell, relate

die **Erziehung** education, bringing up, upbringing

es it

essen to eat

das **Essen (-)** food, meal

das **Etikett (-en)** label

etwa about, perhaps, say

etwas something

so etwas something/anything like that

euch you

euer your

der **Euro (-s)** euro

das **Exemplar (-e)** copy

das **Experiment (-e)** experiment

der **Export (-e)** export

extra extra, on purpose, deliberately

das **Fach ("er)** compartment, subject

fahren to go (not on foot), travel

die **Fahrkarte (-n)** ticket

das **Fahrrad ("er)** bicycle

die **Fahrt (-en)** journey, trip

fallen to fall

falls in case

falsch wrong

fangen to catch

die **Farbe (-n)** colour, paint

der **Februar** February

feiern to celebrate

die **Feile (-n)** file

der **Fehler (-)** mistake, error

das **Fenster (-)** window

die **Ferien (plural)** holiday(s)

der **Fernsehapparat (-e)** television set

das **Fernsehen** television

die **Fernsehzeitung (-en)** TV magazine

fertig ready, finished

das **Fertigessen (-)** oven-ready meal

fest firm

das **Festessen (-)** banquet

das **Feuer (-)** fire

das **Feuerwerk** fireworks

fies nasty
die **Figur (-en)** figure
der **Film (-e)** film
finanzieren to finance
finden to find
der **Fisch (-e)** fish
flach flat, shallow
die **Flasche (-n)** bottle
das **Fleisch** meat
fliegen to fly
fliehen to flee
der **Fliesenleger (-)** tiler
flirten to flirt
der **Flur (-e)** hall
die **Folge (-n)** consequence
der **Fotoapparat (-e)** camera
die **Frage (-n)** question
in Frage kommen to be possible
nicht in Frage kommen to be out of the question
fragen to ask
der **Franzose (PO -n)** Frenchman
französisch French
die **Frau (-en)** woman, wife, Mrs
frech cheeky
frei free, vacant
freihalten II to keep clear
freilich admittedly, to be sure
der **Freitag** Friday
freuen sich auf to look forward to
freuen sich (über) to be pleased (at)/glad (about)
der **Freund (-e)** friend
die **Freundin (-nen)** girlfriend
freundlich kind, friendly
frisch fresh
froh glad
die **Frucht (-̈e)** fruit
früh early
früher earlier, former(ly)
der **Frühling** spring
das **Frühstück** breakfast
fühlen sich to feel

der **Führer (-)** guide
der **Führerschein (-e)** driving licence
der **Fünfzigeuroschein (-e)** fifty euro note
funktionieren to work, function
für for
furchtbar terrible, frightful, fearful
fürchten sich (vor) to be afraid (of)

ganz all, whole
gar nicht not at all
gar nichts nothing at all
die **Garage (-n)** garage
der **Garten (-̈)** garden
der **Gast (-̈e)** guest, visitor
das **Gasthaus (-̈er)** inn
die **Gaststube (-n)** lounge (of inn)
geben to give
es gibt there is/are
der **Geburtstag (-e)** birthday
der **Gedanke (PO -ns)** thought
geduldig patient
geeignet suitable, suited
gefährlich dangerous
gefallen I to please
der **Gefangene (adj)** prisoner
gefroren frozen
gegen against, towards
die **Gegend (-en)** area, region, neighbourhood
das **Gegenteil** opposite
gegenüber opposite
gegenzeichnen II to countersign
gehen to go, walk
es geht um it's about
wie geht's (Ihnen)? how are you?
gehören I to belong
gekocht boiled, cooked
gelb yellow

das **Geld** money
die **Gelegenheit (-en)** opportunity
das **Gelenk (-e)** joint
gelingen I to succeed
das **Gemüse** vegetables
das **Gemüsefach ("-er)** vegetable compartment
das **Gemüsegeschäft (-e)** greengrocer's
genau exact, precise
genieren sich to be embarrassed
genießen I to enjoy
genug enough
genügend enough, suffficient
das **Gepäck** luggage
gerade just, just now
gerade erst only just
geradeaus straight ahead
immer geradeaus (gehen) to keep (going) straight ahead
das **Gerät (-e)** machine, (piece of) equipment
gern gladly
das **Geschäft (-e)** business, shop
geschehen I to happen
geschlossen closed
der **Geschmack ("-e or "-er)** taste
die **Geschwister (plural)** brother(s) and/or sister(s)
gesellig sociable
der **Gesellschaftsraum ("-e)** lounge
gestern yesterday
gesund healthy
das **Getränk (-e)** drink
gewachsen sein to be able to cope with
gewiss certainly
das **Gewitter (-)** thunderstorm
gewöhnen I sich (an) to get used/accustomed (to)
das **Glas ("-er)** glass, jar
der **Glaube (PO -ns)** belief
glauben to believe, think

gleich straight away, immediately, at once, same, similar
das **Glück** luck, happiness
golden gold, golden
das **Gramm (-e)** gram
gratulieren to congratulate
es graut mir (vor) I have a horror (of)
die **Grenze (-n)** frontier, border
grillen to grill
groß big, large, tall
die **Größe (-n)** size
die **Großmutter (")** grandmother
der **Grundpreis (-e)** basic price
die **Gruppe (-n)** group
grüßen to greet, wave
grüß Gott! hello!
gucken to look, peep
gut good, well
na gut! (oh) all right!
guten Abend! good evening!
guten Morgen! good morning!
guten Tag! hello!
meine Güte! my goodness! good heavens!

haben to have
das **Hackfleisch** minced meat
das **Hähnchen (-)** chicken
halb half
die **Hälfte (-n)** half
hallo! hello!
halt just, simply
halten to hold
halten (von) to think (of/about)
die **Hand ("-e)** hand
der **Handball** handball
handeln sich um to be about
das **Handgelenk (-e)** wrist
harmlos harmless, innocuous
hart hard
hast (you) have
der **Haufen (-)** heap, pile

das **Haus (¨er)** house
nach Hause (to) home
zu Hause at home
die **Hausbesitzerin (-nen)** house
owner (female)
der **Hausschlüssel (-)** house key,
front door key
die **Haustür (-en)** front door
heiraten to marry
heiß hot
heißen to be called
das **heißt** that is (to say)
der **Held (PO -en)** hero
helfen to help
die **Helferin (-nen)** assistant
hell light, bright
herausnehmen II to take out
der **Herbst** autumn
der **Herr (PO -n, plural -en)**
gentleman, Mr
herrlich splendid, glorious
das **Herz (PO -ens, plural -en)**
heart
heute today
heute Abend this evening
heutzutage nowadays, now
hier here
die **Himbeertorte (-n)** raspberry
tart/flan
hin und her backwards and
forwards, to and fro
hin und zurück there and
back, return
hingegen on the other hand
hinlegen II sich to lie down
hinten at the back, behind
hinter behind
hinterher afterwards, later
der **Hinweg (-e)** outward journey
historisch historic, historical
hoch high
am höchsten highest
die **Hochzeit (-en)** wedding
hoffen to hope
hoffentlich hopefully

höflich polite
holen to fetch, bring
der **Honig** honey
hören to hear
das **Hotel (-s)** hotel
die **Hülle** case
der **Hund (-e)** dog
der **Hunger** hunger

ich I
ihm to/for him/it
ihn him
ihnen to/for them
Ihnen to/for you
ihr her, their, to/for her
Ihr your
immer always
immerhin after all
immer wieder again and
again, repeatedly
in in, into
indem by
die **Inflation** inflation
infolgedessen consequently
informieren to inform
inklusiv inclusive
innerhalb inside of
installieren to install
das **Instrument (-e)** instrument
interessant interesting
interessieren to interest
interessieren sich (für) to be
interested (in)
interessiert (an) interested
(in)
irgendein some or other, any
irgendwo somewhere,
anywhere
ist is

ja yes, of course
das **Jahr (-e)** year
jahrelang for years
der **Januar** January
jawohl! certainly!

je each, ever
jed. . every, each, any
jedenfalls at any rate
jedoch however
jemals ever
jen. . that
jenseits on the far side (of), beyond
jetzt now
jeweils each time
der **Juli** July
jung young
der **Junge (PO -n, plural often -ns)** boy
der **Juni** June

der **Kaffee** coffee
die **Kalorie (-n)** calorie
kalt cold
kaputt broken (down), exhausted
die **Karotte (-n)** carrot
die **Kartoffel (-n)** potato
der **Käse** cheese
der **Kassenbon (-s)** till receipt, sales slip
die **Katastrophe (-n)** catastrophe
die **Katze (-n)** cat
der **Kauf (¨-e)** purchase
kaufen to buy
kaum scarcely, hardly
kein not a, no, not any
der **Kellner (-)** waiter
kennen to know (people, things)
das **Kind (-er)** child
der **Kinderarzt (¨-e)** paediatrician
das **Kino (-s)** cinema
die **Kirche (-n)** church
klagen to complain
die **Klarinette (-n)** clarinet
der **Klassenbeste (adj)** best in the class

der **Klassenkamerad (PO -en)** classmate
das **Klavier (-e)** piano
der **Klavierlehrer (-)** piano teacher
das **Kleid (-er)** dress
klein small, little
klingen to sound
klopfen to knock
klug clever
der **Koffer (-)** suitcase
der **Kohl** cabbage
der **Komfort** comfort
kommen to come
kommen zu to happen
die **Konferenz (-en)** conference
können can, to be able
kontrollieren to check
das **Konzert (-e)** concert
der **Kopf (¨-e)** head
der **Kopfsalat** lettuce
der **Korken (-)** cork
kosten to cost
der **Krach** noise, racket, quarrel, row
krank ill, sick
die **Krankheit (-en)** illness, sickness, disease
die **Kreuzung (-en)** crossroads, junction
kriechen to creep, crawl
kriegen to get
die **Kritik (-en)** criticism
die **Küche (-n)** kitchen
der **Kuchen (-)** cake
der **Kühlschrank (¨-e)** refrigerator
der **Kunde (PO -n)** customer
die **Kusine (-n)** cousin (female)
der **Kurs (-e)** course, rate of exchange
kurz short
kurz danach shortly afterwards
kurz davor shortly before

lachen to laugh
landen to land
lang(e) long
langsam slow
langweilig boring
lassen to let, make, leave
laufen to run, walk
laut loud, noisy
die Leberwurst (¨e) liver sausage
lecker tasty, delicious
leer empty
legen to put, lay (flat)
die Lehrerin (-nen) teacher
  (female)
leicht easy
leiden to suffer
leider unfortunately, (to be)
  sorry (that)
leihen to lend, borrow
leisten to achieve, manage,
  accomplish
lesen to read
letztens recently, lately
die Leute (plural) people
das Licht (-er) light
die Liebe (-n) love
lieben to love
lieber rather
das Lieblingsreiseziel (-e)
  favourite destination
liegen to lie, recline, be
  (situated)
liegen lassen to leave (lying)
  about/behind
die Limonade (-n) lemonade
losfahren II to set out, come
  out, drive off
loslassen II to set off
der Löwe (PO -n) lion
lügen to lie (fib)
der Luxus luxury

machen to make, do
machen sich nichts daraus
  not to worry about it

es macht nichts it doesn't
  matter
das Mädchen (-) girl
mager lean, thin
der Mai May
mal just
das Mal (-e) time, occasion
malen to paint
man one, you, people
manch. . quite a few, a fair
  number of
manchmal sometimes
der Mann (¨er) man, husband
manuell manual
die Manteltasche (-n) coat
  pocket
der Markt (¨e) market
der Marktkauf (typical
  hypermarket name)
der Marktplatz (¨e) marketplace
der März March
die Maschine (-n) machine, plane
der Maurer (-) bricklayer
die Mayonnaise mayonnaise
das Mehl flour
mehr more
mehrer. . several
mein my
meinen to think, mean, say
meinetwegen on my account,
  as far as I am concerned
die Meinung (-en) opinion
am meisten most of all
der Mensch (PO -en) person,
  human being, (plural) people
merken to notice
messen to measure
das Messer (-) knife
der Meter (-) metre
der Metzger (-) butcher
mich me, myself
die Miete (-n) rent
der Mieter (-) tenant
die Milch milk
die Milchkanne (-n) milk jug

der **Minister (-)** minister
misslingen I to fail
mit with
mitbringen II to bring
(with one)
mithelfen II to assist, help,
co-operate
das **Mitleid** sympathy, pity
das **Mittagessen (-)** lunch
die **Mitte (-n)** middle
das **Mittelmeer** Mediterranean
mitten in the middle
die **Mitternacht (⁻e)** midnight
der **Mittwoch** Wednesday
mögen may, to like
die **Möglichkeit (-en)** possibility,
opportunity
möglichst as far as possible
der **Moment (-e)** moment
im Moment at the moment
Moment mal! just a moment!
momentan at the moment
der **Monat (-e)** month
der **Montag** Monday
morgen tomorrow
müde tired
die **Musik** music
müssen must, to have to
die **Mutter (⁻)** mother

nach after, to, according to
der **Nachbar (PO -n)** neighbour
nachdem after
nachher afterwards
nachholen II to catch up
der **Nachmittag (-e)** afternoon
nächst next, nearest
am nächsten nearest of all
die **Nacht (⁻e)** night
der **Nachttisch (-e)** bedside table
nahe near
nähern sich to approach
nämlich for, you see
nass wet
natürlich naturally, of course

neben next to, alongside
nehmen to take
nein no
die **Nelke (-n)** carnation
nett nice, kind, good
das **Netz (-e)** net
neu new
das **Neujahr** New Year
das **Neujahrsfrühstück (-e)** New
Year's (Day) breakfast
der **Neujahrstag (-e)** New Year's
Day
neulich recently
nicht not
nichts nothing
nichts los nothing happening/
doing
nichts mehr no more,
nothing more
nie never
niedrig low
niemand no one, nobody
noch still, yet, even, nor
die **Nordsee** North Sea
der **November** November
na gut! all right (then)!
null nought, zero, nil
das **Nummernschild (-er)**
number plate
nun now, well (now)
nur only

ob whether
oben upstairs, at the top
ober. . top, upper
obwohl although
oder or
offen open
offensichtlich obvious,
evident, clear
öffnen to open
oft often
ohne without
ohnehin anyway, as it is
der **Oktober** October

das Öl oil
das Orchester (-) orchestra
die Ordnung order
der Orthopäde (PO -n)
  orthopaedics specialist
der Osten east
  östlich east, eastern

das Paar (-e) pair, couple
  ein paar a few
die Packung (-en) pack, packet
die Palette (-n) palette
das Papier (-e) paper
  parken to park
  passen to fit, suit
  passieren to happen
der Patient (PO -en) patient
die Pause (-n) break, interval,
  pause
das Pech bad luck
  Pech haben to be unlucky
die Person (-en) person
  persönlich personal
der Pfeffer pepper
  pfeifen to whistle
der Pfeifton (-e) whistling sound
der Pflaumenkuchen (-) plum
  tart
das Pfund (-e) pound
das Picknick (-s) picnic
der Pinsel (-) brush
der Plan (-e) plan
  planen to plan
der Platz (-e) place, room, space,
  seat, square
  plötzlich sudden
der Politiker (-) politician
  politisch political
der Polizist (PO -en) policeman
die Popmusik pop music
  praktisch practical, handy
der Präsident (PO -en) president
der Preis (-e) price
  preiswert reasonably priced
  pro per

probieren to try
das Problem (-e) problem
das Programm (-e) programme
  prüfen to test
die Prüfung (-en) test,
  examination
der Pullover (-) pullover

das Quintett (-e) quintet

der Rahmen (-) frame
  rasen to rush
  rasieren sich to shave, get
  shaved
  raten to advise, guess
das Rathaus (-er) town hall
  rauchen to smoke
der Raum (-e) room, space
  Recht haben to be right
  rechts to/on the right
der Rechtsanwalt (-e) lawyer
die Rede (-n) speech, talk
  reden to speak, talk
das Regal (-e) shelf
  regelmäßig regular
der Regenschirm (-e) umbrella
  regnen to rain
  reich rich, wealthy
  reichen to pass, hand, reach
  reichhaltig varied,
  comprehensive, extensive
der Reifen (-) tyre
die Reihe (-n) row, series
  reintun II to put in
der Reis rice
der Reiseleiter (-) courier
der Reisepass (-e) passport
die Reklamation (-en)
  complaint, refund
die Revolution (-en) revolution
das Rezept (-e) recipe,
  prescription
  riechen to smell
  richtig correct, right, proper
  röntgen to X-ray

die **Rose (-n)** rose
der **Rosenkohl** brussels sprouts
rostig rusty
rot red
der **Rotwein** red wine
die **Rückfahrt (-en)** return
journey
der **Ruf (-e)** call, reputation
rufen to call (out)
ruhig quiet, calm

die **Sache (-n)** thing, item
sagen to say, tell
die **Sahnesoße (-n)** cream sauce
die **Salami** salami
der **Salat (-e)** salad
das **Salz** salt
der **Samstag** Saturday
satt full, satisfied
sauer sour
schaffen to manage, do, make,
create
schämen sich to be ashamed
der **Scheibenkäse** cheese in slices,
sliced cheese
scheinen to seem, shine
schenken to give (as a present)
schicken to send
der **Schinken (-)** ham
schlafen to sleep
das **Schlafzimmer (-)** bedroom
schlagen to hit, beat
die **Schlagsahne** whipped cream,
whipping cream
schlecht bad, poor
schließen to shut, close
schließlich finally, after all
das **Schloss (¨er)** lock, stately
home
der **Schlüssel (-)** key
schmecken to taste (good)
der **Schmerz (-en)** pain, ache
schmutzig dirty, filthy
schneiden to cut
schnell quick, fast

schon already, even
schön nice, lovely, pretty,
beautiful
schonen to spare, save
der **Schrank (¨e)** cupboard,
wardrobe
schrecklich terrible, awful
schreiben to write
der **Schuh (-e)** shoe
der **Schulanfang (¨e)** start of
school
die **Schuld (-en)** fault, debt
die **Schule (-n)** school
die **Schüssel (-n)** dish
schwach weak
der **Schwager (¨)** brother-in-law
die **Schwägerin (-nen)**
sister-in-law
schwarz black
schwatzen gossip, chatter
schwer heavy, serious, grave,
difficult
die **Schwester (-n)** sister, nurse
die **Schwiegertochter (¨)**
daughter-in-law
schwierig difficult,
awkward
die **Schwierigkeit (-en)** difficulty
schwimmen to swim
sehen to see
sehnen sich (nach) to long
(for)
sehr very
sein to be, his, its
seit since, for
seitdem since (then)
die **Seite (-n)** side, page
die **Sekretärin (-nen)** secretary
(female)
das **Sektfrühstück (-e)**
champagne breakfast
die **Sekunde (-n)** second
d. . **selb. .** the same
selbst -self, even
selten seldom, rarely

der **Semmelknödel (-)** dumpling
der **September** September
servieren to serve
die **Show (-s)** show
sicher sure, certain, reliable
sie she, her, they, them
Sie you
die **Silvesterfahrt (-en)** New
Year('s Eve) trip
das **Silvesterfestessen (-)** New
Year's Eve banquet
sind are
singen to sing
sinken to sink
sitzen to sit
das **Skelett (-e)** skeleton
das **Skifahren** skiing
die **Skimöglichkeit (-en)**
opportunity for skiing,
(plural) skiing facilities
so so, like this/that
so (et)was something/anything
like that
so ... wie as ... as
sobald as soon
sofort immediately, straight
away
der **Sohn (¨e)** son
solch. . such
der **Soldat (PO -en)** soldier
sollen must, ought to, is/
are to
somit therefore, thereby
der **Sommer (-)** summer
sondern but
der **Sonderpreis (-e)** special price
der **Sonnabend (-e)** Saturday
die **Sonne** sun
sonnen sich to sunbathe
der **Sonntag (-e)** Sunday
sonst otherwise, at other
times, or else
die **Sorge (-n)** worry, concern
sorgen (für) to see (to),
take care (of)

die **Sorte (-n)** sort, type, kind
sowieso anyway
sparen to save
die **Sparsamkeit** thrift, economy
der **Spaß (¨e)** joke, fun
viel Spaß! enjoy yourself!
(zu) spät late
später later, afterwards
spazieren gehen to go for
a walk
spielen to play
der **Sportler (-)** sportsman
der **Sportwagen (-)** sports car
sprechen to speak, talk
springen to jump
die **Stadt (¨e)** town
der **Stadtführer (-)** town guide
stammen (von/aus) to
originate (in), come (from)
stark strong
starten to start, take off
statt instead of
stattdessen instead (of that)
das **Steak (-s)** steak
stecken to be (situated), put
(inside), insert
stehen to stand
stehlen to steal
steif stiff
steigen to climb
die **Stelle (-n)** place
stellen to put, place
(upright)
sterben to die
im Stich lassen to leave in
the lurch
stoppen to stop, halt
stören to disturb
stoßen to bump
der **Strand (¨e)** beach
die **Straße (-n)** street, road
streiten to quarrel
das **Stück (-e)** piece, item
der **Student (PO -en)** student
studieren to study

die **Stunde (-n)** hour
stundenlang for hours
suchen to look for
der **Supermarkt (⁻e)** supermarket

der **Tag (-e)** day
guten Tag! hello!
die **Tageszeitung (-en)** daily
(news)paper
tagsüber during the daytime
die **Tante (-n)** aunt
der **Tanz (⁻e)** dance
tanzen to dance
die **Tasche (-n)** pocket
in die Tasche greifen to dip
into one's pocket
das **Taschengeld** pocket money
die **Tasse (-n)** cup
der **Teilnehmer(-)** participant
das **Telefon (-e)** telephone
telefonieren to phone
die **Telefonnummer (-n)**
telephone number
der **Tennis** tennis
der **Teppich (-e)** carpet
teuer dear, expensive
wie teuer? how much?
das **Theater (-)** theatre
der **Theaterplatz** Theatre Square
die **Theke (-n)** counter
die **Tiefkühltruhe (-n)** (chest)
freezer
die **Tischdecke (-n)** tablecloth
die **Tochter (⁻)** daughter
die **Toilette (-n)** toilet
die **Tomate (-n)** tomato
der **Ton (⁻e)** sound, tone
das **Tor (-e)** gate, gateway, goal
der **Tourist (PO -en)** tourist
die **Touristeninformation (-en)**
tourist information office
tragen to carry, wear
treffen to meet
treiben to drive
trennen to separate

die **Treppe (-n)** stairs, staircase
treten to step, kick
trinken to drink
der **Tropfen (-)** drop
trotz in spite of
trotzdem in spite of (that),
nevertheless
das **T-Shirt (-s)** T-shirt
die **Tube (-n)** tube
tun to do, put
die **Tür (-en)** door

über over, across, about
überdies besides
das **Übergewicht** excess weight
überhaupt in general, at all,
altogether
überlassen I to leave
der **Überlebende (adj)** survivor
übermorgen the day after
tomorrow
die **Übernachtung (-en)**
overnight stay
überreden I to persuade
die **Überstunde (-n) (plural)**
overtime
überweisen I to transfer
übrigens by the way,
incidentally
überübermorgen the day
after the day after
tomorrow
die **Uhr (-en)** clock, watch,
o'clock, time
um round, about, at
um ... zu in order to, so as to
umgehen II mit to handle,
deal with
der **Umzug** move, removal
unangenehm unpleasant,
embarrassing
unbedingt absolute, really,
without fail
unberechtigt unjustified
und and

die **Unruhe (-n)** disturbance,
noise
uns (to/for) us
unser our
unsympathisch unpleasant,
uncongenial
unten downstairs, at the
bottom, below
unter under, below, beneath
unterbringen II to
accommodate
die **Unterhaltung (-en)**
entertainment, conversation
die **Unterkunft (¨e)**
accommodation
unterschreiben I to sign
untersuchen I to examine
unterwegs on the way
unwichtig unimportant
der **Urin** urine
der **Urlaub (-e)** holiday(s)

die **Vase (-n)** vase
der **Vater (¨-)** father
veranstalten I to arrange,
put on
die **Veranstaltung (-en)** item of
entertainment, event
die **Verantwortung** responsibility
der **Verbrecher (-)** criminal
verbringen I to spend (time)
die **Vereinigten Staaten (plural)**
the United States
vergessen I to forget
das **Verhältnis (-se)** relationship,
(plural) means, circumstances
verheiratet married
verirren I sich to get lost
verkaufen I to sell
verlassen I to leave
verlaufen I sich to get lost
verletzen I to injure, hurt
verletzen I sich to get hurt
verlieren I to lose
der **Verlust (-e)** loss

vernünftig sensible
verrückt mad, crazy
verschieden different
verschulden I sich to get into
debt, go into the red
versprechen I to promise
verstehen I to understand
der **Versuch (-e)** attempt
versuchen I to try
vertun I sich to make a
mistake, slip up
der **Verwandte (adj)** relative
verzeihen I to forgive, pardon
der **Vetter (-)** cousin (male)
viel much, a lot
viel. . much, many
vielleicht perhaps
das **Viertel (-)** quarter
die **Viertelstunde (-n)** quarter
of an hour
voll full
vollkommen perfect
von from, of, by
vor before, in front of, ago
vorbeischauen II to look in
vorbereiten II to prepare
die **Vorbereitung (-en)**
preparation
vorbeugen II to avert
vorfinden II to find, discover
vorgestern the day before
yesterday
vorhaben II to intend, have
planned, have (got) on
der **Vorhang (¨e)** curtain
vorher before (that)
vorhin a little/short
time ago
vorig. . last
vorkommen II to happen
vornehmen II to undertake
vorn at the front
vorrätig in stock, to hand
vorschießen II to advance
(money)

der **Vorschlag** (-e) suggestion, proposal
vorschlagen II to propose
der **Vorschuss** (-e) advance
vorsichtig careful, cautious
vorstellen II to introduce
vorstellen II sich to imagine

wachsen to grow
der **Wagen** (-) car
die **Wahl** (-en) choice, election
wahnsinnig crazy
während in the course of, during, while
währenddessen during that
wahrscheinlich probably
der **Wald** (-er) wood, forest
wann(?) when(?)
warm warm, hot
warten (auf) to wait (for)
warum? why?
was(?) what(?)
was = etwas
was für (ein)? what sort of (a)?
waschen to wash
waschen sich to wash, have a wash, get washed
das **Wasser** water
das **Wassersystem** (-e) plumbing, water system
weg away, gone
der **Weg** (-e) way, path
wegen on account of, because of
weggehen II to go away
dabei wegkommen II (mit) to get away (with)
wegwerfen II to throw away
weich soft
das **Weihnachten** (-) Christmas
die **Weihnachtsferien (plural)** Christmas holiday(s)
weil because

der **Wein** (-e) wine
die **Weintraube** (-n) grape
weiß white
weiß knows
das **Weißbrot** (-e) white bread/loaf
weiter further
weiterdrehen II to turn on/further
welch. .(?)(!) which(?), what(?)(!)
der **Weltkrieg** (-e) world war
wem? (to/for) whom?
wen? who(m)?
wenig little
wenig. . little, few
wenigstens at least
wenn if, when, whenever
wer? who?
werden will, shall, to be going to, to become
werfen to throw
wesentlich essential, significant, substantial
wessen? whose?
der **Westen** west
das **Wetter** weather
wichtig important
widersprechen I to contradict
wic(?) how(?)
wie (bitte)? pardon?
wieder again
auf Wiedersehen! goodbye!
wieso (denn)? how's that?
wieviel? how much?
wieviele? how many?
der **Wille** (PO -ns) will
der **Winter** (-) winter
der **Winterprospekt** (-e) winter brochure
winzig tiny, minute
wir we
der **Wirt** (-e) landlord
die **Wirtin** (-nen) landlady

wissen to know (facts)
witzig funny, amusing
wo(?) where(?)
die Woche (-n) week
das Wochenende (-n) weekend
wohl well, probably, no doubt
wohnen to live, reside
die Wohnung (-en) flat, dwelling
der Wohnwagen (-) caravan
das Wohnzimmer (-) living room,
  lounge
der Wohnzimmertisch (-e)
  living-room table
wollen to want, intend
das Wort (¨-er or -e) word
worüber over/about which
wundern sich to be surprised
wunderschön beautiful
der Wunsch (¨-e) wish
wünschen to wish, desire
die Wurst (¨-e) sausage

der Yoghurt (-s) yoghurt

die Zahl (-en) number
zahlen to pay
zählen to count
der Zähler (-) counter
der Zahnarzt (¨-e) dentist
der Zehneuroschein (-e) ten
  euro note

zeigen to show
die Zeit (-en) time
vor einiger Zeit some time ago
in letzter Zeit recently
eine Zeit lang for a time
die Zeitung (-en) newspaper
zerstören I to destroy
ziehen to pull, move
ziemlich fairly, rather, pretty
das Zimmer (-) room
zögern to hesitate
zu to, at, too
der Zucker sugar
zudem besides
zufällig by (any) chance
der Zug (¨-e) train, draught,
  procession
zuhören II to listen
die Zündkerze (-n) spark plug
zunehmen II to put on weight
zurück back
zusammen (al)together
der Zuschlag (¨-e) surcharge
zustehen II to be due
zwar to be sure, admittedly,
  und zwar namely
zweimal twice
der Zwilling (-e) twin
zwischen between
das Zypern Cyprus

Index

The numbers refer to section headings, not pages.

'a/an' 17
adjectives 25, 29
  as nouns 61
adverbs 25
affective words 73
alphabet 2
attached phrases 54, 55, 56, 62
attached sentences 62, 63
  enclosed 82
auxiliary verbs 34, 35, 45

'to be' 16, 27, 37, 38
'by … -ing' 74

case 14, 17, 20, 50
comparison of
  adjectives/adverbs 25,
conditional sentences 71
consonants 5

'der, die, das' and related
  words 11, 12, 14, 20, 28,
    41, 50
'da(r)-' 40
dates 48
days of the week 48
direct object (DO) case 14,
  17, 26, 29, 41(c)

'ein' and related words 17,
  28, 50
'-en' non-finite verb ('-en'
  form) 34, 54, 72, 77
enclosed attached sentences
  82
'-end' non-finite verb ('-end'
  form) 61, 74, 82

finite verb 33, 53
friends, addressing 31, 76
future 33, 42

'ge_(e)t' non-finite verb
  ('ge_(e)t' form) 44, 46,
    47
gender 11
'es gibt' 27
greetings 10

'to have' ('haben') 16, 31,
  59, 76

identifiers 60
impersonal expressions 78
indirect citation of speech
  80, 81
indirect object (IO) case
  20, 21, 26, 29, 41
inseparable prefixes 47
instructions 24

joiners 62, 63

line-of-thought pointers 75
location, expressing 37, 38

measurements 36, 60
months of the year 48

negative sentences 23
non-finite verbs 33, 34, 47,
  53, 54, 72, 74, 82

nouns 11
  IO case plural ending 29
  irregular masculine 52
  plural 13

PO case singular ending 50
numerals 18, 30, 37

oblique tenses
  past 69, 70, 71, 80
  present 79, 80
obverse process ('passive')
  57, 72
'ohne ... zu' 56

past tense 59, 66, 67
  oblique 69, 70, 71, 80
possessor (PO) case 50, 51
pre-past 68
prepositions 26, 40, 51,
  63
pre-present 44, 45, 46, 47,
  58
present tense 16, 31, 35, 42,
  43, 76
  oblique 79, 80
prices 19
pronouns 15, 20, 31, 76
  reflexive 64, 65
pronunciation 1–7
  consonants 3, 5
  vowels 4
punctuation 8, 80
'to put' 39
quantifiers 60
quantities 36
questions 22

reflexive pronouns 64, 65
reflexive verbs 65
requests 24

sein 16, 31, 37, 45, 59, 69
separable prefixes 47, 53
'statt ... zu' 56
stop (hiatus) 6
subject (SU) case 14
superlatives of adjectives/
  adverbs 25, 29

tags, reassurance 49
'the' 11, 12, 14, 20, 50
'there is/are' 27, 37
time, expressions of 48
'trotzdem' 74
'um ... zu' 55

verbs 16
  reflexive 65
  requiring IO case 21

'werden' 34, 35, 57
'without ...-ing' 56
'wo(r)-' 63
word order 9, 32, 33,
  53, 54, 63